Nicodemus

Post-Reconstruction Politics and Racial Justice in Western Kansas

CHARLOTTE HINGER

UNIVERSITY OF OKLAHOMA PRESS : NORMAN

Library of Congress Cataloging-in-PublicationData

Names: Hinger, Charlotte, 1940- author.
Title: Nicodemus : post-Reconstruction politics and racial justice in western Kansas / Charlotte Hinger.
Description: Norman : University of Oklahoma Press, 2016. | Series: Race and culture in the American West ; volume 11 | Includes bibliographical references and index.
Identifiers: LCCN 2015042752 | ISBN 978-0-8061-5217-2 (hardcover) ISBN 978-0-8061-9033-4 (paper) Subjects: LCSH: Nicodemus (Kan.)—History—19th century. | Nicodemus (Kan.)—Politics and government—19th century. | African Americans— Kansas —Nicodemus—History—19th century. | Kansas—Race relations— History—19th century.
Classification: LCC F689.N5 H56 2016 | DDC 305.8009781/16309034—dc23
LC record available at http://lccn.loc.gov/2015042752

Nicodemus: Post-Reconstruction Politics and Racial Justice in Western Kansas is Volume 11 in the Race and Culture in the American West series.

The paper in this book meets the guidelines for permanence and durability of the Committee on Production Guidelines for Book Longevity of the Council on Library Resources, Inc. ∞

Copyright © 2016 by Charlotte Hinger. Published by the University of Oklahoma Press, Norman, Publishing Division of the University. Paperback published 2022. Manufactured in the U.S.A.

All rights reserved. No part of this publication may be reproduced, stored in a retrieval system, or transmitted, in any form or by any means, electronic, mechanical, photocopying, recording, or otherwise—except as permitted under Section 107 or 108 of the United States Copyright Act—without the prior written permission of the University of Oklahoma Press. To request permission to reproduce selections from this book, write to Permissions, University of Oklahoma Press, 2800 Venture Drive, Norman OK 73069, or email rights.oupress@ou.edu.

To the memory of my beloved husband, Donald R. Hinger

Kansas will not place a sentinel at her portals to ascertain before permitting those who desire to enter what political party they belong to, where they were born, whether they have been sprinkled or plunged, or what particular shade their skin happens to be.
John Pierce St. John, governor of Kansas

Contents

List of Illustrations	xi
Acknowledgments	xiii
Introduction	3
1 Passing into a New Civilization	11
2 Ho for Kansas!	26
3 Kansas—Sure but Slow Poison	42
4 Unconsidered Trifles	55
5 Black Republicans	67
6 The Needs of the Race	83
7 Leave This Godforsaken Country	96
8 Give No Aid to the Sharks	110
9 The Colored People Hold the Key	128
10 One Tree Bore Bread, Another Bore Lard	147
11 I Will Not Touch the Unclean Thing	170
Epilogue	199
Notes	207
Bibliography	237

Illustrations

Figures

Lulu Craig on homestead in Manzanola, Colorado	8
Nicodemus promotional poster	13
Nicodemus, Kansas, 1885	15
Map of early Graham County	17
Benjamin "Pap" Singleton	23
Senator Daniel Wolsey Voorhees	28
"Ho for Kansas!" poster	33
W. R. Hill	36
Abram Thompson Hall, Jr., c. 1910	57
John Lewis Waller	73
William Bolden Townsend	75
Frederick Douglass	101
Senator William Windom	104
Elizabeth Leslie Comstock and Laura Smith Haviland	118
Edward Preston McCabe	124
Kansas governor John Pierce St. John	136
Abram Thompson Hall, age ninety-two	145
Senator John James Ingalls	168
Lulu Sadler Craig, age 102	203

Acknowledgments

I WISH TO THANK a number of people who have made substantial contributions to my understanding of Nicodemus and black intellectual history. This book began as a master's thesis about a unique town, Nicodemus, Kansas, the first post-Reconstruction all-black town on the High Plains. As more information became available about three influential residents of Nicodemus, I became convinced that the contributions of Abram Thompson Hall, Jr., Edward Preston McCabe, and John W. Niles had been critical in shaping the growth and development of this colony. The focus of this manuscript changed from the town itself to a study of Hall's, McCabe's, and Niles's differing philosophies and the methods they used to influence local, state, and national politics.

Angela Bates, Nicodemus's premier historian, generously gave unique insights into the community. She has become a dear friend and I admire her tireless work to preserve the precious history of Nicodemus. I have encouraged her to write a book about the development of Nicodemus focusing on the interaction between its various families.

I am grateful for the research assistance of Lowell Beecher, who helped me locate material at the Graham County Historical Society in Hill City, Kansas. His book *The Spring Creek Valley* provides unique insights on communities in Graham County. I appreciate the numerous patient country clerks and staff in historical societies in western Kansas who opened their archives. They helped me and then stood by while I literally raised the dust in old areas of courthouses that contained obscure documents.

Throughout my studies, the following outstanding academics at the Fort Hays State University made history exciting and relevant: Robert Luehrs, Ann Liston, Alan Busch, Robert Rook, Raymond Wilson, Jan Wilson, and David Goodlett. I thank them all for their contributions to my education.

I owe a special debt to Dr. Virgil Dean and Melissa Tubbs Loya for sharpening my understanding of academic writing and for guiding me through my first article in *Kansas History*. The Kansas Historical Society was formed in 1875, early in the state's history, and has an extensive collection of documents. The quality of Kansas's trove of material is known to scholars worldwide.

This book would not be possible without resources obtained through interlibrary loan. Librarians in Goodland, Hays (Fort Hays State University), and Hoxie, Kansas, became very familiar with my constant requests for microfilm, as did librarians in Loveland, Colorado. Archivist Darrell Garwood of the Kansas Historical Society patiently sent reels of old newspapers. I appreciate the work the State of Oklahoma has done to track the contributions of African Americans there. The staff at the Oklahoma Historical Society sent me their entire vertical file on E. P. McCabe.

Charles Robinson, a descendant of Abram Thompson Hall, Jr., provided access to family material. He read my article in *Kansas History* and contacted me through Facebook. Deborah Dandridge at the Kenneth Spencer Research Library, University of Kansas, in Lawrence, guided me through the African American collections and put me in touch with Michael Flug at the Chicago Public Library and its extensive Jeanne Borger Jones collection, which includes photos and papers from the Abram Hall family. Regrettably, I did not maintain a list of all the state archivists who located material for me. Without their support I would not have seen obscure primary sources that sometimes supported the ideas in this book and other times helped me realize I was on the wrong track.

The late, great Dr. Charles Leland Sonnichsen, in a single talk at a Western Writers of America convention, shaped my attitude about the levels of research required for different kinds of writing. Sonnichsen talked about informal nonfiction, books with a western setting, and true historical novels, and he said that academics need to locate everything that exists about a subject. Although in the field of African American history that would be a Herculean, multi-century task, I thank him for instilling in me the necessity of taking a formal approach to the interpretation of documents and for fostering constant and lifelong alertness for material that should be brought to light.

I appreciate Charles Rankin's early interest in my topic, and I am grateful for the encouragement of Quintard Taylor, who invited me to contribute articles to BlackPast, the online reference guide to African American history. I am in awe of Dr. Taylor's contribution to scholarship and refer to him as the "Major God of Blacks in the West." His range of knowledge about this subject is unequaled. The works of Dr. Bruce Glasrud and Dr. Cary Wintz validated some of my ideas about blacks in the West. My early correspondence with former University of Oklahoma Press acquisitions editor Jay Dew strengthened my resolve to complete all my research. When Kathleen Kelly assumed the responsibility for the Race and Culture in the West series, she graciously answered all of my questions regarding the editorial process. I also thank her editorial assistant, Bethany Mowry, for time and energy spent helping me with the publication process. Steven Baker's enthusiasm for my research reinforced my belief that western Kansas blacks had made an important contribution to the settlement of the American West. I deeply appreciate his support for the subject.

Chris Dodge has done an amazing job of strengthening this manuscript. His insights into improving narrative construction and calls for clarification in various spots have been invaluable.

I owe a special debt to David Dary, an outstanding Kansas historian, academic, and journalist who generously took the time to read my thesis and offered priceless advice for breathing life into it.

I deeply regret that my late husband, Don Hinger, did not live to see the publication of this book. His constant love and support made my research possible. I cannot put into words my thankfulness for our long marriage.

Nicodemus

Introduction

IN 1877, AFTER RUTHERFORD B. HAYES was elected president, the U.S. government pulled its troops out of the post–Civil War South. Thus ended the era known as Reconstruction, the postwar period during which hundreds of blacks were elected to office in the South, including more than a handful to the U.S. Congress. Now the federal government would no longer set conditions for allowing southern states back into the Union—and now the states of the South had a free hand to enforce anti-black laws they had passed immediately after the war. These "Black Codes" had denied African Americans liberties, curtailed their voting rights, and channeled them into a new system of slavery in all but name.

At the same time that already tenuous political and economic opportunities vanished for freed slaves and other blacks in the South, the federal government launched a campaign to populate the prairie states. Flyers appeared throughout the South advertising lots in towns in the Great Plains region, ads created by speculators who saw an opportunity to exploit black dissatisfaction. Of particular interest was Kansas, a state that southern blacks imbued with mythical qualities. They associated it with John Brown, the militant abolitionist, whom many viewed as a saint and martyr for the cause of their freedom.

Thus the stage was set for the second of two distinct periods of black migration to Kansas. During the first, from about 1873 to 1877, African Americans primarily from Tennessee and Kentucky planned and established colonies in Kansas. Following this, masses of disillusioned African Americans known as the Exodusters left the South in 1879 for political freedom and economic opportunity in Kansas. The Exodusters came mainly from four states: Mississippi, Louisiana, Texas, and Tennessee, with a smaller proportion from Alabama and Georgia.[1] This massive migration, depriving the white community of a dependable labor supply, threatened the economic stability of the South.

Due to the abruptness of the 1879 exodus, and the numbers involved, in 1880 a select committee of the U.S. Senate conducted a formal investigation. The five persons on the committee were Daniel Wolsey Voorhees (Indiana), Zebulon Baird Vance (Pennsylvania), George Hunt Pendleton (Ohio), William Windom (Minnesota), and Henry William Blair (New Hampshire.) They heard the testimony of 153 white and black witnesses and then published a seventeen-hundred-page report that was highly partisan and accusatory. Precisely for its partisan views, the *Voorhees Committee Report* is invaluable. Perhaps no other document so accurately illuminates the post–Civil War controversy surrounding African Americans. The testimonies, often simultaneously honest and skillfully manipulative, attempting to shape opinion, illustrated the depths of the debate over the new citizens' intellectual and political abilities. The leading questions posed by the five committee members reflected their determination to extract testimony in support of their own opinion as to why blacks left the South. Voorhees, Vance, and Pendleton believed it was a massive political ploy on the part of the Republicans to acquire new voters into the state. Windom and Blair believed violence and oppression on the part of southern whites had become unbearable.[2]

Nicodemus, Kansas, one of the pioneer settlements resulting from the black colonization movement, was referred to periodically during the Voorhees Committee debate. Not only was the progress and survival of the town relevant to the political controversy, Nicodemus was also a microcosm representing African Americans nationwide, with residents holding conflicting opinions about settlement in western Kansas. Nicodemus was unique, however, with three resident black leaders, each with differing views, exerting extraordinary influence over county, state, and even national politics. The three were Abram Thompson Hall, Jr., Edward Preston McCabe, and John W. Niles.

This book is not a history describing the founding of Nicodemus but instead an examination of the divergent attitudes of Hall, McCabe, and Niles. The issues that engaged them in Nicodemus echoed the anxieties and prejudices present in the Voorhees Committee. The differing approaches in Nicodemus for relating to white people were typical of emerging black viewpoints nationwide toward racial uplift and civil rights as African Americans from the South grappled with the responsibilities inherent in their new freedom. Hall supported racial uplift, McCabe insisted that equality could only be achieved through politics and legislation, and Niles became a proponent for slave reparations. Although topics discussed in this book are relevant to black history, Kansas history, cultural history, educational history, and western history, my focus is on black intellectual history and the ideas stemming from the African American settlement of western Kansas.

To presume to offer a contribution to scholarship about the nineteenth-century black migration to Kansas is humbling because of the preceding work of two outstanding historians in the seventies, Nell Irvin Painter and Robert G. Athearn.[3] Both became nationally recognized authorities in African American history. Because of their seminal work, it was possible for me to identify unpublished information about blacks in western Kansas.

Nicodemus has been the subject of a number of informal articles. Additionally, scholars of history and sociology have published formal studies about the community. A monograph published by the U.S. Department of the Interior, *Promised Land on the Solomon: Black Settlement at Nicodemus, Kansas*, contains detailed information about the economic development of Nicodemus in a chapter by Kenneth Marvin Hamilton. A chapter by Clayton Fraser traces the architectural development and decline of the town, and a chapter by La Barbara W. Fly focuses on Nicodemus in the twentieth century.[4] Steven Hahn, who won the 2004 Pulitzer Prize for History for his study of the black political struggles in the South, incorporated information about Nicodemus when writing about Kansas propaganda.[5]

Other scholars examined the formation and general history of Nicodemus prior to Painter's and Athearn's work. Nell Waldron's 1932 doctoral dissertation on colonization in Kansas includes a section on the organization of Nicodemus.[6] William J. Belleau's master's thesis in 1943, the first recorded formal study of the community, concentrates on the chronological development of Nicodemus and contains a number of valuable oral histories.[7] Orval L. McDaniel's 1950 master's thesis on Nicodemus focuses on migration aspects of the community. McDaniel gathered records to determine the geographical origins of the emigrants, and he explores the reasons for the migration to Nicodemus and delves into questions surrounding individual land ownership.[8]

Van Burton Shaw completed a doctoral dissertation on Nicodemus in 1951. His work is primarily a sociological study of the isolation tactics used by various black communities to avoid conflict with white communities. Shaw spent the summer of 1949 in Nicodemus, and his principal method was that of "participant observation," as he attempted to become an active member of the community. He conducted formal interviews and kept a diary, making entries daily. Although Shaw had initial reservations about the effectiveness of a white man conducting a field study of this nature in a black community, his detailed work reflects his success in gaining the trust and confidence of the residents of Nicodemus. Shaw credited the presence of his wife and daughter that summer with his unusual success in breaking down racial barriers. It seemed to "represent a pledge of good faith and sincerity that he would trust his family to the community's good will."[9]

Glen Schwendemann, whose 1957 master's thesis explored the general exodus movement to Kansas, published "Nicodemus, Negro Haven on the Solomon," in the *Kansas Historical Quarterly* in 1968. This piece contains insights into the personalities of Hall, McCabe, and Niles.[10] More recent scholarship about Nicodemus includes Claire O'Brien's 1996 article on the biracial aspects of the town and efforts to acquire railroad service.[11]

Belleau, McDaniel, and Shaw completed their studies of Nicodemus over a half-century ago. Present-day researchers can access a wealth of material unavailable to previous generations. Documents can be borrowed through the network of libraries participating in interlibrary loan (ILL). Thanks to the Internet, scholars can view microfilmed letters, diaries, and minutes of meetings without time-consuming and costly travel. Whole journal articles are available online. The Kansas Historical Society has maintained an extensive collection of newspapers since territorial organization, and these publications are available on microfilm. The Library of Congress's Chronicling of America offers a trove of material formerly inaccessible or difficult to access. And due to the increased emphasis on black heritage that emerged in the 1960s,

African American families have since contributed valuable letters and memorabilia to historical societies.

Building on the stellar contribution of previous scholars and incorporating new materials and the *Voorhees Committee Report*, I have concentrated on the political activities of three prominent nineteenth-century black leaders in Nicodemus to explore their effectiveness. Because of the widespread illiteracy of African Americans of the time, previous scholars all too often assumed that the residents of Nicodemus produced few written records. However, a number of colonists were not only literate but also gifted in their ability to write persuasively. Newspapers across Kansas published a number of letters to the editor, political commentaries, and miscellaneous social columns by African Americans. Tracing the black literary contribution is complicated, however, in part because some authors used Greek pen names, a common practice at the time. Moreover, many of the letters were sent to newspapers distant from Nicodemus. Regardless, one thing that became clear to me is that Nicodemus colonists moved quickly to separate their community from the public perception of the "needy hordes," the Exodusters, descending on the state.

I discovered Lulu Sadler Craig's priceless manuscript in the Graham County Historical Society while researching an article for *Kansas History*. Background information about Craig and others in Nicodemus can be found in the various publications of historian Antoinette Broussard, grandniece of Nettie Craig Asberry. Asberry taught school in Nicodemus for a number of years and is believed to be the first African American woman to receive a doctorate. According to Broussard, Lulu Sadler was born in 1868 and moved to Nicodemus with her parents when she was ten years old. She graduated from State Teachers College in Emporia, then taught grades one through eight in Nicodemus. In 1886 she married Sanford Craig, and they remained in Nicodemus for twenty-eight more years. Then the family moved to Manzanola, Colorado where she again taught school. Later her life became the background for a documentary, *Happy Birthday, Mrs. Craig!*, produced and directed by Academy Award–winner Richard Kaplan. Craig died in 1972 at the age of 104, having raised eight children. She had thirteen grandchildren, twenty-five great-grandchildren, and six

Lulu Sadler Craig and grandchildren on homestead in Manzanola, Colorado. Courtesy of Alice Craig McDonald private collection.

great-great-grandchildren. Craig was an indomitable educator and perceptive historian whose topical essays make an invaluable contribution toward understanding Nicodemus. Whenever possible, I have included documentation to reinforce her observations and kept in mind that Craig's recollections were subjective interpretations.[12]

In addition to civil rights issues common to all blacks, African Americans migrating to Nicodemus—whether freeborn or formerly enslaved—were concerned with issues indigenous to settlement of the West. Decisions regarding the formation of local governments, controlling free-ranging cattle herds, and the distribution of public lands were also of critical interest to exclusively white settlements and were not race-related. The most critical political issues in late-nineteenth-century Graham County were local ones: the organization of the county into a formal political entity, the location of the county seat, and the election of county officers; the establishment of schools; the construction of roads and bridges; temperance; and mitigating the perceived immorality of aid appeals.

This book recognizes the following activities as attempts to exert political influence: running for public office; writing letters to editors or state officials; giving speeches or stating political opinions at meetings; and providing columns of political commentary in newspapers, whether negative or positive. Because of the large number of African Americans in Graham County who engaged in these activities, it would be impossible to discuss them all—and the events surrounding them—at length. Therefore, I have limited the scope of this book to Hall, McCabe, and Niles.[13]

Due to the methods used by these skilled politicians to prevail over county, state, and national issues, Nicodemus established a national reputation as an example of the possibilities inherent in African Americans—namely that they could do all the things whites had done. Yet diverging philosophies within the community, held by this trio from the beginning, hinted at the divisions that would divide blacks into the present century. Hall was the first to leave the community, in 1880 after his decisive role in organizing Graham County. McCabe left after he was elected state auditor, and Niles—for a long time just one step ahead of the law—ended up in an Arkansas penitentiary.

The Graham County political drama played out in newspapers, an important source for me. Newspapers were great publicity machines whose purpose it was to establish a town—and thereby the fortunes of stockholders in town companies backing them.[14] The outlandish rhetoric of Kansas editors is an intriguing aspect of the state's heritage. According to historian Don W. Wilson, Kansas led all other states "in terms of numbers of papers, talents of the editors, and interest of the people on a per capita basis."[15] Kansas speculators created newspapers before there was any news to print.[16] The state's editors did not temper their rhetoric until the beginning of the twentieth century, when the Wild West became more civilized.[17] The newspapers published in Nicodemus, *Western Cyclone* (begun in May 1886) and *Nicodemus Enterprise* (August 1887), were both edited by white men in a bald attempt to influence the location of the county seat, but black Kansans, like their white counterparts, were busy newspaper founders, writers, and readers during this time.

Objectivity is required for historical investigation. However, it is difficult to remain detached or even dry-eyed when reading of the courageous actions of Kansas governor John Pierce St. John and African

American journalist Abram Thompson Hall, Jr. These two men were icons of political integrity, and they redefine heroism. St. John's evenhanded intervention to secure civil rights for African American immigrants was fearless and far-sighted.

My biggest regret with this book is that I am leaving out the achievements of so many African American men and women in Kansas by focusing on Hall, Niles, and McCabe. On a state level there were a number of outstanding orators, writers, administrators, ministers, lawyers, educators, and blue-collar citizens who buoyed their communities.

Finally, I must admit that synthesizing and assessing the multitude of relative documents at the Kansas Historical Society and the Spencer Research Library was at times overwhelming. I welcome corrections and contributions to my perceptions.

Chapter 1
Passing into a New Civilization

> [T]he condition of things that prevails in the South, bad as they are . . . are but incidental to the revolution by which these people are passing from one civilization to another . . . the abolition of slavery was not the establishment of freedom. The falling down of one house is not the building up of another.
>
> Testimony of Isaiah Wears (colored)

IN APRIL 1878 the northwestern Kansas prairie was greening up after a cold, miserable winter. Enthralled by the lure of the West, three young African American men, Abram Thompson Hall, Jr., Edward Preston McCabe, and John W. Niles, sat atop wagons loaded with supplies donated by groups in Leavenworth, Kansas. The trio had arrived at Ellis, Kansas, on the Denver Express, a Missouri Pacific train, and spent the night with Mr. and Mrs. Phillip Hayden. That morning Henry Smith, Grant Harris, Charles Page, and John DePrad, men from Nicodemus, had greeted them and loaded three borrowed wagons with the life-saving donations.

Hall, McCabe, and Niles had headed north and crossed the Saline River, and now before them lay the south fork of the Solomon River. Hall and McCabe, political buddies from Chicago, jumped from the wagons and hiked to a promontory to gain their first glimpse of the Promised Land—Nicodemus, Kansas. They gazed across the valley at a network of what Hall would later call "anthills" (dugouts) extending some eight miles north. Stunned, they turned to the smiling, charismatic con artist Niles, who had lured them from a small black colony in Hodgeman County, about a hundred miles to the south to this unpromising beginning. Nicodemus was not at all the thriving settlement Niles had described.[1]

To African Americans, Nicodemus—an all-black settlement situated amid scattered mounds of earth—teemed with symbolism bordering on the magical. The hopes of blacks for the development of this town were comparable to whites' expectations for Jamestown, Virginia, in the early seventeenth century. William Eagleson, editor of the Kansas-based *Colored Citizen*, wrote that if the colony at Nicodemus was successful, then the question of "what shall become of the colored race in this country is solved." He maintained that immigrants from Tennessee and Kentucky could come into Kansas and "go upon land away from railroads, towns, and almost beyond the limits of civilization itself, and succeed in placing themselves in a comparative state of comfort, and could make a living," and that "there is no longer need for our people to remain in the abominable South, to be the slaves of the rebels and targets for the muskets of white men." Craig Miner writing in *West of Wichita* quoted the *Atchison Champion*'s prediction that "if Nicodemus failed, it would darken the whole future of the colored race in the country."[2]

Indeed, with the establishment of Nicodemus, for the first time in the history of the United States enough black voters had gathered in a region to affect critically important decisions regarding the settlement of the West. Approximately six hundred African Americans migrating from the South to the High Plains—in organized colonies, clusters of family groups, and small trickles of courageous individuals—had responded to intensive publicity campaigns luring disillusioned ex-slaves to a better life.[3]

Just as Nicodemus would soon become a microcosm representing political activity by African Americans in the trans-Mississippi West, Hall, McCabe, and Niles—each with distinctive appearance, style, and temperament—were archetypes of contrasting political philosophies that emerged among blacks following the failure of Reconstruction.

Hall, a well-educated freeborn northern journalist, easily melded his racial agenda through intelligent cooperation with the white population and led the campaign to organize Graham County. Governor St. John appointed him census taker, an office whose functions were essential for county organization but a precarious position for a black man who would be visiting isolated whites. Hall subsequently served as a federal census taker. His editorials were quoted nationwide, and he would write on a broad range of subjects throughout his long life.

All Colored People
THAT WANT TO
GO TO KANSAS,
On September 5th, 1877,
Can do so for $5.00

IMMIGRATION.

WHEREAS, We, the colored people of Lexington, Ky,. knowing that there is an abundance of choice lands now belonging to the Government, have assembled ourselves together for the purpose of locating on said lands. Therefore,

BE IT RESOLVED, That we do now organize ourselves into a Colony, as follows:— Any person wishing to become a member of this Colony can do so by paying the sum of one dollar ($1.00), and this money is to be paid by the first of September, 1877, in instalments of twenty-five cents at a time, or otherwise as may be desired.

RESOLVED, That this Colony has agreed to consolidate itself with the Nicodemus Towns, Solomon Valley, Graham County, Kansas, and can only do so by entering the vacant lands now in their midst, which costs $5.00.

RESOLVED, That this Colony shall consist of seven officers—President, Vice-President, Secretary, Treasurer, and three Trustees. President—M. M. Bell; Vice-President—Isaac Talbott; Secretary—W. J. Niles; Treasurer—Daniel Clarke; Trustees—Jerry Lee, William Jones, and Abner Webster.

RESOLVED, That this Colony shall have from one to two hundred militia, more or less, as the case may require, to keep peace and order, and any member failing to pay in his dues, as aforesaid, or failing to comply with the above rules in any particular, will not be recognized or protected by the Colony.

Nicodemus promotional poster. Courtesy of Kansas Historical Society.

McCabe, also freeborn, and who could have passed for white, eventually became a black separatist and hoped that Oklahoma would become an all-black state. McCabe became the first African American in the North elected to a state office. He served as state auditor for Kansas and later founded Langston City and Langston University in Oklahoma. He was elected assistant chief clerk of the Oklahoma Territorial Legislature.

The formerly enslaved Niles, one of the founders of Nicodemus, was controversial and flamboyant. He differed from both Hall and McCabe in believing that African Americans deserved compensation for their years in slavery. Through this assertion he later defeated a cadre of the best lawyers in Kansas while defending himself in a criminal case following his mortgaging of a nonexistent corn crop. He went on to persuade one of the most esteemed legislators in Kansas, James Legate, to back his demands for restitution for blacks. Then, through his considerable oratorical skills, Niles gained national notoriety because of his aggressive demands that whites atone. He was the first black man to persuade the U.S. Senate to consider a petition for slave reparations. It was introduced by Senator John Sherman, brother of General William Tecumseh Sherman.

The thoughtful, philosophical Voorhees Committee testimony of Isaiah Wears, a freeborn African American real estate broker living in Philadelphia, encapsulated the most critical task of the settlers of Nicodemus. How might they shape liberty while in a raw, wounded state, still reeling from the Civil War? Should they woo the approval of surrounding whites? Could they live apart? Indeed, as Wears testified, "the falling down of one house was not the building up of another."[4]

Defining liberty has divided African Americans from the time of the Emancipation Proclamation into the twenty-first century. W. E. B. Du Bois, historian and founder of the National Association for the Advancement of Colored People, and Booker T. Washington, educator and founder of the Tuskegee Institute, would starkly delineate the division.

Abram T. Hall later wrote of his initial disappointment at seeing Nicodemus. He had left a well-paid job as city editor for the *Chicago Conservator*, a prestigious black newspaper. While working there, early settler Lulu Sadler Craig writes in her unpublished history of

Nicodemus, Kansas, 1885. Courtesy of Kansas Historical Society.

Nicodemus, Hall had read articles about the "movement to locate Negro Americans on United States Government lands in the west during the winter of 1877–1878." According to Hall, reports of "boundless acreage, fertility of soil, equable climate and golden opportunity to acquire and own a home on lands west of the Missouri river, in the State of Kansas" lured black people into a great migration from the South. Excited by the opportunity to acquire free land, he and McCabe decided to join the exodus.[5]

Hall and McCabe were not the only ones disillusioned by the sight of Nicodemus. At the age of ninety, Willianna Hickman recalled her first impression when she arrived in the spring of 1878: "When we got in sight of Nicodemus, the men shouted, 'There is Nicodemus.' Being very sick, I hailed this news with gladness. I looked with all the eye I had. 'Where is Nicodemus? I don't see it.' My husband pointed out smokes coming out of the ground and said, 'That is Nicodemus.' The families lived in dugouts. . . . The scenery was not at all inviting, and I began to cry."[6] Adding to her tribulation, her six children were recovering from measles, which had caused a two-week delay in Ellis for a number of the families.

In fact, sixty families in the colony arriving in September headed back to the South the day after they arrived in Nicodemus. As with the exaggerated portrayals of Kansas to future homesteaders, town promotion on the frontier had been raised to an art form, and Nicodemus was no exception. When the exhausted colonists arrived, they found a vast, empty, treeless prairie. The Solomon River, described in circulars as "having an abundance of excellent water," was little more than a creek to people who had lived next to the Ohio River. The promised "abundance of fine Magnesium stone for building purposes" lay under a carpet of tough, nearly impenetrable sod. A magnificent herd of wild horses with black flowing manes, mentioned repeatedly in the personal narratives of early Nicodemus settlers, always remained at a distance. Certainly they could not be captured on foot or with the weary work horses the ex-slaves had brought to Kansas.[7]

Despite their initial shock, Hall wrote Craig that he and McCabe filled their "lungs to capacity with the dry, invigorating atmosphere and returned to the waiting wagons."[8] They pushed on toward the colony, where Hall would soon make his mark as an extraordinarily competent politician. In fact, his involvement in Nicodemus politics had begun before his arrival in Graham County. In the narrative Hall sent Craig he expounded on how Niles had lured him to Nicodemus. After he left Chicago, upon reaching Leavenworth, he overheard a conversation between women in a café regarding the plight of the Nicodemus settlers, who were in need of supplies to tide them over until their crops matured. He later explained that his "newspaper instinct instantly apprised that here was a human interest story fairly crying out loud for investigation and publication." He tracked down John W. Niles, who was soliciting aid for the colony. Hall learned that despite the presence of "articles in the daily newspapers, emanating from a disgruntled group back in the colony [Nicodemus], impeaching his right as a solicitor," Niles had been quite successful.

A month earlier, Niles had called on the editor of the *Leavenworth Daily Times* and presented himself as the president of the Nicodemus colony and claimed he was in charge of some six hundred souls, all of whom were in dire straits. The editor wrote a column admiring Niles's commendable work on behalf of his race. A couple of weeks later, the

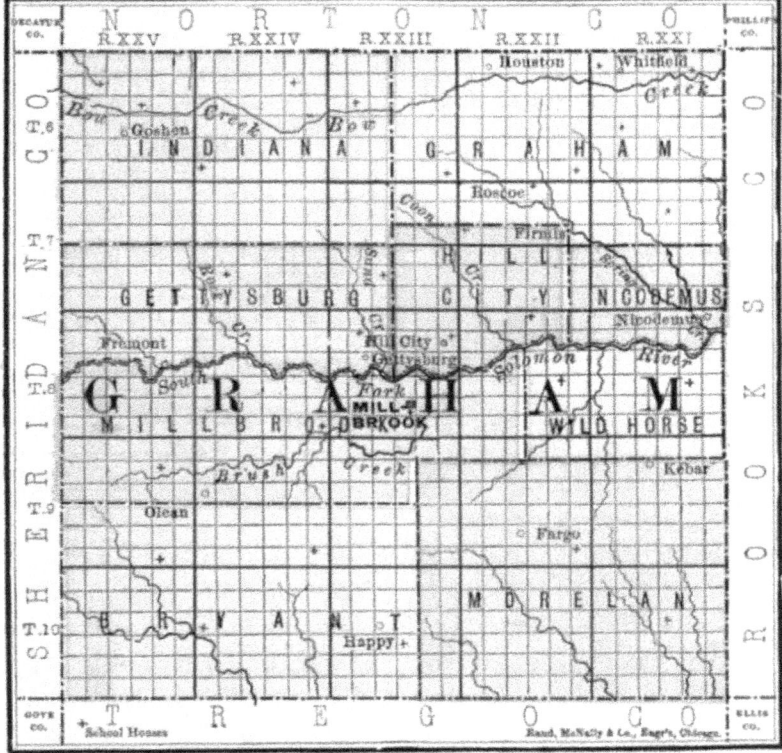

Early Graham County.

Times reprinted a column that had appeared in the *Atchison Champion*, stating that "Chas. Gossaway, a colored minister" representing Nicodemus was also soliciting aid.[9]

On April 7, the *Times* printed a scathing letter from the real president of Nicodemus Town Company, W. H. Smith. In a sharp rebuke, Smith said that there was no suffering in Graham County and that Niles had no authority to solicit for the colony. Smith also accused Niles of falsely claiming that he had the endorsement of the governors of Colorado and Kentucky "to carry on the begging business." Naturally, as an investor in the Nicodemus Town Company and active in propaganda to attract more people to the colony, Smith insisted that Nicodemus was "abundantly able to take care of itself and all of its members."

The residents of Leavenworth responded generously to Niles's appeal. However, two groups that Hall referred to as "local race [Negro] politicians[,] one faction led by W. B. Townsend and the other by William Matthews," had tied up the aid because they doubted Niles's authority. In Hall's opinion, Townsend and Matthews, "seeing the success of the donation," were "eager to be given credit or glory for what they had had no part in bringing about." Since it was Hall's first day in Leavenworth, he was not aware of the background for the controversy that would come to a head that very evening at the African Methodist Episcopal (AME) church, Hall's own denomination. He could not have known that by confronting Townsend and Matthews he was challenging two of Kansas's most prominent African Americans.[10]

Captain William Dominick Matthews, a Republican at the time, who later became a Democrat, owned "Waverly Place, a boarding establishment," which previously had been a station on the Underground Railroad, harboring fugitive slaves. As captain of Company D, he had actively recruited for the famous First Kansas Colored Regiment organized by Senator James H. Lane. In August 1878, in his role as "Most Worthy Grand Master" of the King Solomon Grand Lodge of the Prince Hall Masons, he published a letter in a Lawrence, Kansas, newspaper, tracing the "history of Colored Masonry down to the present day" and denouncing the formation of a rival group, the "so-called States Rights Masons."[11]

William Bolden Townsend, also a Republican, shared Hall's belief in the importance of racial uplift. He too had achieved status a politician, journalist, and attorney, and like Hall was a "spell-binding orator." He built "one of the most beautiful and costly houses in Leavenworth" and would later become one of Kansas's most effective voices against racial violence.[12]

Prior to a meeting to be held at the AME church that evening to determine custody of the supplies, Hall met with church officials, Reverend Phillip Hubbard, chairman, and John Banks, secretary, to see if they supported Niles. They did, so he hatched a plan that worked to perfection. At the outset of the meeting, after Niles again described the destitute conditions of the colonists, Hall thwarted the opportunity for the brilliant debaters Matthews and Townsend to state their views by jumping to his feet and immediately moving to release the goods to Niles. Banks promptly seconded the motion. "Our program," wrote Hall, "went through almost unanimously," and Niles was "elated over the outcome." Hall, McCabe, Matthews, and Townsend would cross paths many more times in their political careers.[13]

Impressed with Hall's abilities, Niles persuaded Hall and McCabe to accompany him to Nicodemus. Hall later wrote that their "approach must have been seen" because after they forded the Solomon River the "entire population met us on the other bank with a greeting much like that accorded homecoming victors loaded with the spoils of war."[14]

Hall immediately used his political skills to settle the controversy in Nicodemus about Niles's self-appointed role as the colony's agent. Those who had supported Niles from the beginning wanted to keep the supplies for themselves, but Hall persuaded that faction to share with all who would sign the following statement he drew up authorizing Niles to solicit aid on behalf of the colonists: "To All Whom it May Concern: Greetings: We the undersigned members of a Negro Colony, located at Nicodemus, Kansas, being in destitute circumstances, due to the lack of food, clothing, shoes, garden and farm seeds do hereby and herewith appoint and empower John W. Niles, one of our number, as an agent and solicitor before the public in our behalf until such time as our crops are ready to be planted shall mature and be ready for harvest."[15] That same night, the colonists elected Hall clerk of the colony and McCabe disbursing clerk, and they decided to dole out goods every Friday. All but seven signed Niles's authorization document at once. The remaining seven signed by "ration day."

After negotiating cooperation over aid, Hall immediately addressed an equally critical problem. The settlers wanted to stay clustered in town. Witnesses in the Voorhees Committee hearing would spar over the advisability of ex-slaves living apart from a community on individual claims. Milton W. Reynolds, a fiery journalist from Parsons, Kansas, who often used the pseudonym "Kicking Bird," wrote, "The colored people are gregarious. They move in squads, in companies, battalions, in regiments." Lulu Craig also commented on the issue.

There was no building large enough to accommodate large groups, and Craig noted, "They being people who liked to get together, that was a hardship for them." Also, the first settlers had built shelters around the town site and were daunted by the idea of carving out a second dugout on their land outside of Nicodemus. There was safety in numbers, and the community had created a central storage facility and shared labor, supplies, tools, and food.[16] Nevertheless, Hall immediately took charge of officially recording the settlers' preemption, homestead, and soldiers' claims at the district land office in Kirwin, Kansas. Warned by land officers there of an impending rush of white settlers, Hall urged the colonists to move out of their temporary residences in Nicodemus and onto their own property because the law required "whole or partial residence and a certain amount of cultivation" to legitimize a claim. The Kirwin land agent, W. C. Don Carlos, helped secure Hall's appointment as deputy district clerk of Rooks County for the unorganized area known as Graham County, and he helped secure McCabe's commission as a notary public.[17]

Hall's assistance was critical. Tragedy loomed if the settlers lost their claims through ignorance of the laws. The availability of homestead land had been a prime motivation for these settlers to leave the South and move to Kansas. Nell Irwin Painter writes that "whatever the importance of the new race relations of the postwar South, the issue of land remained one of the most crucial, to both blacks and whites."[18]

Friction over the allocation of land has exasperated lawmakers from the country's founding. Both formerly enslaved and freeborn African Americans understood the importance of political influence in getting and keeping land. The preliminary report of the American Freedmen's Inquiry Commission found that the "chief object of ambition among the refugees is to own property, especially to possess land, if it be only a few acres, in their own State."[19] Southern whites, meanwhile, were outraged at the thought of ex-slaves acquiring control of land previously owned by their masters. African American mass migration from the South deprived planters of a cheap and dependable labor force. Consequently, the third part of the *Voorhees Committee Report* focused on the movement of African Americans into Kansas.

Benjamin "Pap" Singleton, the African American credited with beginning the colonization movement to Kansas, originally hoped that blacks would be able to acquire land in the South. He organized the Tennessee Real Estate and Homestead Association to assist African Americans in buying land there but abandoned this plan when he realized it would fail. When questioned by Senator William Windom (R-MN) as to why blacks had moved to Kansas, Singleton replied that they had left the South for "want of land—we needed land for our children . . . pity for my race, sir, that was coming down, instead of going up." Singleton declared he was "the whole cause of the Kansas immigration."[20] He testified that his people would rather have stayed in the South but realized it was impossible: "Allow me to say to you that confidence is perished and faded away; they have been lied to every year. Every year when they have been going to work the crops, [whites] have said "I will do what is right to you," and just as soon as that man sees everything blooming and flourishing in the flowers and cotton blooms, he will look at that negro who has been his slave, and when he see him walk up to take his half of the crop it is too much for him to stand, and he just denies his word, he denies his contract."[21]

Former slaves were bitterly disappointed when they did not acquire land after the Civil War. Historian Steven Hahn writes in *A Nation under Our Feet* about the factors leading to the expectations of African Americans that they would be gifted with parcels of land. The ubiquitous black grapevine had promised them possession during the war, and the very visible signs of chaos in the region of their former masters reinforced the rumors. Certainly the federal government now controlled massive tracts of land, and former black Union army officers mentioned redistribution in speeches.[22] Hahn maintains that the "expectation of land distribution expressed almost universally held notions of just compensation for the travail of enslavement, of what was rightfully due those who tilled the soil, and of what would provide meaningful security in a postemancipation world."[23] Niles exploited the disillusionment of African Americans in his movement for slave reparations.

Singleton, who was astute and attuned to reality, was one of the first to realize that the aspirations of African Americans for land ownership in the South would never be met. However, free blacks had been operating small farms in Kansas since 1869.[24] In 1871, an organization of blacks in Alabama, the State Labor Union, asked George F. Marlow to visit Kansas. He reported that Kansas was "much more productive than other states. . . . The weather and roads enable you to do more work here than elsewhere, . . . The climate is mild and pleasant. . . . Winters short and require little food for stock. . . . Fruits of all kinds easily grown and sold at large profits."[25] If Marlow had visited Kansas during a mild winter, considering that the lush prairie he would have viewed in 1871 was far different from relatively grassless plains of today, it is easy to understand how he might have regarded the area as a paradise. Marlow's assessment that "the population is enterprising, towns and villages spring up rapidly, and great profits rise up for all investments" certainly characterized the activities of the white settlers already in northwestern Kansas.[26]

Singleton led colonizing groups into Kansas until 1879. When Van Burton Shaw conducted his sociological study of Nicodemus in 1949, he reported that he had "checked all the sources" and could not find a "specific connection between the activities of Singleton and the Nicodemus Colony."[27] Nevertheless, Nell Waldron asserted that the news of Singleton's success with colonization had stimulated interest in Negro immigration, which resulted in the organization of the colored people of Lexington, Kentucky.[28]

Although the movement to Nicodemus is often erroneously associated with the later Exoduster movement, in the beginning it comprised colonization groups. Nevertheless, a number of Exodusters found their way to Nicodemus. In a poster advertising Singleton's Real Estate and Homestead Association, he promoted the benefits of blacks moving as a group: "This association was gotten up for the benefit of the Colored Laboring Classes, both men and women, to purchase them large tracks of land, peaceful homes and firesides, undisturbed by any one. To do this we must be prudent and save our little means and blend together as a band of brothers and sisters; when we do this we will then march onward to peace and prosperity."[29]

Senator Windom spoke at a Washington, D.C., church on March 21, 1879, entitled "The Future of the Colored Race," and said that "the

Benjamin "Pap" Singleton. Courtesy of Kansas Historical Society.

westward movement of Negroes was not a new thing, that they had left Kentucky, Tennessee, and Missouri at a rate of from two to three thousand annually for some years."[30] Historian Robert Athearn pointed out that "Kansans had no objection to the arrival of black colonists, provided that they either paid for their land in the manner of other settlers or took government homesteads without asking their neighbors for financial assistance."[31]

Ironically, the black settlers' view of Kansas as the "Promised Land" belied the state's violent cultural history. Dubbed "Bleeding Kansas," the state attracted attention from the moment of territorial organization because of border wars with Missouri. With the passage of the Kansas-Nebraska Act in 1854, allowing the people in new territories to decide for themselves whether to allow slavery, the future state exploded. This period in Kansas's history introduced the national perception of the territory as being volatile, unpredictable, and occupied by unstable fanatics such as militant abolitionist John Brown.

Craig Miner, in his book *Kansas*, quotes Congressman William Seward as saying that "the circumstances of Kansas, and her relations toward the Union are peculiar, anomalous, and deeply interesting."[32] The journalist Noble Prentiss, who once visited Nicodemus, commented on the media's tendency to see "'something extraordinary, striking and unheard-of' in everything coming out of Kansas." The prestigious New York–based *Harper's Weekly* dramatized Kansas politics and exacerbated the state's reputation for extremes. The notorious instability of Kansas weather, with temperatures ranging from −40° to 121°F, provided local editors with opportunities to attract national attention. Some of these inflated images were based in fact: Kansas politics were turbulent and incomprehensible to outsiders, the erratic weather played havoc with an economy that depended on agriculture, and even mentioning John Brown in mixed political company was likely to provoke a fight.

Other dramatic stories coming out of Kansas did not require embellishment to horrify the reader. In 1867 Theodore Davis, an embedded reporter for *Harper's New Monthly Magazine*, filed daily notes about his harrowing journey across Kansas on the ill-fated Butterfield Overland Despatch Express. Although his trip report began benignly enough with physical details about the landscape, bullwhackers, messengers, and drivers, it soon became a macabre account of burned stage stations, Indian massacres, ruined waterholes, and scenes of tortured, staked-out stockmen.[33]

Although points in Kansas had been well-known stations for the Underground Railroad, the state had a very mixed history in attitudes toward African Americans. A number of slave-owning Missourians had moved into the territory before the passage of the Kansas-Nebraska Act, but an influx of New Englanders following the Civil War overwhelmingly outnumbered this group. In fact, before the failure of Reconstruction, only Union men—those who had not borne arms against the United States—could claim homestead land. At the time when Nicodemus was founded, African Americans were granted the right to vote through the passage of the Fifteenth Amendment and freely exercised their franchise. However, the Kansas constitution still had an outdated section stating that only "white males" had suffrage. This restriction, overruled by federal law, was not removed until 1888.[34]

There are no extant writings by the early settlers of Nicodemus that indicate any awareness of Kansas's troubled history. On the contrary, letters and speeches reflect enchantment with John Brown, a belief that they would soon own homes and land, and an expectation that they would be coming to a state that honored their humanity. Excited by the opportunity to create a new civilization, Abram T. Hall, E. P. McCabe, and John Niles would thrive on the challenges inherent in settling western Kansas. Their ability to influence Graham County politics discredited Isaiah Wears's belief that "if the United States Government cannot protect me in my rights in South Carolina, North Carolina, Alabama, and the other Southern States, I do not see how it can protect me in Kansas or Indiana."[35]

Although Wears believed that blacks would be better off staying in the South and fighting for their rights there, the forcefulness of residents of the Nicodemus colony proved that place could make a difference. The colonists united to acquire and keep land and affect regional politics. The white population of northwestern Kansas reluctantly assimilated this new energy and together with the African American newcomers fumbled toward a new concept of civilization on the prairie.

Chapter 2
Ho for Kansas!

Q. About what time did you lose all hope and confidence that your condition would be tolerable in the Southern States?

A. Well, we never lost all hopes in the world until 1877. . . . [E]very State in the South had got into the hands of the very men that held us slaves . . . holding the reins of government over our heads in every respect almost, even the constable up to the governor. . . . Then we said there was no hope for us and we had better go.
                                            Testimony of Henry Adams

THE LENGTHY AND RIVETING TESTIMONY of Henry Adams, a man described in the Minority Report of the Voorhees Committee as "an uneducated colored laborer, but a man of very unusual natural abilities," bore witness to the factors pushing the formerly enslaved out of the South and pulling them toward Kansas.[1] With the failure of Reconstruction, they had indeed lost "all hopes in the world."[2]

Although African Americans believed Kansas to be a place of racial harmony, the state had never been free of racial violence. Nevertheless, as historian Brent M. S. Campney has pointed out, Kansans were internalizing a narrative that identified their state as a fearless champion of universal freedom regardless of ethnicity. The belief grew that only the South collectively was capable of atrocities, while racial incidents in Kansas were anomalies perpetrated by deviant individuals.[3] The myth was bolstered by Kansas editors who fed on affirmation by the former abolitionists who flocked to the state. James N. Leiker has explored the writings of a number of contemporary historians who have challenged the myth that the state has been free of racial antagonism.[4] Graham County newspapers during settlement and Kansas newspapers statewide during McCabe's campaign for state office offer blatant examples of prejudice against African Americans.

The quest for political freedom was a motivating factor in establishing Nicodemus. Blacks left the South in droves as they were losing, not gaining, rights. The hopes of African Americans, as expressed by Henry Adams, were that the land promised by the federal government would materialize, that they would be truly free to exercise their constitutional right to vote, that they would be safe in their own homes; and that they would be able to establish schools and have access to education.

Loaded with political allegations, the third part of the *Voorhees Committee Report* focused on Kansas. The Senate committee's majority members, Daniel W. Voorhees, Zebulon B. Vance, and George H. Pendleton, believed that a vast Republican conspiracy accounted for the exodus of blacks from the South. In their summary of the investigation they charged that members of the extremely active aid societies operating in Kansas were all also active members of the Republican Party. Furthermore, they alleged that the whole purpose of luring ex-slaves to Kansas was to "remove a sufficient number of blacks from the South, where their votes could not be made to tell, into close States in the North, and thus turn the scale in favor of the Republican Party."[5]

However, the two minority members, William Windom and Henry W. Blair, asserted that "a long series of political persecutions, whippings, maimings, and murders committed by Democrats and in the interest of the Democratic party extending over a period of fifteen years, has finally driven the negro to despair and compelled him to seek peace and safety by flight."[6]

Consequently, the *Voorhees Committee Report* contains numerous references to blacks' despair over deprivation of voting rights. Jacob Stevens testified, "They shot my father because he was a radical. . . . On election days if a black man got a Republican ticket to vote they would say he was spotted, and that meant they were going to kill you."[7] Another man, Emile Auspitz, said that on election days armed Democrats at the polls "prevent the colored men from voting."[8] The volume of testimony about atrocities committed against blacks who dared to vote or affect political decisions stunned the Voorhees Committee.

After the Compromise of 1877, through which the South was permitted to "redeem" the former Confederate states, whites moved

Senator Daniel Wolsey Voorhees (D-IN). Courtesy of Library of Congress, Prints & Photographs Division.

immediately to secure their hold over ex-slaves. The two Republicans writing the Minority Report for the Voorhees Committee, Windom and Blair, reported in their final document that nearly all the witnesses who were asked to testify as to the causes of the exodus included denial of political rights as a major factor. African Americans were willing to die for their rights, and many of them did. Windom and Blair contended that beginning in September 1868, in Caddo Parish, Louisiana, over three days, there had been a "massacre of colored people" during which whites had killed "between two and three hundred colored people."

Henry Adams even wrote a letter to President Rutherford B. Hayes that contained a strong and moving appeal for protection based on natural rights. Adams informed Hayes that since he had not enforced the U.S. Constitution relative to the "amendments that [guarantee] protection to our race and color in the exercise of our rights, after twelve years we find the colored race of the South in worse condition than they were before."[9]

Not all blacks who came to Kansas before the Civil War were sympathetic to the plight of their southern kin. Intraracial hostility was present even during the colonization movement and accelerated during the massive migration into Kansas in 1879. William Twine, an African American minister from Atchison, Kansas, who was also engaged in "real estate, house-renting, and employment business," stated that Kansans "are not pleased with these people, not because they are colored people, but because they are of that class that Kansas has no use for in the world, whether black or white."[10] Twine further stated that there were two classes of immigrants and that "the class of men from Kentucky and Tennessee is of a different class from those of the other Southern States." Nevertheless, Twine, who had lived there since 1862, insisted that the allegedly better class of blacks were not welcome either, because cheap labor threatened the livelihoods of longtime Kansas residents.

The first groups to arrive in Nicodemus came from Kentucky. Modern-day descendants of these settlers maintain that white slaveholders often treated their ancestors like family.[11] Historically, slaves in Kentucky and Tennessee often developed superb skills as carpenters, blacksmiths, brick masons, coopers, and factory workers, and they freely hired out to individuals other than their white owners. This inherent sense of independence might account for the bold approach of the newly arrived settlers of Nicodemus—atypical of ex-slaves—to relationships with the white population.

However, even with this "better class," the cold truth was that they had been owned body and soul and subject to their owners' will.

Kentucky and Tennessee were active participants in the lucrative and brutal internal slave trade. White owners often cruelly separated families. Even though most Kentucky slaves lived on small farms averaging about five slaves each and participated in fairly diverse agricultural operations, they lived in fear of being sold "down the river"—that is, to new owners from southern states such as Alabama and Mississippi whose vast cotton plantations depended on slave labor.

Even though the United States no longer imported slaves, W. E. B. Du Bois wrote that there was a "widely organized slave trade between the Border States [the Upper South] and the Cotton Kingdom of the Southern South; it led to neglect and the breaking up of families." Interstate slave marketing led to "commercial breeding" in the owners' search for profit. Du Bois noted that "cotton planters were supplied with laborers from the Border States" and said the selling of blacks "was a nasty business."[12]

After the Civil War, whites often took advantage of former slaves to provide human fodder for the barbaric system of convict labor that was nearly indistinguishable from slavery. When a black man came close to achieving his goal of owning land, he lived in fear of being jailed on a trumped-up charge, sent to work on a chain gang, and having his property confiscated. Nell Painter wrote that whites believed that if blacks were "not allowed to acquire property or become landholders, they must ultimately return to plantation labor, and work for wages."[13] But many of the formerly enslaved were too bitter to return to their previous owners as paid laborers.

One narrative collected by Lulu Craig, attributed to "an ex-slave who came from Kentucky to Graham County in one of W. Hill's parties," bore witness to the shock, exultation, but then despair with which African Americans reacted to emancipation. Born on Willis Viley's plantation in Scott County, Kentucky, the narrator showed tremendous empathy for his owner, describing when the old man called all the slaves to gather around the big house and "with his white hair blowing in the breeze" announced they were all free. He looked "sad, so sad; we knew why. Only one of the three boys who had gone to war returned and he was heart-broken and sick." The freed people sang and shouted, and "many of the older people dropped down on their knees" to "thank God for deliverance."[14]

The next day, reality dawned, when Viley kicked them out, telling them, "You must go. Get out and find places for yourselves and make homes of your own." The narrator says that they "stood speechless": "Leave home! Where could we go? Everyone went slowly back to the quarters. I tell you, that was a sad, sad, time. That was our home. We had never known any other. Yet we must go, and as we could claim nothing nor demand anything, we prepared to depart." Years later the narrator told Craig that he thought often about that day:

> Of our leaving with nothing when we had raised and put up such a great quantity of crops and foods. There was a big smoke house, full of meat; barrels of lard, sugar, molasses and flour, in the storehouse. There was plenty of everything on the place; yet he sent us away without giving us so much as a slice of bacon or a spoonful of flour or meal. . . . My gaze wandered on up to the slope to where the brick mansion stood in beauty and security, offering comfort to those inside. While I looked I was almost overpowered by sadness, lonliness [sic], and humiliation.
>
> To think that here I had spent my life, working faithfully, interested at all times in the success and progress of the plantation. . . . Now to be driven off as if I had committed a crime. It was distressing.[15]

One of the freedman's children died of exposure during his attempt to find work, food, and shelter. However, in ten years the narrator adapted to his new circumstances and learned to read and write. He even managed to save enough money to make the trip to Kansas and secure the "home we had wished for all those years by homesteading here in Graham County and sticking to it through thick and thin." He declared that he "never wished to return to the plantation."[16]

Other Nicodemus settlers regretted moving to the colony. The former editor of the nearby *Rooks County Record*, W. L. Chambers, wrote that he met "one old mammy who hungered for the fleshpots of the plantation, and anathematized Abe Linkun [sic] for setting her free from her good old Massa." But some who left Nicodemus regretted not sticking it out. One such man, whom Craig met in Emporia twenty-six years later, told her: "I did not think anyone could live in a place like that. There was nothing to be seen, not a tree, not a house, not a drop of water, except away down to the river. I have never dreamed of seeing any one from that desolate place." He asked Craig a number of questions about the community. After she told him that there were now comfortable homes, good farms, and a lot of stock, he said, "I wish I had stayed; because I have worked hard here and have saved nothing. But, Oh Lord, it was the barest place I ever seed. I thought I could not stay. I walked away."[17]

In addition to escaping an increasingly hostile political environment, Kentucky African Americans were pushed westward by an "unprecedented depression in business." The *Kentucky Gazette*, an influential paper based in Lexington, Scott County, home to the first and second groups of emigrants to Nicodemus, reported in January 1877, "A severer winter or a more protracted one has not been experienced within a century."[18]

There is little to indicate in the *Kentucky Gazette* that the social climate there was any more amenable to blacks post–Civil War than the Deep South during harsh economic times. The editor, discussing the harsh winter, wrote, "It is painful to witness the suffering among the poor negroes who were thrown out from good homes and kind masters by abolition cruelty to freeze and to starve, and thousands are now bitterly regretting the change from human slavery, to a cold and hungry freedom that is gradually, but surely extinguishing their unhappy race."[19] These words from a "moderate" southern state indicate barely a whit of empathy for the yearning of African Americans to exercise their political rights and realize the goal of owning land.

"Ho for Kansas!" urged Pap Singleton in the widely circulated flyer distributed by his Real Estate and Homestead Association.[20] With the increasing violence, the treachery involved in the sharecropping system, and the hostility of whites who were often preempting jobs formerly held by skilled black workers, Kentucky African Americans were highly susceptible to such propaganda.

Ho for Kansas!

Brethren, Friends, & Fellow Citizens:

I feel thankful to inform you that the

REAL ESTATE
AND
Homestead Association,

Will Leave Here the

15th of April, 1878,

In pursuit of Homes in the Southwestern Lands of America, at Transportation Rates, cheaper than ever was known before.

For full information inquire of

Benj. Singleton, better known as old Pap,
NO. 5 NORTH FRONT STREET.

Beware of Speculators and Adventurers, as it is a dangerous thing to fall in their hands.

Nashville, Tenn., March 18, 1878.

"Ho! for Kansas"—Benjamin Singleton's real estate poster. Courtesy of Kansas Historical Society.

Although the surge into Kansas of ex-slaves known as Exodusters was separate from the carefully planned and organized colonization, the two movements occasionally overlapped. Nicodemus began as a planned colony, but Exodusters sometimes trickled into the town. In 1879, a Topeka paper reported that "there are three men from Virginia here who want to get to Nicodemus." The wives of two of the men were still in Brazil, Indiana.[21]

Moreover, some of the witnesses during the Voorhees investigation stated that whites made had violent attempts as early as 1877 to prevent blacks from moving to Kansas, which was two years before the label "Exodusters" was attached to the massive black migration in 1879. John Cummings, in an affidavit introduced by Charlton H. Tandy, swore:

> They would not let me vote; the men at the polls told me they would shoot me if I voted the Republican ticket; they said if I did not vote the right ticket I would vote none at all. . . . I saw four men killed at a Republican speech at Vicksburg; we had been in the house hearing speeches and four men came in the back door and said, "Get out of here all you damn sons of bitches," and fired right into the crowd and killed four of the colored men; don't know who they were; that was in December, 1877. . . . All the negroes South are Republicans, or most of them. I have heard of other colored men being killed for political reasons. About forty killed out on the Jackson road, and about four out on the Valley road; these four I know of myself; one of them was a minister; after they were killed they would not be allowed to be removed, but they were left there and the buzzards ate them up. This was about the same time, in 1877.[22]

In another affidavit, Edward Parlor reported that a "white club was stopping the colored people from going to Kansas." When the members of the club went to a black man's house, the man escaped, and when they asked his pregnant wife if she was going to Kansas, "She said she was, and they took her and hung her, and while she was hanging she had a baby right under the gallows."[23]

W. R. Hill, a white speculator from Indiana, launched the initial campaign to lure blacks to Nicodemus. Through the cooperation of several black ministers, he presented his plans in churches in Lexington and Georgetown, Kentucky. Hill incorporated Nicodemus on July 1877 with six African American men: W. H. Smith, Ben Carr, S. P. Roundtree, Jerry Allsap, William Edmunds, and Jeff Lenze. Lulu Craig's manuscript history of Nicodemus also lists an advisory board composed of Anderson Boles, John Scott, John Anderson, Henry Buckner and Charles Page. She credits the following people as being instrumental in founding the colony: Thomas and Henry Johnson (father and son), Mr. and Mrs. Hugh Brown, Charles Williams, Charles Reynolds, Jacob Martin, William Stemmons, S. P. Roundtree, Rev. Silas Lee and Willis Lee (father and son), John DePrad, Beverly Herring, Grant Harris, George Dorsey and his mother (Mrs. Tabitha Dorsey), Mrs. Patterson and her daughter Georgiana, Maria Miles, Margaret Jackson, Jefferson Lindsey, Ben Dorsen, Rankin Booker, and John Scott.

Urban black settlements in Topeka and Wyandotte, Kansas, were growing rapidly at the time. In the spring of 1877, W. H. Smith, S. P. Roundtree, secretary of the town company, and Zachary T. Fletcher, one of the investors, organized thirty African Americans living in Topeka who were originally from Kentucky.[24] They became the founding fathers and organizers of Nicodemus. The only woman in the group was Jenny Fletcher, daughter of W. H. Smith and wife of Zachary (Zack) Fletcher. She became the first schoolteacher. This first colony arrived in Nicodemus in July. Historian Kenneth Hamilton wrote that those who wanted to live in Nicodemus paid the town company five dollars and those who wanted homestead land paid Hill a location fee of between two dollars and thirty dollars.[25] In autumn 1877 another 350 arrived from Kentucky. In March 1878 the *Ellis County Star* reported, "Some two hundred colored people, headed by Agent Hill, arrived in Ellis this morning from Kentucky, enroute for the Nicodemus colony." The editor went on to observe that when "this re-enforcement reaches Nicodemus, it will swell the number of that colony to considerably over five hundred."[26]

Most of the migrants traveled by rail. However, some colonists migrating from Kentucky boarded "packet" boats and began their journey on the Ohio River. Although these riverboats were sturdy and had

W. R. Hill, land speculator, founder of Hill City, Kansas. Courtesy of Kansas Historical Society.

majestic names, such as *Grand Tower* and *Belle of Memphis*, their conditions were squalid, crammed with migrants and all their possessions. Packet boats had four decks. From bottom to top these were the main deck, which housed the boiler room, engine room, and cargo space; the passenger deck; the crew's quarters; and the pilothouse, which contained all the navigation equipment.[27] The Kentucky emigrants' cargo included animals and tools they needed to start their new lives. Leaving the Ohio, they then went up the Mississippi River, and finally they transferred to another boat to travel up the Missouri to Wyandotte, Kansas (now Kansas City).

From Wyandotte, the first group of settlers went on to Topeka, where they benefited from the largesse of the extremely active Kansas Freedmen's Relief Association, which paid their $21 per person railway fare to Ellis.[28] It was forty more miles to Nicodemus. Guided by a compass and the stars, they walked and drove their meager assortment of livestock.

Hill had filed the 160-acre town plot with the federal land office in Kirwin on June 8, 1877. When the colonists arrived, the founders allowed them to purchase a membership certificate in the Nicodemus Town Company for a mere five dollars. This fee was in addition to the five dollars paid up front for the cost of transportation and inclusion in the group migrating to Kansas. Few of the settlers had any use for membership in the town company. Their goal was to acquire land. In the early years of Kansas's town-building mania, lots could go as high as $600, and speculators got rich.[29] Historian Kenneth Marvin Hamilton in his study of the origins of the settlement asserted, "The desire for profit inspired the founding and early promotion of Nicodemus, Kansas."[30] But Hill also had a political motive, and ultimately his political maneuvering dovetailed with economic considerations. Hill wanted these new African American settlers to vote for Hill City, his proposed white community, as the county seat. County seats were a guaranteed source of wealth, and their citizens often voted bonds to finance construction of railroads. Often county seats were the only towns that survived.

The economic return from funding black communities was unknown, but Hill aggressively courted the new black voters. Hill's courtship of black voters differed little from the targeting of specific interest groups in elections today. Foolishly insensitive, he stated in 1879 in the *Gettysburg (Kans.) Lever*, "We will have to make concessions to the niggers and give them a few offices, but when we get the county seat at Hill City, they may go to hell."[31]

However, Hill had not counted on the atypical psychological makeup of the African Americans who flocked to Nicodemus. Both freeborn people and freedpeople demonstrated an unusual degree of assertiveness from the beginning. When the first group of colonists realized the extent to which Hill's propaganda had misled, they tried to hang him.[32] Hill fled to a friend's dugout, and the lady of the house, a Mrs. Lawlis, was said to have hidden Hill behind her shawl. He was later smuggled to Stockton under a load of hay. Sixty disillusioned families in that first colony headed back to Kentucky the next day.[33] Another group, arriving in 1879, claimed that Hill had told them that their freight bill would be paid in advance, when in fact it was not. The blacks were forced to camp out in WaKeeney, and Hill tried to pawn some of their goods to pay the bill. This same unfortunate colony lost a team of horses at that time, when an approaching train frightened them. Nicodemus historian Orval McDaniel wrote that there was no record of "what happened over this affair" and said the "freight bill trouble came up every time Hill brought a group by rail." Moreover, Hill collected "as much as thirty dollars for locating on a hundred and sixty acres of land that was being given free by the government."[34]

Hill's motive for founding Nicodemus provoked a lively discussion in the local papers. A column in the *Hays City Sentinel* criticized a "deadbeat, named Hill, who is anxious to induce a sufficient number of people to emigrate to that county to enable him to perfect an organization of the county, and then vote school district and county bonds, for his personal benefit."[35] While Hill clearly underestimated the resourcefulness of the collection of people he had gotten to colonize Graham County, so did the surrounding white community. In April 1877, before the founders began their intense promotion of Nicodemus, the *Stockton News* reported: "Hillsdale has just received reinforcements. Two lineal descendants of Ham passed through this place last Friday.... The outfit with which they traveled was an old spring wagon occupying both sides and the middle of the road, drawn by an old gray horse that voted for General Jackson, and a three-legged mule that served in the Revolutionary War."[36] Yet a mere two years later, the same editor would refer to black men from Nicodemus by using "sir" and "mister" and "distinguished residents of Nicodemus."

Abram T. Hall quickly reversed his initial impression of Nicodemus. By June he was writing letters to the editors of various newspapers with positive accounts of life in Kansas.[37] Since he and McCabe had arrived in the spring of 1878, they had escaped the extreme hardships of the first winter. His appraisal jibed with Henry Adams's assessment that blacks would receive better treatment in northern states and that it was time for African Americans to leave the South for a region where they could claim their natural rights as humans. While their first year would be extremely trying, the colonists who established the first black community on the Great Plains would exert remarkable control over local, county, and state affairs from the beginning of settlement. It would have been impossible for ex-slaves to achieve this degree of influence and authority in the South. The magnitude of their success would not have been possible in any state other than Kansas because of their substantial land ownership, made possible through the Homestead Act, coupled with the capable leadership of Hall, McCabe, and Niles.

The formerly enslaved John W. Niles blossomed in this new setting. As secretary of the Nicodemus colony and one of its seven founding officers, he exploited his status within the colony and the state, and he clearly was more controversial than any other person in Nicodemus. About half a century later, in 1925, the former editor of the *Rooks County Record*, W. L. Chambers, published *Niles of Nicodemus*, a monograph bearing the subtitle *Exploiter of Kansas Exodusters, Negro Indemnity and Equality of Blacks with Whites His Obsession, Beats Bankers, Bench and Barristers; Counter League to Post War K.K.K. Riots and Finally Prison*. In it Chambers describes Niles as "a flamboyant figure, well fed and groomed, rotund, flashily clothed in garments of fine texture, wearing heavy rings on hands uncalloused by manual toil." Some Nicodemus colonists had accused Niles of pocketing donated cash during the Leavenworth trip, but Lulu Craig defended his role in securing supplies for the colony and insisted that Niles had withheld only a small sum to defray his expenses. In Kansas historian George Root's "A Biographical Sketch of Daniel Hickman," Root quotes Hickman as declaring that Niles would always be "remembered with veneration by the older members of the colony," because he was able to obtain assistance after the colonists' first terrible winter on the plains. But Chambers's take on Niles is more nuanced. Chambers recalls that when he first met Niles, before Hall and McCabe arrived, the man's leadership was undisputed. As Niles "strode down the path," then about thirty-five years old, he was greeted deferentially by all. Chambers remembers Nile as having a smile that was "gracious though condescending," and his greetings as effusive: "full of vitality, poise and self-conceit."[38]

According to a letter that Niles sent to Governor St. John February 25, 1880, he had come from Kentucky, where he had left behind a wife and four small boys. He told St. John that his family was starving and begged for assistance to get them to Kansas. However, he may have invented the information. He had been in Nicodemus for two and a half years without returning to his native state when he wrote the letter. If he had a family at all, he would not have known how they fared. St. John politely replied in a letter dated March 2 that he had "no means" which he could use in "bringing your family from Ky. to Kans., otherwise I would gladly do so."[39]

Other than this letter, there is no evidence that Niles was concerned about his family. The record suggests the opposite. Recalling Niles in Nicodemus "sporting a fine white team of ponies and a shining buggy," Chambers writes that Niles "beguiled many dusky damsels of the colony into relations that did not comport with the strict notions of the devout elderly people composing its substantial citizenry; and in time he lost his hold on them." Chambers quotes a *Stockton Record* editor who was more crude, calling Niles was "a fat mass of black ignorance and conceit, carrying 250 pounds of odoriferous averdupois [sic] and less than an ounce of brains or common sense."[40]

However, such information, it must be considered, was filtered through an all too prevalent patronizing racial bias. For instance, Chambers writes: "I never met in those days a darkey who wasn't grinning, singing or praying. Life was ever sweet to him. With progress, education and greater creature comforts, has come the white man's care; and now the colored folk are serious and often sad in facial expression."[41] Regardless of Niles's questionable character, he played a vital role in creating and insuring the survival of the community. Having been a slave himself, he was a passionate advocate of civil rights.

The "Ho for Kansas!" flyer encapsulated the hopes of an oppressed citizenry that life would be better in another part of the country, away from the upsurge in murder, rape, property destruction, theft, swindling, and annihilation of civil rights. Yet the federal government thought the flight of former slaves from the South so perplexing that it called for formal investigation by a special Senate committee. The *Voorhees Committee Report* would illuminate attitudes of white people toward race and migration, as it would also provide a glimpse into the differing opinions held by African Americans. What is certain is this: the desire for political freedom pulled ex-slaves into a region formerly viewed as uninhabitable. Residents of Nicodemus would demonstrate that blacks were as capable of making a life on the plains as their white counterparts, and they would quickly seize political opportunities. And some ex-slaves, such as John Niles, would achieve a status on the Kansas prairie that would have been impossible in the South.

Chapter 3
Kansas—Sure but Slow Poison

Q. What are you going to say to the people down there about going to Kansas?

A. I will tell them it will be a race which they will do first, starve to death or freeze to death. . . . I tell you this Kansas business is just like rot-gut whisky; it is slow but sure poison to a negro. The fact is, I was out of heart, because I was out of money: and a man without money in Kansas totes a low head.

Testimony of Philip Brookings

IN HIS TESTIMONY to the Voorhees Committee, Philip Brookings, an African American from Yazoo, Mississippi, accurately summed up the main sources of disillusionment for both black and white immigrants lured to Kansas by the aggressive publicity campaigns. There were few jobs, the extremely variable weather frightened immigrants who came from gentler climates, and it was difficult to obtain food and fuel on the Great Plains. Hence, as Brookings pointed out, a man without money in Kansas "totes a low head." Southern blacks continued to praise Kansas's potential and rejoiced when families and friends immigrated to the state, but some hedged their bets. One group headed for Nicodemus was "accompanied as far as Topeka by a brass band that gave concerts to raise money for transportation back to Kentucky."[1]

The notoriously inflammatory western Kansas editors paid a great deal of attention to Nicodemus from the beginning of its settlement. As historian David Dary says, they had been "outspoken crusaders on differing sides of the slavery question since before the Civil War."[2] However, since their papers were usually subsidized by town companies, their commentary tended to skew in favor of attracting people of means to the plains, rather than destitute immigrants who would be a burden. Thus, the *Hays City Sentinel* reported that when the "residents of Graham County saw the 210 colored people surging over the Solomon bluffs like an ominous cloud, they were perturbed in spirit."[3]

The second group of Nicodemus settlers came from Kentucky, where cash was not necessary for survival. Cheap lumber was available for fuel and building homes. It was easy to trap game and grow crops. Jobs were plentiful, and there was a market for ex-slaves' manual labor. In Kansas, however, there was little farm work available. A. J. Allen, a railroad attorney living in Ottawa, Kansas, testified before the Voorhees Committee that most of the farms there consisted of "smooth bottom land and upland prairie, and the farming is done by machinery." He assured the senators that blacks could acquire free land only in the western part of the state, and he said that it would not be possible for them to survive there, as it was as much as "many good white men could do." Some blacks agreed with the attorney's assessment. The *Kentucky Gazette* smugly reported, "Cage Banks, colored, late of Brandon Mississippi, writes from Kansas to say that he had rather live in the Mississippi penitentiary than in Kansas."[4]

Blacks bore an added burden of racial prejudice, although, as promised, white Kansans were much more likely than whites in the South to give immigrants of all ethnic origins a chance to prove themselves based on character. A number of European settlers in the western half of the state were determined to "treat the colored people exactly the same as if they were white people in like circumstances," historian Craig Miner writes.[5] To Kansans, the determining factor for assessing the quality of newcomers to the Great Plains was whether they could prevail against the environmental odds. Kansans took perverse pride in their state motto, "*Ad astra per aspera*" (To the stars through difficulties), as if that which could be acquired easily lacked merit.

However, coping in a strange land requires adequate information and preparation. W. R. Hill had stated in his handbill of 1877 that the first colonists coming to Nicodemus would find buildings erected, an abundance of supplies, houses, well-platted streets, and business.[6] Instead they found a barren, treeless prairie, and with winter coming they struggled to survive. There was not even a well yet—water had to be carried from a creek.[7] A correspondent from the *Atchison Daily Champion* later wrote, "The valley of the south fork of the Solomon is not, beyond Stockton, the most fertile or beautiful body of land on earth. There is a proneness to sand; a tendency to cactus."[8]

During the Voorhees Committee hearings a number of witnesses expressed concern about blacks moving to a cold climate. When Senator Voorhees, who doubted the ability of African Americans to survive in western Kansas, questioned A. S. Johnson, a land commissioner of the Atchison, Topeka and Santa Fe Railroad, he asked if Kansas was the frontier. Johnson replied that indeed it was "the extreme frontier, outside of civilization." He added, "Of course they have got to have fuel—coal. Coal is gold, money, cash, out there. They have got to have homes. If they got there and have not homes, they have got to have fire and protection from storms, and if they have not the means to get it they suffer and freeze to death out on those prairies in winter. They cannot expect to live without some means, and it is absolute folly to send them out on the frontier. It is inhumanity, and they ought to know it."[9]

However, others thought differently. The editor of the *Ellis Standard* reported the arrival in Nicodemus of the first group of blacks from Lexington, Kentucky, and noted several carloads of "goods, furniture, and provisions." Thus, the editor wrote, "We conclude that these dusky sons and daughters of the South who, as the Israelites of old, have wandered in search of a new home, have enough of everything to make a decent start in this land."[10] A correspondent to the *Hays City Sentinel* refuted this optimistic assessment in a letter to the editor signed "Bismark," asserting that "Mr. Hill, or any of his associates at Topeka, or elsewhere, cares no more for the colored man or his welfare than they do for the smallest insect that crawls. . . . As we look on the surface of that affair, it looks to an outsider perfectly honorable: but underneath that honest appearance, lies a plot that when once brought to light, well can the people say "lo, the poor Negro! . . . Many of them haven't money enough to last one month, to say nothing of the coming twelve months that will have to pass before they can raise a crop for the market."[11]

As "Bismark" suggested, the amount of cash that would have enabled settlers of any ethnicity to survive in other climates simply was not enough on the Great Plains. Lulu Craig wrote that most of the settlers had "a little money," but it didn't help because "the markets were too far away." The nearest town with a market, Ellis, was forty miles distant.[12]

W. H. Smith, president of the Nicodemus Town Company, immediately fired back that Bismark's words had "the sound of the old Democratic whiskey party" and that "although not over-burdened with money, we do not want the public to labor under the impression that we are paupers." Smith pointed out that despite the distance, the colonists' trade in "Ellis alone in the past sixty days has not been less than three hundred dollars."[13] Nevertheless, by the time winter arrived in late 1877, the colonists who had arrived in September had very little cash and indeed "hung a low head."

In addition to the shock delivered by the misleading propaganda handbills no one had prepared the immigrants for the extreme weather and natural disasters they would face in western Kansas. For instance, in 1880, the *Stockton Record* would report a temperature of 107 degrees in the shade in May.[14] A little over a month later the *Stockton News* reported a hailstorm with an eighteen-inch accumulation, which nearly destroyed the town of Roscoe.[15] The *Roscoe Tribune* classified it a cyclone and reported one citizen's stone building in ruins "and his residence removed to the center of the street."[16] By late December that year the thermometer would drop to eighteen degrees below zero.[17] Elam Bartholomew, a Rooks County botanist whose collections later became famous worldwide, faithfully tracked the region's weather. Bartholomew said that he gave only "comparative temperatures of the weather and not the absolute as our common thermometers vary so much that they are of scarcely any practical value."[18]

During the summer of 1878, a prairie fire killed two men from the Nicodemus colony, Peter Jackson and Henry Blackman.[19] The fire also destroyed hay and corn residents had counted on to see them through the winter of 1878–79. Kansas stood in stark contrast to their gentle Kentucky, with its predictable and moderate climate. Nevertheless, most of the African Americans who migrated to Kansas adapted. J. W. Wheeler, a contractor in St. Louis who inspected tobacco, testified before the Voorhees Committee that he had warned newcomers that they could not "live through the weather, clothed as they were: they would have to go back South." The immigrants had responded, however, that "they had only one death to die, and they might as well die in the North as in the South."[20]

An unanticipated problem during the colonists' first weeks after arriving in September 1877 was the lack of light after the sun went down. No one had thought to bring candles or lanterns, as they had expected to find an established town. Although a few had grease lamps, there was no grease to burn. Lulu Craig wrote, "Even the beasts cower in the darkness." For a people used to working hard in the evening and nighttime, the absence of light was profoundly unsettling. The families were confined to their dugouts from sundown to sunup. At first a few men had ventured out at night with the intention of visiting a neighboring dugout, but they had often lost their way and had to wait until dawn to find their way home. After their first trip to Ellis for supplies, men brought back "gallon jugs of coal oil, matches, some lamps and four lanterns," Craig writes. A box of two dozen matches cost ten cents.[21]

As A. S. Johnson testified, new arrivals had to have shelter. Time was of the essence for the colonists who came in September, as the weather often turns in October on the plains. Clayton Fraser wrote that the colonists first erected lean-to tents, but the wind blew the sheets from the frames.[22] Then they resorted to dugouts, working quickly, in common, to finish as many as possible before winter cold arrived. Dugouts constructed by their white counterparts were often about five feet underground, with three-foot sod walls above ground.[23] Unfortunately, Nicodemus settlers lacked the equipment needed to cut sod. They covered the tops of their dugouts with poles from "timber growing along the river, cottonwood, hackberry," says Craig, placed brush on the poles, and then "grass was put on top to support a generous cover of dirt and magnesia, a lime stone composition, supposed to prevent leaking." They leaked anyway. Those who had bedding used it to shield the doorways, while others placed tall grass or willow branches in the entries to check the wind.[24]

Nicodemus colonists hacked away at the sod with hoes until they had hollowed out burrows where they could survive the frigid Kansas winter. Since this type of construction depended on hills and ravines, the settlement was "scattered over an area twelve miles long and six miles wide."[25]

As the weather turned colder, discouraged by the constant quest for fuel, families often went to bed early to keep from freezing. They gathered sunflower stalks, grass, and willow, but these "flashed out as fast as they could be put on the fire," Craig writes. Buffalo chips were a slower burning source of fuel, but before long the chips were covered by snow. There was an abundance of game, but the colonists lacked long-range rifles.[26]

Reverend Daniel Hickman later recalled his anxiety over shelter and the difficulty of constructing a dugout with "spades and grubbing hoes."[27] His wife, Willianna, said that her family had hated to see her leave for the West, so her brother, J. A. Lewis, had been persuaded to go with her to help.[28] The Hickmans came with the third group of colonists, arriving in March 1878, and stayed in the dugout of Mrs. Hickman's good friend, Raz Kirtley, who had come with the group from Kentucky in September 1877.[29] Mrs. Hickman would recall being heartsick from the death of some of the migrant children and exhausted by the long trip: "No words can describe the suffering and heartaches of the ones that had to lay their children into bare graves with not even a box to protect their little bodies. They could not spare any of their clothes or bedding as they did not have enough to care for the sick children and make them comfortable. So the ones that passed away were wrapped in anything they could find or spare. Some gathered grass or leaves to put under and over them for some protection from the bare earth." After her husband filed papers on a claim west of Nicodemus, she felt very "homesick and unhappy in this strange bare country," but she "finally became reconciled to her western home."[30]

There was no easy way for the settlers to obtain food. Without horses to chase down the "abundant game" promised by the circulars, the settlers depended on contributions of food and clothing during the first terrible winter. Friends in Topeka sent aid, as did sympathizers living in Leavenworth, Kansas. The *Manhattan Enterprise* reported that citizens of Leavenworth gave $25.75 in cash and 2,400 pounds of provisions. Kansas City also sent a carload of goods.[31]

Two men from Salina, the Reverends W. A. Simkins and J. H. Lockwood, representing the Presbyterian church there, visited the colony to assess the condition of the settlers and reported that the people of Nicodemus were living "merely on bread and water" and that "sharpers" had "defrauded them of considerable money." However, Simkins and Lockwood were amazed at the setters' progress, saying, "We found them in better shape than we feared. They have shown much industry and considerable skill in constructing their cabins or half dugouts; they have indeed done a great deal of hard work since they sat down upon the raw prairie forty miles northwest of Ellis six months ago. They have had to do most of the work in getting material for their homes with their hands and backs, 'toting' it together on their backs, as there is but one little pony team in the whole colony." The two ministers concluded that in addition to food and clothing the church would send chickens and invest in two teams of oxen and loan them to the settlers, with the intention of selling the teams later. With typical Kansas prudence, they added, "Our aim shall be to give them only such help as they absolutely need, and help that will put them in shape to help themselves."[32]

Then assistance came from an unexpected source: American Indians. Oral tradition within the Nicodemus community credits the Osage Indians, returning from their annual hunt, with supplying buffalo meat to the settlers, and Hamilton's research supports this account.[33] Historically, however, the Osage people had divisive dealings with whites over the dark-skinned people they referred to as *Nika-Sabes* (black men). The Civil War had split the tribe in two, with the Great Osage band fighting with the Confederate army and the Little Osages fighting with the Union. Also, the Osages had been forcibly moved by the federal government close to the Kansas-Missouri line, where they were exposed to the excesses of the border wars, and, as historian John Joseph Matthews writes, "They couldn't see any reason for these wild, unthinking men murdering each other, burning houses and whole communities, and shouting themselves into uncontrollable emotionalism."[34] Therefore, it is quite likely the Osages gave the Nika-Sabes a wide berth. There is conflicting evidence that the Potawatomi people, rather than the Osages, helped the settlers.

The *Stockton News* noted on August 9, 1877, that "last Saturday about seventy-five Pottawatomie Indians (men, women, and children) passed west through this place, en route for the buffalo range." Their route would have taken them through Nicodemus on the way back. The website of the Prairie Band Potawatomi Nation contains an account of helping the settlers, based on a story handed down to William Mzhickteno: "On the return trip through Graham County, the hunting party came across the crude settlement of Nicodemus. They found a black settlement whose members were 'helplessly stranded, hungry and without any means of shelter.' . . . They decided to return the next day and help the settlers cut slough grass from a nearby creek, teaching them to build shelters similar to their own tribal homes. . . . The Great Spirit touched the hearts of the hunting party, and they agreed to give the Nicodemus settlers half their buffalo meat."[35]

McDaniel's "History of Nicodemus" contains information supporting the Osage account, saying that Nettie Craig, one the early schoolteachers in the colony, stated that the Osages had just received their quarterly subsistence supplies at Fort Ogallah, and they "shared with the negroes."[36] Perhaps both tribes assisted the colonists.

Philanthropic institutions across Kansas were aware of Nicodemus. John D. Knox, treasurer of the Relief Board of Kansas, testified before the Voorhees Committee that the Nicodemus colony had refused aid from his organization. He claimed that he had spoken with a man there who said that "it was wonderful how they were getting along." Knox added that eventually the Nicodemus settlers did need help and the conference sent teams of horses.[37] In October 1879, Elizabeth Comstock of the Orthodox Friends Society planned to visit Nicodemus with her daughter, Carrie De Green. Comstock had a worldwide reputation for good works. She had advised and assisted President Lincoln during the war and, according the *Topeka Capital*, "addressed women's meetings at Belfast, Dublin and London."[38]

J. W. Wheeler testified that most of the African Americans continuing to Kansas from St. Louis did not entertain ideas of Kansas "flowing with milk and honey." He said that they had no expectations of receiving "forty acres of land and a mule and that all they expected was a "chance to make a living."[39] The problem for the Nicodemus settlers was that there was no one hiring laborers for agricultural work.

In addition to the large formally organized colonies populating Nicodemus, families and individuals arrived in the community who were not part of any group. African Americans freely moved in and out of

Nicodemus on a temporary or permanent basis. Some of the residents returned to towns in eastern Kansas during the winter. The *Atchison Champion* noted that "a considerable number of colored Kentuckians who went out to Graham County last fall and took claims, returned to this city for the winter, and when spring fairly opens will go back to their locations."[40] However, most of the settlers, did not have Eastern Kansas relations who could take them in during the winter months.

The first Christmas in Nicodemus was trying, as it was preceded by a heavy snowstorm. Traditionally Christmas had been the most joyous time of the year for slaves. In the words of historian Kenneth Stampp, "Even the severest masters gave their slaves Christmas day to celebrate." There was more food in abundance than usual, and often planters relaxed their policy of keeping alcohol away from blacks.[41]

As Christmas 1877 approached in Nicodemus, however, there was no food for the starving colonists. Lulu Craig writes that they recalled Christmases past with "goose, duck, chicken, shoat, or 'possum," but, though they still had a little money, they had no way to travel through heavy snow to the store in Ellis. Miraculously, two days before Christmas, young men from nearby Bow Creek came by, and the colonists bought some wild turkeys from them. And the next day another party passed through the settlement and "peddled some deer and antelope meat to them," and "by dividing, exchanging and planning, each family was able to prepare a holiday feast that baffled criticism, and that dinner was never forgotten by those pioneers." Craig concludes this narrative with a testimony about the ex-slaves' gratitude for the "gift of the Babe of Bethlehem, that came to be the light of a darkened and saddened world." The colonists held a prayer service and sang "Deck the Halls," "Joy to the World," "Oh Little Town of Bethlehem," and "other songs of equal beauty."[42]

Adding to the stress of environmental challenges, there were a number of violent incidents over the colonists' claims in and around Graham County during their first year of settlement. According to the Daniel Hickman, one murder might have been racially motivated. Hickman's account is related by George Root, archivist and historian at the Kansas State Historical Society, who compiled Hickman's biographical information. Root recorded Hickman's following account of the murder of John Landis who surveyed land for the colonists:

> The first job of the colonists on arriving at the new location was to secure the services of a surveyor who could survey the lands up in tracts in such sizes as would suit the needs of the various colonists. Some opposition developed in this and adjoining counties, at the settlement of the Negroes in the vicinity, and no surveyor in Graham county could be induced to take the job of making the survey. The difficulty was overcome by the colonists securing the services of a surveyor named John Landers [Landis] who lived at Norton. This man met the party at Ellis and accompanied them to Graham county, where he finished the job in a manner satisfactory to the colonists. Shortly afterwards he was killed in Norton county by some unknown person who shot him in ambush.[43]

Two men, Henry Gandy and Dr. William Cummins Jr., were arrested for the death of the surveyor, but they were acquitted due to insufficient evidence. There had been earlier attempts on Landis's life. The first had been in April 1878, when his house had been set on fire. Four months later, someone fired shots through the windows of his house while his family was sleeping. On August 1, 1878, the Norton paper reported of "another little case of unpleasantness occurring on the Solomon." A man had "jumped a claim belonging to a negro woman and the difficulty arose in reference to the possession of the claim." Apparently the African American settlers did not hesitate to defend their rights, as "the man who was claiming possession got pretty badly used up in the melee that followed." Then the man came to town and had the woman and "another party or two" arrested. About a month later, on September 4, 1878, Landis was murdered.[44]

The *Hays City Sentinel* commented, "There is a small colony of Missourians settled in the vicinity, who are said to have been rebel bushwhackers during the war. Landis had no love for this class of men; and they were not on the best of terms."[45] A year later, the editor of the *Millbrook Times* made a comment that sheds further light on the affair, referring to an attempt to get rid of another editor, Thomas Beaumont, as "a ku-klux measure, the cause of which is about the same as that that prompted the killing of John Landis."[46] Western Kansas newspapermen supported Hickman's belief that the Landis killing was racially motivated.

W. E. B. Du Bois, civil rights activist and cofounder of the National Association for the Advancement of Colored People, wrote that it should be kept in mind that before the Civil War most southerners were not slaveholders but "white peasant-farmers, artisans, [and] merchants and professional men," and many of these displaced Confederates bore an intense hatred of black men who were now competing for their jobs.[47] James Shortridge's demographic studies support the *Sentinel*'s claims about the concentrated settlement of "Missourians" in Graham County.[48] Nevertheless, Daniel Hickman also remembered positive encounters with the colonists' new white neighbors. He recalled the assistance offered by a white man he called Uncle Johnny Furrow, who "time and again" went as far east as Beloit, nearly ninety miles away, "where he stocked up with a load of provisions, and going back sought out the more needy ones."[49]

Most white newcomers arriving in Graham County were from the upper Midwest and New England. They had a strong tradition of self-reliance and were inclined to live in isolation. The number of displaced white southerners was small in the county. Voorhees Committee testimony and Lulu Craig's narrative support Du Bois's arguments that African Americans were willing to help one another. Nicodemus had a strong sense of community from the beginning. It was the settlers' primary strength and enabled them to survive. The colonists already in residence immediately helped other families when they arrived, and they maintained a communal building to house supplies. They were also linked by religious faith and a shared musical heritage. Lena Hicks Penny, who came to Nicodemus with her parents in September 1877, recalled the meetings that took place in Scruggs Grove, the 160-acre farm south of Nicodemus originally homesteaded by R. B. Scruggs, and the sound of banjo music that accompanied their plantation songs. They met around communal fires and ate food prepared in pots suspended over cooking trenches.[50]

Nearby white settlers endured the same hardships as the settlers of Nicodemus. Many of them were also victims of the same propaganda campaigns that had lured blacks to the plains. In his history of the state, Craig Miner writes that "one Kansas town bought 5,000 copies of the Bible, printed a map of the city on the fly leaf, ran a description of the county around the margins of the book of Genesis . . . and sent the volumes back east as boom literature."[51] Whites too found, when they arrived, entirely different circumstances than the balmy, plentiful scenes they had imagined.

John Ise's book *Sod and Stubble*, based on his mother's memories, expresses the range of trials simultaneously experienced by black settlers in Kansas: deaths in childbirth, injury, illness, and starvation; snowstorms, drought, floods, tornados, and grass fires; and confrontations with claim jumpers and other unsavory strangers.[52] Ruth Kelley Hayden, writing in *The Time That Was*, describes a Bohemian immigrant in Rawlins County who had to seek work, and who wrote, "With grief I left my family, as our youngest child, a girl, was only five days old. . . . My wife walked three miles for water, holding the younger child while the other five hung on to her dress.[53] He found work picking corn and eventually received a letter from his wife saying that snow had fallen and that they didn't have a stove. By then he had enough money to buy a pig and a stove, and he headed back. Later, when giving an account of working "from one place to another for several years," he said without a trace of irony, "My wife worked at home." The settlers in Nicodemus were buoyed by a tradition of communal assistance and aware that if they did not master the Great Plains there was no place else to go. The frontier shaped their psyche, and in turn they shaped the frontier. Frederick Jackson Turner later wrote: "The stubborn American environment is there with its imperious summons to accept its conditions; the inherited ways of doing things are also there; and yet, in spite of environment, and in spite of custom, each frontier did indeed furnish a new field of opportunity, a gate of escape from the bondage of the past; and freshness, and confidence, and scorn of older society, impatience of its restraints and its ideas, and indifference to its lessons, have accompanied the frontier."[54]

Scott G. McNall wrote in his forward to Howard Ruede's *Sod-House Days* that there was "almost a religious belief" in the promise of progress if resilience was backed by hard work.[55] Men who put forth maximum effort were greatly admired. Survival was the only goal of the courageous and resourceful settlers—black and white—during the brutal Kansas winter of 1877–78.

The people of Nicodemus were hungry, exhausted, dirty, daunted by the monotony of their lives, worn down by their efforts to compensate for inadequate sanitation, and irritable from coping with the excruciating tension of parents and children living in a single room fourteen feet square. Their houses leaked and let in fleas that tormented them. A solitary team of horses survived that first winter, and one lone roan horse belonging to Jake Martin, referred to by Lulu Craig as their "Pegasus Célèbre."[56]

Although the African Americans who settled Nicodemus did "hang a low head" in the beginning, those who made it through the first winter alive had developed systems for survival. As was the case with their white counterparts, those who could not tolerate the harsh conditions on the plains died or left. As a racial group, through hard work and ingenuity, they neutralized much of the initial prejudice of white settlers.

Chapter 4
Unconsidered Trifles

I do not believe that there are any objections on the part of the people of Kansas to colored people coming there, as such: that is, simply on account of their color. If they come there and behave themselves well, and sustain themselves by their own industry, as the rest of us there have to do, they would be entitled to all the privileges that white people coming there would be.
Testimony of T. C. Sears

SPRING CAME. HOPE SURGED. Shouts of gratitude greeted John W. Niles, Abram T. Hall, and Edward P. McCabe, who sat atop wagonloads of food and other provisions. The exuberant settlers formed a corridor from the north bank of the Solomon toward the stovepipe-pocked grassy knoll they called Nicodemus. Charles Williams offered to store the supplies in an "unoccupied stone [*sic*] up on the Stockton Trail."[1] Hall and McCabe would bring a far more lasting contribution to the community than food and supplies. The two had impressive educational credentials and formidable political skills with which to confront the increasingly treacherous racial animus in Kansas.

Hall's political skills were put to use immediately when he and McCabe arrived with Niles. Because Niles had left the community a couple of times previously to solicit donations, some of the colonists believed that Niles was keeping the money. Those who had supported Niles wanted to keep the provisions for themselves. Hall settled the conflict by drawing up a petition that empowered Niles to solicit on their behalf. All who signed it would share in the provisions: "To all Whom it May Concern: Greeting: We the undersigned members of a Negro Colony, located at Nicodemus, Kansas, being in destitute circumstances, due to the lack of food, clothing, shoes, garden and farm seeds do hereby and herewith appoint and empower, John W. Niles, one of our number, as an agent and solicitor before the public in our behalf until such time as our crops are ready and to be planted shall mature and be ready to harvest."[2] Every person but seven signed, and by the first "ration day" these holdouts relented.

Hall was likely the most highly educated person—black or white—in all of Graham County, and E. P. McCabe was a close second. Hall came from a uniquely privileged background. He was born April 15, 1851, in Chicago, to Abram and Joanna (Huss) Hall. His father, Abram Thompson Hall, Sr., was a minister in the African Methodist Episcopal (AME) Church. The elder Hall was the first black man given formal license to preach in Chicago and organized Quinn Chapel, which became one of the largest AME congregations in the country.[3]

Abram Hall, Jr., was educated in public schools and attended medical school for one year at the prestigious College of Physicians and Surgeons in Indianapolis. Although there were one or two African Americans in about every class of twenty-four students, at that time it was unusual for blacks to obtain admission in any school intended for whites. The medical college was formed in 1873 after dissension in the Indiana Medical College that "culminated in a division of the faculty." The institution was short-lived, as in 1878 it joined with its rival, Indiana Medical College, to form the Medical College of Indiana, with a "new charter and faculty selected from the two former facilities."[4] After Hall left college, he worked three seasons as a sailor on the Great Lakes, then began his career as a journalist. Throughout his long life he would at various times work as editor, reporter, and columnist.

Edward McCabe, born October 10, 1850, in Troy, New York, was a fastidious man who could have passed for white. Somewhat of a dandy, there are several extant references to his attire after he was elected state auditor, including his preference for patent leather spats. (Hall would note with some amusement that, on the journey to Nicodemus, McCabe's "aesthetic appetite and city raised stomach" could not tolerate food cooked over a cow chip fire. McCabe "starved in silence; but he later became an adept 'cow chip' cook himself.")[5] McCabe's family moved from Troy to Fall River, Massachusetts, then to Newport, Rhode Island, where he attended the public schools. Following the death of his father, he discontinued his studies and supported his mother and siblings. Later, after serving as a clerk on Wall Street, he moved to

Abram Thompson Hall, Jr., c. 1910. Courtesy Vivian G. Harsh Collection, Chicago Public Library.

Chicago and was a clerk for hotel magnate Potter Palmer. He was eventually appointed a clerk in the Cook County office of the federal treasury.[6]

Although the skills of these two northerners were a critical addition to the community, the common sense and entrepreneurial spirit of those who arrived in September 1877—and decided to stay—were more important. During the long winter, the settlers had figured out what they needed to do to survive. When the ground finally thawed, they dug a well—fifty-seven feet deep—and no longer had to carry water from the river. Some had even broken out an acre or so of their claims with a spade. Those who had money bought oxen from Bow Creek farmers. Soon, Lulu Craig reports, "there were many small fields planted to corn, beans, peas, squash, melons, turnips and rice corn; which would provide food for the next winter." In addition to "Pegasus Célèbre"—Jake Martin's much-admired bony old mare—they acquired a "goodly number of chickens, ducks, and pigs," which were kept in dugouts because there was no lumber available for aboveground pens.[7]

A man from Stockton, James Keeney, started the first store in Nicodemus, during the winter of 1877–78, but then he moved closer to Hays, where he founded another store, with a name (Wakeeney) that combined his name with that of his business partner, Albert Warner. When Keeney left, Z. T. Fletcher opened a store in a dugout in Nicodemus that stayed in business for a long time. Simultaneously Bill Harris opened a store—"in the Wright-Palmer sod-up," Craig says— with what he considered a full line of groceries. He had "ten pounds of bacon; a pound of tea; and three pounds of bulk green coffee." By 1879 Fletcher's general store offered "a few pounds of coffee in bulk, three to five pounds of tea, ten to twenty pounds of cured meat, bacon or salt pork, about a dozen bars of laundry soap, five pounds of salt, fifty to one hundred pounds of corn meal, about ten pounds of sugar, a plug of tobacco and a few packages of smoking tobacco, three gallons of coal oil, three or four boxes of matches, a few packages of soda, some stick candy, [and] some rice or hominy." Sometimes there was molasses to be had. None of the first merchants sold flour or much meal. The supply of this kind of commodity was bought from flour wagons that came by occasionally. No one knew when flour would be available. Often men of the colony walked to Ellis and carried back flour to their families. Since the storekeepers at Nicodemus depended on passing teamsters, their groceries were often exhausted before anyone passed by again to replenish their goods.[8]

The colonists who could adapt to the prairie were quick to take steps to improve their lives. One immigrant described Kansas as "a country infested with rattlesnakes, coyotes, and tarantulas, pestered by fleas and damned by Kansas droughts, but for all that, it was Kansas, a free country with political and economic equality for all."[9] Undaunted by the harsh environment, Hall and McCabe together began a land location business. No doubt they became aware of the potential of this sort of enterprise through their association with W. C. Don Carlos, the land agent at Kirwin, and Lewis Best, registrar of the land office. Hall and McCabe also advertised themselves as attorneys qualified to conduct business in Kansas's fifteenth judicial district.

There are several references to McCabe having had some legal training. However, no training was necessary. At that time, when the requirements for admission to the bar were quite casual and based on "good moral character," both the men's educational backgrounds were considerably above those of most lawyers practicing on the prairie. Hall's letters and speeches contained Latin and French phrases, and he often quoted from the classics and Shakespeare.[10] According to Craig, Hall was appointed deputy district clerk of Rooks County for Graham County, and McCabe was commissioned a notary public through the influence of Carlos and Best. The colonists were then able to "execute contracts, sales and bargains, make affidavits, etc." without making the arduous trip to the Rooks County seat in Stockton, about twenty miles to the east.[11]

Among the several references to Hall's and McCabe's experiences as lawyers, Hall related an incident to Craig describing colonists' dispute over a horse trade. The squire (justice of the peace) drafted the two men to appear for the plaintiff and defendant. In Hall's words, "what those two embryonic pettifoggers did not know about law would have filled several Carnegie libraries; and what that Justice did not know about common jurisprudence was—everything." [12]

Before Hall and McCabe's arrival, occasional legal disputes had been settled within the community. Granville Lewis served as an informal justice of the peace and presided during the first "lawsuit," a case to settle the disputed ownership of two ducks, with storekeeper Fletcher acting for the prosecution and Niles for the defense. Court costs were covered by the sale of the ducks.[13] A later, more serious dispute took place after a white man, William Sheppard, gave rides to three hitchhikers from Nicodemus. When Sheppard, who was drunk, demanded payment, his penniless passengers showed him their empty pockets. Sheppard then shot Erasmus Kirtley in both legs—just for fun, he said. After Sheppard was subdued, taken to Stockton, and fined, the *Kirwin (Kans.) Chief* reported the shooting as a "brutal outrage" and wished Kirtley a swift recovery. This incident, with the white community siding with the blacks, reinforced the belief in the African American community that in Kansas it was possible to obtain justice, even in an unorganized region.[14]

By spring in 1878, many of the settlers had established congenial relationships with the white community. When the weather cleared and the colonists were able to walk long distances, Nicodemians went to work. The women made substantial contributions to the welfare of the settlement. The *Hays City Sentinel* reported, "The females of the Nicodemus colony have made a descent on Ellis in hope of finding situations as house servants." Many of the women were excellent cooks and laundresses and found work more easily than the men. Some worked as far away as Beloit, Osborne, and even Salina and Junction City while the men tended to the homestead.[15] White communities also appreciated the colony's "mechanics," a term used for skilled tradesmen such as carpenters, blacksmiths, masons, and plasterers.[16]

Some of the women had special skills. For instance, Willianna Hickman, who was W. R. Hill's assistant manager of the second colony, had received professional training in dressmaking, tailoring, and millinery when she was quite young. After arriving in Nicodemus, she made hats for men, women, and children in the colony, and she sold her goods to persons in nearby towns, with prices ranging from twenty-five cents to a dollar. She used native bluestem grass and blocked the hats on a form she brought with her.[17]

During the summer of 1878 a good many blacks came to Nicodemus to look over the community. One man, William Yancy, said that he went there "to see how badly off they were, with a view of going back to Chicago to raise funds for them." Yancy instead reported to the *Colored Citizen* that the "many stories about suffering and destitution [in Nicodemus] are base falsehoods."[18] In fact, by early fall, in September

1878, the colony had sixteen teams of livestock brought by newcomers into the township.[19] The *Colored Citizen*, which never ceased to tout the merits of Kansas, reported that an Illinois man had gone to Nicodemus to inspect the settlement, liked what he saw, and was going home to sell his property and return to Nicodemus to stake his claim. There were many such items in Kansas newspapers, telling of individuals and small families finding their way to Nicodemus. The *Hays City Sentinel* editor noted that the March 1878 settlers arrived with "five carloads of stock and agricultural implements" and intended to "start work at once."[20]

The colonists took advantage of every opportunity to improve their claims. They hailed "westward-going caravans, offering shelter and food in return for the use of plows and teams to break their land," and men "often walked thirty or more miles to surrounding towns to find work."[21] Joe Patterson and Billy Smith walked all the way to Denver, over three hundred miles. They were preceded by Nicodemus blacksmith Henry Washburn, who also had suffered an attack of "Colorado fever."[22] Many of the men worked for the railroads or gathered buffalo bones. They carried the bones to WaKeeney, where they received six dollars per ton for them. The colonists also discovered a vein of coal that would relieve their fuel shortage, although it was not in large enough quantities to sell.[23]

Whites in the surrounding communities employed some of the Nicodemus men as laborers, sometimes for dangerous work. Thomas Allison undertook the treacherous job of digging a well and was severely injured when a hundred-pound rock fell on his head. Well diggers were also in danger of succumbing to lethal gases lurking at the bottom of a well, and walls often collapsed. A number of white men too died or were injured while searching for water. J. J. Jewell, a white man who had left his homestead to find work, was buried alive while digging a well. He was found standing up—with sand two feet above his head.

Hall and McCabe had a wider range of employment opportunities than the typical colonist due to their education. Despite his branching out into land location and establishing a law practice, Hall's first love was journalism. Shortly after arriving in Nicodemus, he sent a letter to the editor of the *Colored Citizen*, which was located in Fort Scott, Kansas, at that time but would soon move to Topeka for economic reasons. In his typically lyrical style, with irrepressible optimism, he referred to "the merry laugh of children at play upon the green sward" and assured readers that "what was once a prairie wild will soon take on city airs." He assured the subscribers to Kansas's most prestigious black newspaper that "every week brings its quota of new comers, who come to stay, not to look around—they represent all class of sturdy, enterprising citizens, who have wearied of the hand-to-mouth existence which is all the older states offer, and who have come out to Kansas to make a home, and get their children a start toward that glorious future for *our race* which has already cast up shadows on the horizon of the future."[24]

Two months after his arrival, Hall wrote his first letter to the *Stockton News*:

> As we are too young on this side of the line to afford a paper of our own, and as there will now and then occur something which might adorn a column and prove interesting reading to your many subscribers, I submit the following unconsidered trifles:
>
> A wedding occurred in this settlement, on the 3rd Inst. It was the initial movement in a connubial way among us, and enshrouded somewhat in romance. The high contracting parties were a Miss Mary Robb and Mr. Henry Johnson. Rev. Silas Lee of Ellis, Kan., tied the knot at the First Baptist Church, which the ladies of the colony had decorated very prettily.
>
> The generous-hearted people of Kansas City, Mo., last week sent the colony a car load of provisions.
>
> Sheriff Shaw and deputy Kent, visited our Sabbath School last Sunday, while halting here for dinner. They were making an official call we believe, on a party of riotous herders in the western part of our county. They went about their business with renewed strength after the school adjourned.
>
> Crops are looking very fair and the colonists are hopeful. About 250 acres are under cultivation—mostly in corn and sorghum.

Postmaster Fletcher will begin the work on his new store this week.

Water has been found in the public well at a depth of 45 feet.

The people of Nicodemus intend to celebrate on the 4th of July. The programme as arranged is as follows: Salute in the morning: parade of Co. A. 1st Regt. Rag Muffins at high meridian: reading of the Declaration of Independence from the Post Office steps at 2 o'clock P.M. followed by a festival at the church at night.

Immigrants are continually dropping in and locating claims. Parties from Rockford Illinois are here looking for a mill site. Life is too short to tell it all.

A. T. Hall, Jr.[25]

Hall's "unconsidered trifles" were hardly a trivial communication. Not only was his letter a brilliant piece of propaganda, it was genuinely representative of Hall's genial stance toward whites. The letter immediately established the colony as non-threatening, and in mentioning a church and a minister it was bound to connect. Religious people usually met with approval on the plains, even though, unlike southwestern Kansas, northwestern Kansas was not part of the Bible Belt. Hall's mention of gratitude for the carload of provisions sent by African Americans in eastern Kansas might have eased the minds of whites burdened with feeding their own families. Acceptance of charity was an explosive topic among whites, and aid—in the form of tools, clothes, food, seed for planting, and fencing—would become a divisive issue later in Nicodemus, resulting in Hall and McCabe temporarily severing their relationship with Niles.

Hall's mention of the sheriff and his deputy attending a welcoming "Sabbath school" in Nicodemus would likely have eased the minds of any whites who associated ex-slaves with lawlessness. And the reference to "riotous herders" would have struck a chord with everyone living on the prairie at that time. There was a thinly disguised range war going on between cattlemen and homesteaders. The latter often retaliated by slaughtering cattle that were destroying their crops, and settlers formed self-protection groups that ignored racial and cultural boundaries. Reverend Samuel P. Roundtree of Nicodemus wrote to Kansas governor George Anthony asking for help in ridding the county of the cattle. However, assistance was not forthcoming, and Graham County farmers waged a long struggle with the gun-carrying cattlemen.

In referring to crops and the depth of a well, Hall indicated that the people of Nicodemus were industrious. Well-digging was such an arduous process that it was never attempted unless persons intended to stay in a town or on a claim. The well alone advertised that the Nicodemus colonists intended to remain on the plains, in case the surrounding whites had any doubts. Finally, the inclusion of the agenda for the Fourth of July program and the reference to "immigrants continually dropping in" were hardly unconsidered trifles. Not only would there be a parade and a reading of the Declaration of Independence, but the Independence Day ceremony would take place at a church. Then, as now, patriotism and religion were a magic combination. And clearly these proud black settlers intended to be control their own destiny.

In a very short letter, Hall established Nicodemus colonists as people of faith embracing conventional moral standards in line with white norms. He presented them as law-abiding, religious, industrious, patriotic, shrewd, innovative, and determined to unite with homesteaders in the eternal range war. But the most telling detail was the mention of the town's well. It served notice that African Americans were in Graham County to stay.

Hall was also sending letters to the *Atchison Daily Champion* at this time. There were no newspapers based in Graham County when Hall was first published in the *Champion*. Nevertheless, it is ironic that the first columnist from Graham County was an African American. Atchison had been organized by radical southern pro-slavery advocates, and named for Missouri senator David Atchison, a participant in violent raids on abolitionists during the state's territorial period. And the *Champion*'s progenitor—the *Squatter Sovereign*—excelled in vicious pro-slavery rhetoric. John A. Martin purchased the paper in 1858 and renamed it the *Atchison Daily Champion.* Martin, who would in 1885 become the tenth governor of Kansas, completely changed its tone from pro-slavery advocacy to avid support for civil rights regardless of race.

There is no record of how Hall learned of the paper's interest in information from the western part of the state. Martin could have identified Hall's race just by seeing "Nicodemus" tag in the slug line. Hall's first letter began, "To the Editor of the Champion: From this region of Indian raids and prairie fires, I send you the following." This letter and an entry in the Craig manuscript are the only two extant references to the Nicodemus colonists' reaction to the flight of renegade Northern Cheyennes from Oklahoma through Kansas in 1877. According to Craig, a cowboy warned the settlers, and people rushed from their claims into Nicodemus, while "those on the townsite gathered around the sod-up of Hall and McCabe's asking fearfully what should be done." They decided to send George Dorsey and Henry Smith to Fort Hays asking for "arms, ammunition and a detail of soldiers to protect the settlement." But before the men started off, another cowboy galloped in "bearing the news that the event [the passage of the Northern Cheyennes] had taken place the Thursday before," and the colonists were safe.[26]

Hall's first letter to the *Champion* also contains his account of a lethal prairie fire that began about five miles south of Nicodemus. With meticulous detail, Hall reported on the fire even as he was observing it. "In the room where I am writing lies a victim of the fire fiend," he wrote. Peter Jackson had crawled there after the wind had shifted and set his clothes on fire. Jackson and another man, Henry Blackman, died of their injuries. Hall wrote, "From my window I can look out on one vast sea of red flame. The loss to the settlers in hay, corn, and various other things is very great, coming as it does just before the winter sets in."

Although Hall was a superb journalist, he could not make a living from this in western Kansas. He and McCabe depended on their thriving land location business, which was quite profitable. Obviously Hall had a vested interest in presenting the region in a favorable light. He wrote that "dug-outs and sod-ups spring up on the prairie as if by magic, and with thankful hearts for present and happy ones for the future" the colonists were pressing forward.[27]

Hall reported that Graham County was "growing so rapidly both in business enterprise and population, "that a column a week [in the

Colored Citizen] will hardly suffice to tell the story." He claimed that "many a goodly 'schooner' makes this or adjacent ports in the course of every twenty-four hours; while the white sails of many others can be discerned in the offing, bound for different points of this, our western world." Nicodemus exploded with an influx of new settlers who brought supplies and new energy. Despite the devastating toll the first winter took on their health and physical assets, by spring the settlers pressed forward.[28]

Many years later, Montana-born Taylor Gordon, a musician associated with the Harlem Renaissance, said that his western heritage made all the difference in his attitude toward racial issues.[29] The prairie was a great leveler. Blacks, like their white counterparts, survived by developing "courage, initiative, aggressiveness and industry," historian Walter Webb asserts. "The genius of America is expressed in the word *work*."[30] Because the Nicodemus colonists proved they were capable of working as hard as white people and embraced the same ethic, by the fall of 1878, western Kansas newspaper editors referred to African Americans by their individual names with no mention of their race.

Chapter 5
Black Republicans

They are here not of our seeking, nor on invitation, except as Kansas from the first hour of its birth in tumult and travail of blood, in the first wild, passionate cry of freedom, sent an all-hail and welcome to the oppressed everywhere to come and make these prairies, consecrated in a baptism of fire, "the homestead of the free." . . . They are not needed for political purposes in Kansas. But they are coming all the same.

Testimony of F. M. Stringfield

KANSAS DID NOT NEED to lure blacks to the state to insure the dominance of the Republican Party there. Nevertheless, Kansas African Americans did overwhelmingly vote Republican, and they were a force to be reckoned with during the summer of 1878 and the first nine months of 1879. They resented whites who courted their votes and then ignored their desire for political appointments.[1]

The complaints of Kansas blacks about being slighted politically were trivial compared to the violent treatment blacks experienced in other regions. In the South, Democrats used brutal intimidation and violence to keep blacks from voting, as they were registering in greater numbers than were whites.[2] The Voorhees Committee continued to hear a wealth of horrifying testimony about this. For black colonists in Kansas, "the world of politics assumed special importance, because politicians set the tone of the community," historian William H. Chafe notes. Politicians' actions would "inform both the Negro and white community of the Negro's status."[3]

For instance, John Milton Brown, an African American resident of Topeka, testified before the Voorhees Committee that he had been a teacher in Mississippi, where he had been elected sheriff of Coahoma County in 1873, then served two years without incident. Before the 1875 county Republican convention, however, Brown said that he had learned that "Democrats had the names of all the leading Republicans on their dead-list, and my name was at the head of it . . . [and] when we met they were to come around and take us out and hang or shoot us." Brown gave a long account of murder, rape, and pillage by whites despite some armed resistance from blacks. He said that it had taken an influx of "one thousand to fifteen hundred [white Democrats] from different parts of the county and the State" to prevent the Coahoma blacks and white Republicans from voting. Senator Windom asked Brown if that election was "understood to have been carried out by what is sometimes called 'The Mississippi Policy' "—and Brown affirmed it, saying that "Mississippi Policy" referred to brutal intimidation and murder. Perhaps needless to say, Democrats carried the state.[4]

In Kansas, Republicans had simply ignored African Americans prior to the late summer and early fall of 1878. But in July 1878, three months after they arrived, Abram Hall and E. P. McCabe became involved in state politics. Their land business and legal activities provided money for what became frequent trips to Topeka, the state capital. Topeka was a Mecca for well-educated, freeborn blacks and the center of the state's African American cultural and political activity. It had been an abolitionist center before the Civil War and a major station on the Underground Railroad, but its black population exploded after the war.[5] Topeka's African Americans often brokered sophisticated compromises with white citizens, an approach Hall used again and again to achieve better conditions for blacks.[6]

Leavenworth, the other black community with a significant African American population, had a high concentration of white Democrats. Historian Brent M. S. Campney wrote that this was a major factor contributing to the "high level of localized racism and violence."[7] In 1880, the population of Leavenworth was approximately 16,500. According to the *Colored Citizen*, the black population ranged between four thousand and five thousand.[8] The town's location on the Missouri River had attracted ex-slaves fleeing from the slave state of Missouri. Former slaves wrestled with the residual prejudice of white residents, many of whom retained pro-slavery sentiments and resisted granting suffrage to blacks. The growing frustration of these African Americans may have caused one of their most brilliant advocates for civil rights,

Charles Henry Langston, grandfather of Langston Hughes, to move to more congenial surroundings near Lawrence, twenty miles east of Topeka. While in Leavenworth, Langston would endure prejudiced comments about his light skin color. Newspaper publisher John W. Wright, for one, would assert that Langston, of mixed ancestry, "could not fully comprehend the social wishes of either white or black people" and that the "pure black man can only feel the responsibilities."[9]

During the summer of 1878, the responsibilities of the race were weighing on A. H. Walton, a black man from Leavenworth who visited his parents in Kirwin and toured the surrounding counties. Walton had graduated in 1877 from the State Normal School in Leavenworth and went on to become principal of Leavenworth's African American schools. Since Hall had made a number of trips to Kirwin to file claims for the settlers of Nicodemus, Walton may have learned there of Hall and his abilities. Otherwise he learned of Hall when visiting Nicodemus on July 4. In Walton's account of his visit, published in the *Colored Citizen*, he praised the courage and fortitude of Nicodemus residents in general and lauded the rhetorical abilities of Hall and McCabe. After Hall publicly read the Declaration of Independence, Walton reported, "McCabe traced briefly though beautifully and eloquently the history of the colored man in America." Walton described Hall and McCabe as "able, energetic, and working young men" who managed the affairs of the colony and were destined for future eminence.[10] Coupled with Hall's optimistic letters to the press, Walton's glowing words about Nicodemus ensured a warm welcome for Hall and McCabe from the leaders of Topeka's African American community.

When they visited Topeka, Hall and McCabe attended the St. John AME Church, which had started as a prayer circle but would grow to become a powerful advocate for racial uplift and civil rights. The church supported the arts and enjoyed an array of musical performances by its talented members. The members met in a rented barn and sponsored a literary society hosting dynamic speakers who addressed issues concerning African Americans. In 1879 the congregation began construction of a new building. Black churches such as St. John filled many needs, offering mutual aid and assistance as well as inspiration, and their pastors, often powerful orators, were considered the primary leaders of their communities.

Even in its infancy the congregation of St. John was Topeka's foremost champion for civil rights. In the late 1870s, church members protested against segregation in "education, in public accommodations, and common carriers," writes Thomas Cox, historian of blacks in Topeka from the end of the Civil War to 1915.[11] AME pastors from other Kansas communities visited St. John when in the city and were often invited to deliver sermons or lectures, and the church's members included some of the most prominent black politicians in the state, including William L. Eagleson, editor and publisher of the *Colored Citizen*.[12] A former slave, born in 1835, Eagleson had trained as a barber and a printer and would practice both trades all his life. Before moving the *Colored Citizen* to Topeka, Eagleson had been a member of the Wayland Chapel at Fort Scott, Kansas.

Even before having met them, Eagleson was already quite taken with Hall and McCabe, who had advertised extensively in his paper and mailed in well-written letters. No doubt his admiration increased with their acquaintance. Hall and McCabe's joint visits to Topeka in 1878 preceded the massive influx of Exodusters that would overwhelm the resources of St. John AME the following year. Their visits came as St John and the larger African American community focused on Republican Party politics. Specifically, they wanted a black man elected to state office. The *Colored Citizen* spearheaded this campaign and focused on the office of lieutenant governor.[13]

Eagleson's first choice for the position was J. C. Embry, the AME pastor of Wayland Chapel in Fort Scott, Kansas. Embry, national commissioner of education for the AME Church, was a powerful editorialist known for his insightful, well-reasoned opinions on all matters regarding race. He frequently published columns and letters in Kansas newspapers, and his book *Upon the Past, Present and Future of the Colored American*, was sold at the J. B. Bayless book store in Fort Scott.[14] Earlier in 1878 he had proposed that blacks ("colored laborers and businessmen") hold an industrial convention to devise plans for developing the business talents of African Americans.[15]

To Eagleson's dismay, not only did Embry refuse to be considered for nomination, he wrote a stinging letter to the *Colored Citizen* dismissing the whole proposal as a "joke." Embry argued that "any future of the race worth living for depends on the solution of the caste problem. . . . But I do not believe it can be solved in political conventions. It must be done in the field, in the Shop and in temples of trade." He ridiculed African Americans' fanciful visions of political equality with whites and bolstered his argument for succeeding through racial uplift by concluding:

> So long as colored men are practically excluded from celebrating the Fourth of July, our national holiday[,] with white men and marching in the same procession; so long as they are obliged to send their children to school in tumbling horse stables, so long will it be impossible to elect a colored man, however worthy, to the office of Lieut. Governor, or any other high position of honor in this State . . . this whole question turns upon the social status of the race. Wealth, intelligence and character will bring us office and honor without the seeking. . . . More farms, gentlemen, more big houses in the city, more lots, more business, more money, more brains, and the honors connected with them, will come as naturally as apples when full ripe, come to the ground.[16]

T. W. Henderson—a staunch Republican, pastor of St. John, and Eagleson's associate editor—then consented to become the first Kansas African American candidate for a state office and entered the Republican primary. Unlike Embry, Henderson had no reservations about the role electoral politics could play in bettering conditions for the race. The selection of the lieutenant governor nominee would take place August 23, 1878, at the party's state convention.

Embry's provocative letter was followed by a number of responses refuting his claims that a black man did not have a chance. Eagleson, for one, asserted that if "the doctrines in this remarkable letter are true, then we colored people had just as well make up our minds to forever be hewers of wood and drawers of water." Eagleson stated that if Henderson were not to be nominated it would be due to lack of effort within the black community to "throw aside petty jealousies and personal feuds and unitedly demand proper recognition from the party."[17] Writing from Nicodemus, E. P. McCabe accused Embry of influencing those "without towns, big city houses, business, money, etc." to lose sight of their duties as citizens. McCabe argued that "if the caste problem is not to be furthered toward an amicable solution in political conventions where officers are made; where on earth shall we commence the same?" He believed that the "colored vote of the state cuts a very important figure, and . . . by forcing upon the conventions who cater to the colored vote, delegates who will use their influence and votes in their races' influence, unconditional recognition will be the result in the near future." The "caste problem," said McCabe, had to be "commenced and settled at the ballot box."[18]

A young African American lawyer named John Lewis Waller agreed with McCabe. Waller had moved to Leavenworth in May that year from Cedar Rapids, Iowa, arriving two weeks after Hall and McCabe had arrived in Nicodemus. Waller believed that "once Negroes were excluded from voting and holding office, they would be vulnerable both economically and legally, to those who wanted to reintroduce slavery." He and McCabe would become fast friends, and Waller matched McCabe's political ambitions. After a number of political appointments, he would eventually serve as U.S. consul to Madagascar. In the interim, he soon became "discouraged by the prejudice and opposition he encountered in the white community" in Leavenworth, and he followed Charles Langston's example by moving to Lawrence in 1879.[19]

Newspapers as far away as New Orleans lauded Henderson's candidacy.[20] He emphasized his loyalty to the party in his announcement but campaigned on a platform that he was not to be considered merely for his personal service, saying that the Republican Party owed his race recognition for its support.[21] Most blacks endorsed him, but Eagleson accused some of being in tandem with whites who had promised them favors for disrupting Henderson's campaign.[22]

Shortly before the convention, William Bolden Townsend weighed in on Henderson's nomination. He was one of black Leavenworth's

John Lewis Waller. Courtesy of Kansas Historical Society.

favorite citizens because of his fearless stance against racial violence. In addition to being a lawyer, he was one of the prison guards at the state penitentiary.[23] Townsend had been one of those holding up community aid to Nicodemus, questioning John W. Niles's credentials. Now he called attention to the Republican Party's unjust past distribution of patronage and official appointments "so far as the colored race is concerned," saying that after victory was secured with the help of the "17,000 colored votes," white men filled all the offices. The Republican Party may have had a role in freeing slaves, but African Americans needed more. They needed employment—and wages that would enable them to support their families, acquire homes, and educate their children. Townsend suggested that the Republican Party was likely to lose black voters if it failed to put up "a representative colored man on the state ticket this fall" and pay attention to racial issues. Starkly illustrative of Townsend's criticism is the fact that the most prestigious paper in Leavenworth, the *Leavenworth Daily Times*, did not print any information about Henderson's candidacy.[24]

Townsend's comment about black voters leaving the Republican Party was connected to their increasing involvement in the Greenback Party. The Greenbacks objected to the U.S. standard of "hard money"—then based on a gold standard—which they believed benefited the rich. They wanted more paper currency in circulation, "greenbacks," as issued by the federal government during the Civil War, which they believed worked in favor of laborers. In Nicodemus, however, Hall and McCabe nominated themselves as "official" delegates from the yet-to-be organized Republican Party from the yet-to-be organized county of Graham. Graham County was named after John L. Graham, a Union soldier who died in the Battle of Chickamauga. The geographical boundaries had been designated by the state legislature in 1867.

Hall and McCabe paid their way to the convention and were applauded by the *Colored Citizen* as being "among the noble and true colored men in the State of Kansas" who "worked like true heroes for the recognition of the race." Eagleson wrote that he expected to see the day "when these young men will be occupying places of trust and honor."[25]

William Bolden Townsend. Courtesy of Kansas Historical Society.

The *Wichita Eagle* referred to the 1878 Republican state convention as "the largest, wildest and most exciting that ever assembled in the state."[26] Much to the surprise of many in the party, the Republican candidate for governor would be John Pierce St. John, one of the country's fiercest defenders of civil rights. St. John was elected on the seventeenth ballot. He had received a mere fifty-six votes on the first ballot (John A. Martin, who would be a Kansas governor in the future, received 119 votes, and George T. Anthony, the incumbent governor, received 114).[27] St. John won on the seventeenth ballot after Anthony withdrew. On the final ballot, St. John received 156 votes and Martin received 129.²⁸ L. C. Humphreys won the nomination for lieutenant governor.

Not all of the blacks in attendance at the convention worked on behalf of Henderson's nomination for lieutenant governor. Henderson received the largest number of votes on the first ballot (seventy-two) but would lose the nomination, and the *Citizen* pointed out that if the men who voted for him had stood firm on subsequent ballots Henderson would have received the nomination.²⁹ Eagleson was furious, publicly deploring the "great lack of backbone among the republicans of this state," and he predicted that if they continued to snub their strongest allies they would neither be "troubled by colored candidates nor colored voters."³⁰ However, the Valley Falls *New Era* called "laughable in the extreme" the idea of "a colored man demanding to be put upon the ticket, as essential to the best interests of the party." The paper referred to Henderson as a "pretty starchy looking negro," whose "co-laborers were everlastingly polite."³¹

As it had promised in a previous issue, the *Colored Citizen* published the names of the "Noble 72"—those who had voted for Henderson on the first ballot. Hall was numbered among these men. McCabe had not been able to vote because the number of official representatives awarded voting status was based on a county's) population. The unorganized county of Graham was granted a vote despite lacking formal status. J. C. Embry, who had scoffed at the idea of a black candidate, did not hesitate to exacerbate blacks' dissatisfaction with the Republican Party. He wrote another provocative letter to the *Colored Citizen*, this one asserting that the party had changed and there was a great deal of difference now between its "real" and "apparent" attitudes. He repeated his aversion for considering alliance with Democrats, with that party's history of "murders [and] its persistent slanders upon our race," but he also deplored the Republicans' feeble protest against continued anti-black violence in the South. Embry urged African Americans to give serious consideration to the Greenback (Greenback-Labor) candidate for governor, D. P. Mitchell. He said that while very little was known about St. John, he could personally vouch for Mitchell's belief in common humanity.³²

In the same issue of the *Colored Citizen*, Hall's reaction to the convention appeared. Written with his characteristic imaginative imagery, suggestive of a style later used by W. E. B. Du Bois, Hall compared the Republican Party to a diseased patient whose recovery would occur naturally if blacks did not rush in with radical treatments. Hall's cosmopolitan approach to racial issues is clearly evident. He deplored what he saw as the self-absorption of young blacks but also the tendency of the older black man to "imagine every young man as his mortal enemy." He asserted that those marking ballots "vote for candidates on sectional reasons, on race considerations, on [a candidate's] qualifications for office, on his past record, for place, for spite, for fun, for money, for the sake of the party, but, seldom ever for the good of the commonwealth." He called on black leaders to exercise "fairness of spirit" and "maturity of judgment."[33]

In contrast to Hall's call to focus on the national welfare instead of racial issues exclusively, several post-convention correspondents simply attacked Embry's endorsement of the Greenback Party. C. C. James, from Lawrence, urged continued loyalty to the party that had "offered great protection, better school privileges, and more offices to the colored man than any other party ever did." James accused Embry of being in alliance with "wily democrats using their cunning to induce colored men to forsake the only party that ever made it possible to vote at all in the interest of a party who always deprived colored men of their rights."[34]

Embry replied that he was a "far better Republican" than James because James's kind of Republican projected an image of blacks needing care and protection while Embry's kind acted like men capable of "noble, independent action."[35] Embry insisted that his defense of the Greenback Party was because it embraced a belief once held by Republicans that every paper dollar issued by the government should be on equal footing with gold-backed and silver-backed currency and should be legal tender.[36] And he wasn't alone. Many other Kansas blacks were soured on the Republican Party because it had not supported a black candidate. In October, the Shawnee County Republican Club met at St. John AME church and a number of men there spoke in favor of the Greenback Party.[37]

Testimony before the Voorhees Committee verified the *Colored Citizen*'s accounts of Kansas African Americans' dissatisfaction with the party. Major A. J. Allen, a Democrat and a retired attorney for the St. Louis, Wichita, and Western Railroad, told the committee that he did not know "of a colored man holding office that was elected by the Republican Party." Allen testified that the venerated Captain William D. Matthews from Leavenworth, an African American, had been a candidate for the Kansas state senate "with the full sanction" of the convention, but then party members had refused to vote for him. Voorhees asked, "Do you mean to say Republicans in Kansas would rather vote for a Democrat than a respectable colored man?" Allen replied that they would. He said that more Democrats than Republicans had supported Matthews, to the degree that Matthews had since switched parties. Allen insisted that this defection had been caused by "the treachery and falsehood of the Republican party," rather than any favoritism promised by Democrats.[38]

The editor of the *Colored Citizen*, for his part, graciously wished Matthews "long life and prosperity" ("although we don't agree politically").[39] Eagleson had a reason for wanting to retain a genial relationship. Matthews had just been installed as Most Worthy Grand Master of the King Solomon Grand Lodge of the Prince Hall Masons, an organization whose membership included many of the paper's subscribers. The *Lawrence Journal* meanwhile warned that "all roads leading out of the Republican Party have gone directly or indirectly into the Democratic Party."[40] However, very few blacks followed Matthews into that party. With the national election looming, Eagleson was more concerned with squelching blacks' attraction to the Greenbacks.

The *Colored Citizen* kept its readers informed regarding the effectiveness of elected officials, one of whom was Kansas's U.S. senator John J. Ingalls, in office since 1873. Ingalls was supported by his colleague Blanche Kelso Bruce, a Republican from Mississippi, the second African American to serve as a U.S. senator, and the first to serve a full elected term. After Bruce publicly backed Ingalls "because he is a good friend of the colored man," the *Kansas City Times* rejoined that this made Ingalls a "poor friend to the white man."[41]

Bruce was an energetic supporter of equal treatment of African Americans in the military, not only regarding pay but to obliterate the color line when it came to promotions. A former slave, he had become a plantation owner accepted in elite white circles. According to a biography of the senator published on the website of the U.S. House of Representatives, his wife, Josephine Beall Wilson Bruce of Ohio, was "the first black teacher in the Cleveland public schools and the daughter of a prominent mulatto dentist."[42] She had traveled in Europe, and the *Citizen* predicted "the only ones that will find it difficult to receive and treat her well, will be those who have accidentally got up out of a second class clerkship to the exalted positions they now occupy."[43] In the manner of contemporary tabloids, even papers as far-flung as Kansas's *Atchison Champion* in an article entitled "Mrs. Senator Bruce," reported that her husband had "sufficient wealth to gratify any taste she may have." The paper compared "Mrs. Senator Bruce" to the only other "colored senator's wife, Mrs. Pinchback, who was "beautiful and accomplished" and "was made quite a lioness." The writer hoped that "Mrs. Bruce will receive similar treatment."[44]

Most Kansas blacks, however, were much more interested in the Bruce's stance on important issues than in his wife's reception by the Washington elite. Eagleson was wary of Bruce's endorsement of Ingalls, because Ingalls had voted to postpone a proposal for equal treatment of blacks in the military. The *Citizen* called on "colored men" to reject men who would vote for a politician "who ignores our claims, treats our cause with contempt, and willfully insults us by voting against measures of vital importance to us because, we are unfortunately black." Eagleson's militant rhetoric again demonstrated his distance from Hall's appeal to "the higher good of the Commonwealth," which sometimes meant minimizing racial issues. Eagleson's attitude was allied with that of McCabe. They both promoted vigorous racial advocacy through legislation and seemed to have little concern for the wider commonwealth.

Not all blacks were enthusiastic about politicians, and some of the black citizens most dedicated to racial uplift simply did not have the ability to write and speak as well as the contributors to the *Colored Citizen*. Nevertheless, many of these less literate individuals saw issues clearly and could express their views with razor-sharp accuracy. One of the most admired African Americans in the state, Benjamin "Pap" Singleton, who claimed to be the father of the Exoduster movement, snubbed black politicians.[45] When he was called by the Voorhees Committee and questioned by Senator Windom, he testified that neither black politicians nor white men had been involved in the Nicodemus colonization movement: "O no, sir; no white men. This was gotten up by colored men in purity and confidence; not a political negro was in it; they would want to pilfer and rob at the cents before they got the dollars.[46]

The African American men contributing to the *Citizen* certainly were not the "representative colored men" described by Nell Painter in *Exodusters*, whose goal was to emulate Euro-American culture and who often minimized the concerns of uneducated blacks.[47] These writers were neither assimilated nor were they the kind of men, so despised by Singleton, who altered their views to solicit the favor of whites. They carried a distinct racial agenda, although their beliefs varied, some endorsing separation and a few others integration. Nearly all were bitter over the type of "exclusion," as discussed by Randall B. Woods in his essay on the color line in late-nineteenth-century Kansas, in which blacks were arbitrarily turned away from applying for white-collar jobs, attending certain schools, or being seated in restaurants. However, the contributors to the *Colored Citizen* were articulate, educated African Americans who advocated a path of "parallel development" to the accomplishments of whites. Racial uplift embraced hard work, education, and accumulation of wealth.[48]

On November 4, 1878, as expected, Kansas elected its entire Republican state legislative ticket and sent only Republicans to Congress. However, the Greenback Party did surprisingly well nationwide as it acquired thirteen seats in the House of Representatives, with the Democrats losing nine seats and the Republicans four seats. After the 1878 election campaign some in the African American community then turned their attention to acquiring political appointments. J. C. Embry left for Washington, on November 26, 1878, as both an official correspondent for the *Colored Citizen* and a forerunner of modern-day lobbyists.[49] His dispatches from Washington would continue to reflect his bitter discontent with the Republican Party. He asserted, for example, that over half the party's leaders were "insincere about protecting the rights of the Colored South."[50] Back in Topeka, Eagleson hoped that "as all the colored men in the State are Republicans," black men would have a chance at gaining some of the available offices and positions controlled by the Kansas legislature.

In the months ahead, Kansas African Americans received at least token political appointments. On January 15, 1879, Eagleson himself was nominated for the position of first assistant doorkeeper for the Kansas House of Representatives. He was elected on the second ballot with sixty-seven votes, defeating the two white candidates, John J. Donahue and John Carter. Failed lieutenant governor candidate Henderson was nominated for the position of chaplain but lost on the third ballot, by a mere three votes, to J. G. Eckles, a white man from Rice County. Although the *Leavenworth Weekly Public Press* predicted that Reverend Henderson's prayers would no longer ascend very high for the Republican Party, the *Colored Citizen* assured its readers that Republicans needed prayers more than ever.[51] Later Eckles stepped down as chaplain, and Henderson assumed the position after all.

According to the *Atchison Champion*, Abram Hall was a candidate for a position as clerk to one of the legislative committees. However, there is no record in the house and senate journals of his election. Judging from his subsequent intense political activity in Graham County, he may have declined the nomination. Hall stood to lose a great deal financially if he abandoned his lucrative land location business and his homestead claim.

W. B. Townsend, the *Citizen*'s Leavenworth correspondent, claimed the title as assistant doorkeeper in the senate. His editorial duties were assumed by J. W. S. Banks, who would also canvass for new subscribers. It is notable that two of these busy new appointees were important contributors to the *Colored Citizen*: Townsend and editor Eagleson himself. Even the votes cast for these minor political offices were scrutinized by Kansas African Americans, and state representatives were monitored carefully. Back in Nicodemus after a visit with Hall to Topeka, where they had attended the St. John AME literary society gathering and observed the legislature in action, McCabe wrote a scathing letter to the *Citizen*.[52] McCabe castigated the performance of the representative from Ellis County, L. F. Eggers, writing: "We were pleased to notice that Ellis Co. is so ably represented in the lower House, as to warrant her representative's appointment as chairman of possibly the most important committee in the House. And while we acknowledge that the sudden elevation to which he has been raised over the heads of abler and more experienced men, is sufficient to have turned the brain of cooler men . . . we at the same time feel an emotion akin to pity for the speaker, who allowed himself to err in judgment." Eggers's sin had been to vote with the Democrats rather than with the Republicans for the "three colored men who aspired to minor positions in the lower House." McCabe speculated that Eggers "has forgotten or, perhaps, never knew that the black vote of Northwestern Kansas cuts, or soon will cut, an important figure in the political arena of the near future."[53]

McCabe's words should have put white politicians on notice nationwide. The United States was in transition. Considering the lack of progress by blacks in other parts of the county, Kansas African Americans had made significant political strides. They had unified to nominate a black candidate for lieutenant governor, discussed issues in a paper that boasted a national readership, insisted that white Republicans take their racial agenda seriously, and had achieved their main goal of securing legislative appointments for worthy African Americans. However, blacks' attraction to the Greenback Party during the elections of 1878 portended a developing chasm among Kansas Republicans. It soon manifested itself in class warfare rather than as a racial divide, and it led to the rise of Populism. McCabe's warning, although prescient, was unheeded. Disenchanted African Americans teamed with rebellious whites, and the Kansas Republican Party was indeed under assault.

Chapter 6
The Needs of the Race

A good many of them don't know A from B when they see it but they have their share of mother-wit, and know that the great thing their children need is an education. We can clearly see that the colored people must be educated or they must go to the wall.
                                                        Testimony of H. Ruby

AFRICAN AMERICAN PASSION FOR EDUCATION following the Civil War cannot be overstated. Blacks regarded education as one of their most precious rights, and black schools sprang up all over the South. Booker T. Washington wrote: "Few people who were not right in the midst of the scenes can form any exact idea of the intense desire which the people of my race showed for education. It was a whole race trying to go to school. Few were too young, and none too old, to make the attempt to learn. A[s] fast as any kind of teachers could be secured, not only were day-schools filled, but night-schools as well. The great ambition of the older people was to try to learn to read the Bible before they died. With this end in view, men and women who were fifty and seventy-five years old, would be found in the night-schools."[1] In the Voorhees Committee hearing, R. C. Badger, a lawyer from North Carolina, testified that blacks "have shown a desire for knowledge that is remarkable," predicting that "in twenty-five or thirty years there will not be one person of color in all of North Carolina who can't read and write."[2]

On January 2, 1872, Alabama blacks met at a statewide labor convention in Montgomery to discuss the advisability of staying in the South. John B. Simpson, chairman of the convention's committee on education, stated, "We find that the free schools of this State are well patronized by the children of colored people, and thousands are today merrily and prosperously tramping down the school house paths who four years ago had never seen the inside walls, or even the outside wall of a free-school building." Simpson added that "the board of education seem to have done all in its limited power to provide for the education of the colored children of the State."³ Former slave Gilbert Meyers, a farmer in Caddo Parish, Louisiana, acquired extensive property after the war and sent his thirteen children to private schools. Meyers was proud that he had managed this on his own and declared before the Voorhees Committee, "I am going to school my children if I have to eat bread and water."⁴ Another Louisiana man, John G. Lewis, a legislator and teacher, testified to the Voorhees Committee that Sunday schools where he lived "are not run on the ordinary system, but are run the same as you would a day school, in order that the grown people that cannot get out in the daytime may have an opportunity to educate their children and themselves."⁵

In Kansas, on January 21, 1879, Abram Hall presented a paper, "The Needs of the Race," to the St. John literary society, and the *Colored Citizen* published his entire talk. Although McCabe and Townsend also spoke at this meeting, their comments were not recorded. Hall's ability to think, speak, write, and persuade are evident in this essay, which confirms his stance that the most effective path to racial uplift lay in education and seizing economic opportunities. He began by asserting that blacks were "mendicants of the bounty of their fellow races" and said that this was a shameful state. However, Hall thought the future looked bright. Craftsmen were teaching apprentices, professions were lowering the bars, and the avenues of trade were opening. But "we need first all, Education," he said, "for it is the key which will unlock the door of caste, of trade, and consequently of wealth, will bring us home, and make those homes the abode of intelligence. . . . Wise legislation has provided schools the length and breadth of the land, where neither race or nationality is held as a barrier to admission. And I hold it to be the duty of parents, next to serving their God[,] to see that their children attend them."⁶

Hall tied education to material progress and asserted that wealth would command respect. He gave a personal example about being in a Chicago department store with Pinckney Benton Stewart Pinchback, who had served as acting governor of Louisiana for over a month, the first black man in the United States to hold a governorship. The store clerks had not given Hall and Pinchback even minimal help or courtesies. However, after Pinchback selected items for purchase and "the time arrived for my friend to give his name and the address where the goods were to be sent, courtesies were showered on us until we left the establishment." Hall believed that "what our color robbed us of, my friend's name and position restored," and he asserted that that "wealth and intelligence, or position . . . are the 'open sesame' to recognition in every walk of life." But education was necessary to get to that point. Education was the "key to the entire situation; which if the race will only seize and use, will go far toward solving or allaying all of the evils under which the race is now laboring."[7]

Kansas African Americans were united on the importance of education more than they agreed on any other issue, although their reasons varied. From a purely practical standpoint, blacks were often cheated in transactions with landlords—they did not know what they were signing, and without an education they were helpless in understanding simple arithmetic. Voorhees Committee witness Lewis reported that one ex-slave had said, "I wants my children to be educated . . . because then I can believe what they tells me. If I go to another person with a letter in my hand, and he reads it, he can tell me what he pleases in that letter, and I don't know any better. I must take it all for granted; but if I have got children who read and write, I will hand them the letter, and they will tell me the contents of that letter, and I will know it's all right as he says it."[8]

Hall's philosophical ally in advocating for liberal arts education for blacks was none other than the fractious J. C. Embry, who supported Hall's passionate belief in education as the path to upward mobility. As was clear in his letter to the *Colored Citizen* when he declined the nomination for Kansas lieutenant governor, Embry believed that political power would come with economic status. Hall's "Needs of the Race" talk showed that he concurred:

> We need Ministers who will preach more and pound less. We need Leaders who will buy more and sell less. We need Doctors who can cure; Lawyers who can advise; Merchants who can trade; Architects who can plan; Builders who can construct; Capitalists who have money to invest; Mechanics who can invent;

Professional men who can teach; Farmers to till the soil; Authors, Editors, Astronomers; men to build railroads, and men to run them; men to build ships, and men to sail them; Manufacturers to make our clothing; Millers to grind our grain. . . . Wealth will clear the way; and life's arena will spread wide its gates and welcome us into the enclosure of nations as a peer if we will only remember that.[9]

Schooling was crucial. There were no public schools in the South before the Civil War. When free schools were instituted, after the war, many whites believed them inferior to private schools and not proper places to send their children. But that prejudice was gradually overcome. Not only were public schools a boon for African Americans, they provided the first educational opportunities for many white children from poor families.[10] In the postwar period there were passionate pleas for public education all over the country. Grosvenor Clark Morse, a Congregationalist minister and early emigrant to Kansas, gave an address in Kansas during the Civil War tying public education to a nation's effectiveness. Stating that "the condition of the common schools is the true index of general intelligence," Morse insisted that education was the only intelligent foundation for participation in the affairs of government." In sum: "Knowledge is power."[11]

Despite blacks' enthusiasm for education immediately after the war, by the time John Simpson delivered his report in Alabama in 1872 public schools were under assault in many southern states and school systems were not receiving enough funds. Simpson regarded this as class warfare and accused capitalists of hating both poor whites and blacks, saying that both would suffer equally.[12] Many whites, however, were outraged by blacks' educational ambitions. Members of the White League army went so far as to post a warning in the *Franklin (La.) Enterprise*, of St. Martin's Parish, Louisiana, stating, "We own this soil of Louisiana by virtue of our endeavor, as a heritage from our ancestors, and it is ours and ours alone. Science, literature, history, art, civilization belong to us, and not to the negroes."[13] In some cases throughout the South, white supremacists physically destroyed black schools. H. Ruby testified before the Voorhees Committee, "When we opened the school a party of armed men came to my house, seized me, carried me out, and threw me in Thompson's Creek after they had belabored me with the muzzles of their revolvers." These white men told Ruby that they "did not want to have any damned nigger school in that town, and they were not going to have it."[14]

African American public education nationwide was further complicated because many white legislators controlling funds believed blacks simply were not capable of learning. However, when quizzed about blacks' abilities, J. H. Shepherd, school superintendent of Caddo Parish, Louisiana, insisted to the Voorhees Committee that whites and blacks "learn with equal facility." He found, however, that black teachers were often substandard and that both blacks and whites were far behind in mathematics. Shepherd was "inclined to think that the difference is not in the capacity of the races, but that it is the result of the system, as conducted down there.[15] A Louisiana physician, George E. Gillespie, insisted that "some of the colored children learned very rapidly."[16] Nevertheless, whites' belief in blacks' intellectual inferiority was widespread. The Voorhees Committee's Senator Vance asked James Rapier, a black farmer and landlord from Calhoun, Alabama, if he had said that "a colored child could not be raised in the South, and educated, under any circumstances, without being made to remember continually that he was a negro?" Rapier replied, "In my opinion, no colored child could be developed mentally, and morally, in the South."[17]

Voorhees Committee testimony frequently indicated that the breakdown of educational systems in the South was one of the main factors behind post-Reconstruction emigration. Schools disappeared—failed due to lack of funds or were torched by white supremacists, and in many areas of the South there was no free public school system, even for white children. It was generally acknowledged that in some cases schools funds had been stolen, but there was disagreement as to whether the funds had been stolen by Democrats or Republicans. Andrew Currie, the mayor of Shreveport, Louisiana, insisted that "it is a notorious fact, patent both to the colored people and whites that the Republicans misappropriated the school funds; that it was used for election purposes."[18] Regardless of who made off with the money, school funds deposited in the Freedman's Savings and Trust Company Bank had disappeared, J. H. Shepherd testified, and he afterward did the best he could with limited funds.[19]

Southern blacks were ambivalent about wanting integrated classrooms. Some would have preferred segregation but were acutely aware that with so little money available, blacks would end up with inferior schools, if they were established at all. The prevailing attitude was that if a school was segregated, they wanted an African American teacher. But even blacks' most ardent educational supporters, such as Shepherd, testified to the Voorhees Committee that unless these teachers were educated in the North, they were inferior to white teachers.[20]

While testifying to the Voorhees Committee, John Henri Burch entered a report on the proceedings of the labor convention of Alabama. Mr. James Rapier had addressed this convention, commenting that Alabama allocated such a low amount for education that there was only enough money to keep schools open for two months a year, and consequently "under this system we have some of the most inferior teachers on record; in too many cases it appears that they are in the schoolhouses more to exhaust the funds than to improve the child."[21] John Milton Brown testified that since whites dominated school boards, they made sure that only inferior teachers were hired for black schools. The senators could not resist putting the subject of schools aside long enough to quiz him about Alabama's infamous Coahoma County riot. As the county sheriff at the time, Brown had single-handedly faced between 250 and 300 white men, "all drawn up in a line, with their coats off and armed to the teeth," who had come to kill him and break up a meeting of Republicans. Although he talked these men out of executing him, arguing that he could negotiate peace between the two factions, his subsequent efforts did not stop these whites from a rampage of random killings in the black community.[22]

John G. Lewis entered into testimony pledges made by the Louisiana state legislature and emphasized the state's fourth resolution regarding education, which he insisted had not been honored at all: "The education of all classes of the people being essential to the preservation of free institutions, we do declare our solemn purpose to maintain a system of public schools by an equal and uniform taxation on property, as provided by the constitution of the State, which shall secure the education of the white and colored citizens with equal advantages."[23]

Regarding incompetent black teachers, John Simpson said that "many persons have to be employed as teachers from the fact that no better or more competent person can be procured, who should themselves be students in some primary school, and who are totally unfit to teach.[24] Then too, sometimes blacks simply threw out competent white teachers and replaced them with unqualified teachers from their own race. V. Dell, an editor from Fort Smith, Arkansas, testified regarding black intolerance of white educators. Dell stated that "we employed a white teacher for the colored schools—most excellent man," but he said that blacks "were almost unanimous in requesting his dismissal." Dell regretted this situation, then revealed his own prejudice by saying that "the colored people are clannish; and they need careful training, and they need the white man to train them."[25]

"Competent white teachers" were often shunned in the South when they taught in African American schools. John Henri Burch, who was in charge of the archives of the customhouse in the city of New Orleans, testified that while serving on the school board in East Baton Rouge Parish he had "commissioned a great many teachers" and found that "when I would commission a Republican white man . . . he was immediately ostracized and proscribed; but when I would appoint, as I did in many instances, a white teacher who was a Democrat, or whose family were Democrats, whether he taught a white school or a colored school, in some cases it was all right [and] in other cases all wrong. It depended on politics, not their race, or whether they taught in a white or colored school."[26]

For some blacks, given the precipitous decline of public education in the South from the promising beginning after the Civil War, the solution was to go to Kansas. Affronted by the perception of that state as an educational Mecca, Senator Vance confronted Voorhees witness John Milton Brown, saying, "Did you ever see the constitution of Kansas? . . . Don't you know that the word 'white' is in the constitution yet?" Brown replied, "The word 'white' may be in the constitution, but it is regarded as null and void, it has no effect whatsoever." Brown argued,

"There is no law on the statute books of the State of Kansas against the colored man in any way whatever." When Vance countered that no southern state had the word "white" in its constitution, Brown reminded him that there were nevertheless specific laws against blacks.[27]

The ambivalence of Kansas's white communities toward blacks extended to their views of African American education. The truth was that although the majority embraced blacks in an abstract sense and abhorred slavery, most whites did not want their children sharing a classroom with African American children. In the eastern part of the state, where whites dominated in resolving question regarding education, Topeka flitted back and forth between segregation and integration. In fact, that varied from one school district to the next according to the whims of school boards.

William Eagleson of the *Colored Citizen* was outraged by the segregated arrangement of the majority of Topeka's schools. In an editorial he stated, "The school board has again opened and set into operation two or three little colored schools . . . and offers insult to every colored resident of the city." He pointed out that there were "no Irish schools, no German schools, no Swedish schools," and that all the children in the city could attend the closest school except for "the poor child . . . with a black face instead of a white one."[28] Blacks in upper grades, however, were allowed to attend schools with whites.

When Abram Hall presented "The Needs of the Race" to the St. John AME literary society in January 1879, his statement that "wise legislation has provided schools . . . where neither race or nationality is held as a barrier" was true.[29] But a mere six weeks later, on March 14, Kansas passed legislation that again provided for segregated classrooms in "first-class" cities. A "first class city" had a population over fifteen thousand, and a second-class city had a population of between two thousand and fifteen thousand.[30] In 1868, after the fourteenth amendment to the U.S. Constitution provided a broad definition of citizenship that included African Americans, first- and second-class cities in Kansas could still decide to "maintain either separate or integrated educational facilities."[31] In 1877, the state legislature amended existing educational laws to sharply penalize any district school board "refusing the admission of any children into the common schools." The fine was stiff: one hundred dollars each "for every month so offending." However, this did not apply to first- and second-class cities.[32]

Abram Hall's belief in the value of education was shared by his fellow Nicodemians. One of them, William Kirtley, who came in November 1878, brought with him two Bibles, an elementary speller, and an unabridged dictionary. Despite the obstacles endured by all the colonists during the long winter of 1877–78, they found a way to pursue education. The *Stockton News* reported as early as March 14, 1878, before Hall and McCabe's arrival, that there were already two schools in "flourishing condition" in Nicodemus.[33]

One early settler of Nicodemus, John Samuels, told Lulu Craig how he acquired some of his rudimentary skills. Back in Kentucky he had worked in a hemp factory from the time he was twelve until he was twenty-four and freed. He had toiled from dawn to dusk in a dark room, spinning hemp into rope as part a group of over one hundred slaves, driven by an overseer who applied the lash to anyone who fell short of production quotas. The overseer wrote the names of the workers on a large slate, with a weekly tally of pounds spun, and "anyone falling short of what was considered a week's task would be whipped for his failure." Some of the younger men figured out which values spared the lash, although they had no way of knowing the names of the numbers. They carefully altered the numbers to stop the whippings, without the overseer suspecting a thing. This was possible because many supervisors themselves lacked an education. In fact, since there were no public schools in Kentucky at the time, often even the "masters" were poorly educated.[34]

Samuels's story about his hemp-spinning stint continues. One cold January night, an escaped slave from Tennessee came out of the woods to the factory and pleaded for help. The workers were frightened because of the likely stiff punishment for assisting a runaway. The man insisted he meant no harm, and he was obviously starving. He was terrified and his clothing was in tatters, and he could not hide effectively in the leafless wood. They fed him and let him warm up. He then left before daybreak, but he returned two nights later. This time the workers took a chance, helping the man, whom they called "Tenn," and secretly taking him in till spring. In return, he taught them the alphabet by drawing letters on the stone hearth and showing them how to join the letters to make words. Then he told them the names and values of the numerical figures on the board. Tenn departed when spring came, after urging the men to collect any scrap of printed material they came across. Following his departure, secretive studying continued far into each night, as "the flame that he lighted continued to burn. It blazed on and on and threw its light to generations ahead."[35]

John Samuels would later volunteer to serve on the committee to establish Nicodemus's first official school, saying that "though I never went to school a day in my life, I do know the importance of an education." Reverend Roundtree, another former slave, also volunteered. His owner had branded him on the cheek as punishment for learning to read and write.[36]

Establishing schools had been an uphill battle in Graham County long before blacks arrived. Cattlemen had successfully blocked attempts by white settlers to settle in the area. Ranchers dominated the Kebar District, a large, lush, spring-fed grazing area beginning about five miles south of present-day Bogue, Kansas, and extending for some fifty to seventy miles. Craig wrote of the district, "In some places a man riding horseback could not be seen in the tall grass." Naturally, ranchers were not pleased when whites began to settle there in the early 1870s, and they used a variety of means to try to make things intolerable, from destroying crops to outvoting homesteaders trying to organize a subscription school. In one instance, two cowboys forced a clerk at gunpoint to record votes by forty-five nonexistent persons.

Finally, however, in 1877, just before the arrival of black colonists, white settlers met for another vote during roundup and authorized a school when ranchers were away. Craig calls the voters a "determined group of men[,] each carrying his Winchester."[37] The area was said to have gotten its name from a wooden key with the word "Bar" carved on it. The key was carried around by someone petitioning for a post office in the region, a man who insisted that farmers were the key, "for we bar the cattle out of this fine farming section."[38]

Shortly after Hall arrived in Nicodemus, he observed that "one of the drawbacks of our colony has been the absence of a good school. Several attempts have been made, but in time collapsed." He reported in

July 1878 that steps were underway to start and maintain an organized school.[39] However, by December 1878 he said in a letter to the *Stockton News* that men were "raking into life all the old embers of prejudice against the negro race" over the school question. The majority of "unfortunate people . . . of both races" have children who "attend the same school, and are taught by a colored teacher."[40] His comment suggests that this biracial school was located in the Kebar or nearby Millbrook area, which had a number of white immigrants from the South. Earlier in the year, Hall and McCabe had located claims there for the last large African American colonization group in this region.[41]

Shortly after arriving back from Topeka in early 1879, Hall reported to the *Stockton News* that there was now a night school in Nicodemus with an average of forty-five pupils in attendance, conducted by "Prof. J. W. Niles." Friday nights, he said, were set aside for "general spelling school, at which time the entire orthographical force of the village 'lend a hand.'"[42]

Craig also reported on the difficult attempts to start an official school. No one had an idea where to begin. Most of the colonists had never been inside a schoolroom. Reverend Myers, the newly arrived AME pastor, agreed to organize the effort. He called for volunteers, and Clarence Page, who had had only two months of schooling, and John Samuels, who had only received instruction from a runaway slave, agreed to serve on the committee. Other members were Jerry Meyers, Z. T. Fletcher, and John Scott. Niles agreed to let them use his stone house, which was about fourteen feet wide and twenty-five feet long. They used stone blocks for seats.[43]

School began on Monday, July 14, 1879, in an arbor. The teacher, Jenny Fletcher, took enrollment and then instructed the students to go to Niles's house Wednesday morning for the first official day of classes. She began with no working materials, no books, restless children, and "anxious parents expecting great results." The curriculum was basic: Fletcher started with songs and by passing around letters of the alphabet on cardboard squares. The school would later be moved to Charles Page's sod house, followed by the erection of a frame building in 1886.[44]

That month of its founding, July 1879, this fledgling school became the first official school district in the unorganized county of Graham.

To attain this status, by Kansas law, the district had to elect qualified officers, and their acceptance had to be on file with the county superintendent.[45] There was little immediate tangible benefit in such a move. Schools established in unorganized counties would receive a share of the public funds to be apportioned in 1881, but in the meantime Graham County lacked taxable real estate to fund schools, as homesteaders had not proved up on their claims. "Proving up a claim" meant fulfilling all the requirements for owning 160 acres of land on the testimony of two witnesses. The requirements were that homesteaders had to reside on the land for five years, make improvements, and be the head of a household. There were no race or gender limitations. The total fee amount, including the initial filing fee, was eighteen dollars.[46] Teachers in other regions were paid on a subscription basis by impoverished homesteaders. Nevertheless, despite a complete lack of financial support, Nicodemus could proudly claim the honor of establishing the first official school district in the county. It can be assumed that Hall or McCabe did all the paperwork.

By the end of 1879, Graham County had four school districts, although only three were located on the county map of the superintendent of public instruction: Nicodemus, Graham, and Houston. It would be another thirty years before the first student from Nicodemus completed the exam necessary for one to go on to high school. In fact, in the 1880s there were no secondary schools at all in western Kansas. The examination given to students in eastern Kansas was quite difficult, and there were few teachers competent to train students adequately enough for them to pass.

The lack of well-trained teachers was mentioned in the *Voorhees Committee Report,* but part of that problem was financial. Allen B. Lemmon, the Kansas superintendent of public instruction, stated in his second biennial report that "the great hindrance to the success of common schools in all the frontier counties, whether organized or not, is want of funds." He maintained that unless there were appropriations from the state treasury these areas would be plagued by short terms taught by very poorly paid and generally poorly qualified teachers.[47]

The African American settlers of Nicodemus overcame staggering odds to fulfill their dream of educating their children. In Graham

County they overshadowed the white population by organizing the first school district, and for a short time a black teacher taught white students in the Kebar area. It wasn't easy keeping children in school, as on the prairie both black and white families needed children to stay home during warm weather to help with physical labor. The settlers were correct in believing that if Kansas did not provide better educational opportunities for their race, neither would blacks be hindered from pursuing instruction on their own. Certainly they did not have to deal with violence and the destruction of school property as they did in the South. There was less prejudice and more interracial cooperation. By establishing the first school district in the county, African Americans in Nicodemus demonstrated that they were dynamic contributors to the settlement of Kansas.

Chapter 7
Leave This Godforsaken Country

> *I find that the colored man does not like the idea of going to Liberia . . . he prefers to remain here in this country as an American citizen, and if he cannot secure his right as an American citizen in the South, then he wants to go somewhere in the United States where he can—to Kansas or Nebraska, or Missouri—or to any State he can where he can be a citizen under the American flag without fear or hindrance.*
>
> Testimony of John Henri Burch

THERE WAS A SUBTEXT to the Voorhees Committee investigation of the black exodus or, as the subtitle of its report would phrase it, "the removal of the Negroes from the southern states to the northern states." Could African Americans survive outside the South? Were blacks smart enough, strong enough, or determined enough to endure without the guidance of whites? Were they physically suited to survive the severe northern winters? John Davis, a farmer and the editor of the *Junction City Tribune* believed they could not. Davis testified that "men of exceptional enterprise will go into dugouts and make homes for themselves by their own muscles. . . . Such homes can be made, and are made, but it requires the energy and patience of the Northern European to do it."[1]

The Voorhees Committee hearings were to investigate the reasons for the massive immigration from the South. The senators did not concern themselves with the questions being asked by affluent blacks across the United States. *Should* ex-slaves emigrate from the South? If so, to where? For those who favored emigration, the choices were to go north, head west, leave the United States for another country, or ask the government to create a new protected territory as had been done with American Indians. Blacks also debated the advisability of emigrating as colonies, families, other groups, or individuals. A few simply wanted the government to leave them alone and let them rise or fall on their own merits. All of the issues explored during the Voorhees Committee investigation were deliberated widely in newspapers across the nation, but the internal black debate was made public mostly in the African American press. The black newspapers, which surged as subscribers became better educated and more affluent, "countered the stereotypes perpetuated by the communities as a whole, which were often fostered by the white-owned press."[2]

Indiana attracted southern black immigrants who wished to settle in the North. Jobs were plentiful there for mechanics and laborers, and the established school system was a strong draw. In his testimony before the Voorhees Committee, John C. New, chairman of the state's Republican Central Committee, vehemently denied that there had been any effort to bring blacks into the state to bolster votes, saying that "we were earnestly and vigorously opposed to it as a party movement and as a political movement." However, New testified that most blacks coming into the state easily found employment, especially as farm laborers. Estimating that 80 percent found jobs, he gave the impression that Indiana welcomed blacks as long as there weren't too many women and children.[3]

Indiana's school system was somewhat integrated, with separate schools for blacks unless the distance was too great for easy access or regions could not afford two systems. In the latter cases, races attended together. Indiana blacks were also pleased that their children received an education six months a year rather than the scant three months then normally provided in the South.[4] However, many blacks found Indiana's racial attitudes intolerable. Senator Voorhees (of Indiana) asked Samuel L. Perry a leading question—"A man like you, you don't find social equality any more in Indiana than you did in North Carolina, do you?"—and Perry replied that he did not, adding, "If I owned a lot in Indiana and one in hell, I would rent out the one in Indiana and live in hell."[5] Not many blacks in Indiana did own lots: the state could not deliver the main incentive for blacks leaving the South—free land. For that, Kansas still reigned.

Some of the Voorhees Committee's black witnesses who advocated going west into Kansas mentioned the poor conditions for agriculture in the South. In many areas there the land had been overworked and had lost its fertility. O. S. B. Wall, a black real estate agent whom President Abraham Lincoln had once commissioned as a colonel and who had later worked for the Freedmen's Bureau, was quizzed extensively about the treatment of blacks in his home state of North Carolina. He conceded that whites in North Carolina treated African Americans "better and with more consideration, even in the old times, when slavery was still in existence, than any other state in the Union." Still Wall urged blacks to "leave this poor wretched God forsaken country, where the soil does not seem able to sprout black-eyed peas, and go out into the broad, rich, fertile West. It is not from any hostility to the white people, but for the good of the black people, that I urge them to get up and get out from that state." He reiterated, "The trouble is in the sod."[6]

Henry Adams, another Voorhees Committee witness, represented blacks who had given up on America and believed they would only find full acceptance in another country. During Adams's testimony, Senator Blair read aloud a letter sent by Adams to President Rutherford Hayes and Congress on September 15, 1877, on behalf of the National Colored Colonization Society. It was sent when Adams was still living in Shreveport, Louisiana. The letter beseeched that "unless some protection is guaranteed to our race . . . we will cease to be a race of people." It concluded, "Our only hope . . . is the exodus of our people to some country where they can make themselves a name and a nation and be happy and prosperous." Adams urged Hayes and Congress "to assist us . . . by using your power or influence to aid us either by appropriating some Territory in which we can colonize in Liberia or some other country, as we feel that for us to remain in the South will be the destruction of our race."[7]

The Voorhees Committee grilled Adams longer than any other witness. His testimony began March 13 and continued for three days, not concluding until the senators adjourned for the day on March 15. Some of the questions were personal because of the senators' curiosity about Adams's reputed physical strength. He was capable of cutting and splitting three to seven cords of wood a day. He was also well known as a faith healer. The record of his testimony is over one hundred pages long—pages 101–214 of part two. After the Civil War, Adams had toured the South and collected memorandums of atrocities. He produced these records during the hearing. There were 682 documented accounts of brutal crimes against African Americans.[8] Murder was rampant as well as rape, deadly beatings, and senseless destruction of property. Blacks were helpless against mob action. At the conclusion of his testimony Adams said, "To my own knowledge there was over two thousand colored people killed trying to get away, after the white people told us we were free, which was in 1875."[9]

Samuel L. Perry, an African American, testified that when whites in North Carolina believed all blacks were going to Liberia, "They gave us schools, and that stopped the movement."[10] Adams, however, argued that in some areas whites retaliated and seized blacks' assets when they were not able to quell black interest in Liberia.[11] Clearly whites felt threatened by the thought of black emigration. They saw African American labor as crucial to their well-being.

Kansas blacks turned their attention to the national debate over the advisability of migration from the South after the intense activity of the 1878 elections died down. During late 1878 and early 1879, migration into the state from the South was increasing, but it had not yet become the deluge that would come in the fall of 1879. The lull in politics afforded black communities an opportunity to develop new strategies for racial uplift, and the *Colored Citizen* continued to be a major forum for diverse opinions nationwide.[12]

Three prominent Kansas blacks were absorbed with additional issues—E. P. McCabe and William Eagleson battled for civil rights and political power, while William Matthews struggled against a rebellious branch of black Masons—but migration was the foremost subject of their writings. And throughout the country essays poured from the pens of articulate African Americans asserting arguments more nuanced than much of the oral testimony taken during the Voorhees Committee hearings (where many of the witnesses were men who had always been laborers). Many believed that the only hope for blacks was to leave the South for new territory where their rights would be respected. Others regarded the South as their birthright, their natural home, and believed their best hope lay in achieving equality there. Frederick Douglass, a former slave whose writings were often published in the *Colored Citizen*, was one of the latter. Widely admired for his superior ability to write and speak, Douglass wrote an autobiography that inspired blacks and amazed whites with its story of cunning and determination to acquire an education. Douglass was adamantly opposed to the exodus, writing, "There is in my judgment no part of the U.S. where an industrious and intelligent colored man can serve his race more wisely and efficiently than upon the soil where he was born and reared and is known." Douglass asked rhetorically, "Shall we, who have borne so many hardships and outrages and seen so many changes in our favor now throw up the sponge, abandon our vantage ground of possession . . . and go among strangers in pursuit of homes in a cold and uncongenial climate, rather than remain on the soil of birth, where we may live down persecution and oppression?"[13]

Some blacks endorsed Douglass's reasoning, while others, such as Isaiah Wears, a real estate broker from Philadelphia, strenuously objected to the blacks' exodus for other reasons. In his testimony before the Voorhees Committee, Wears warned against blacks becoming "unsettled" and "losing their place." He found the idea of moving to foreign countries especially worrisome and believed that liberty could be best realized in the South. He believed the federal government had a duty to protect African Americans and further opposed the exodus on the grounds that it led to northerners feeling released from their duties. Now they thought, as Wears viewed it, that any anytime blacks were experiencing unendurable oppression they could just "get up and go to Kansas, or somewhere else."[14]

In Topeka, *Colored Citizen* editor Eagleson took strong exception to Douglass's views, although he noted in print that Kansas's own Captain Matthews agreed with Douglass. The *Colored Citizen* assured its readers that Douglass did not represent the views of "the best thinkers."[15] Matthews was distracted with his duties as a Prince Hall Mason, otherwise he might have been more involved with the migration debate. Editor Eagleson, who was also a Prince Hall Mason, always treated Matthews with the utmost respect, while he seemed to more

Frederick Douglass. Courtesy of Kansas Historical Society.

freely challenge the arguments of other correspondents who advocated blacks remaining in the South.[16]

A differing opinion came from J. C. Embry, who argued that "the present menaced situation of the blacks of the South threatens also the peace and well-being of the whites." He had decided that "owing to the long habit of complete domination of whites over blacks the natural incompatibility of race has become so exaggerated that the prevailing aspect is, and has been for some years past, practically a state of war. . . . The blacks of the South must be wholly free or re-enslaved."[17] Embry thought the best way for blacks to be "wholly free" was to live apart from whites. He insisted it would be cheaper for the nation to give lands to African Americans in the "Southwestern territories and the unsettled portions of the Southwestern states" than to "spend millions in fruitless efforts at protection in the South, and at length drift into a new Civil War."[18] Embry suggested that the small number of African Americans who did not want to leave the South and were prospering would have greater security without tensions between the races. He urged blacks to emulate suffragists and petition Congress. Although the "woman suffrage" movement began in England, after the Civil War women in the United States increased their lobbying for the right to vote. Embry reminded the readers of *Colored Citizen* that suffragists "give the country no rest for years" and "they make their wants known.[19]

John S. Waller of Leavenworth "heartily approved of the idea."[20] Eagleson was intrigued by what he saw as the practicality of the proposal and urged his readers to give the plan careful consideration.[21] But J. W. S. Banks, the *Citizen*'s new editorial correspondent from Leavenworth, representing the views of many, no doubt, opposed Embry's idea. Banks said that he was already dismayed that blacks were being persuaded to "leave their native homes hard-earned by them through troubles, hardships, much suffering under the lash, and by the sweat of their brows." He asked, "If America is our country, and if we fought and toiled for it, and above all made it what it is . . . and helped to save it, why should we try to persuade a part of our nation to leave any State and go to another? America is our native country; why be driven from one State to the other?"[22]

Despite the opposition in Kansas, Embry pressed on with his agenda and snagged a lengthy interview with Senator Windom, who would in 1880 lead the minority faction of the Voorhees Committee. While Embry conceded that his plan tended to separate the races, he insisted that "no law framed by Congress for the protection of colored citizens, can be enforced in the face of united hostility by the Whites of the South." Windom agreed with Embry and introduced a congressional resolution promoting the partial emigration of blacks from the South to other areas of the United States.[23] Shortly after Embry persuaded Windom as to the merits of the "Embry Plan," he reported having called on Kansas senator John J. Ingalls at his residence and "favorably influenced his feelings toward our down trodden and hated, but really noble, race." At this meeting, according to Embry, Ingalls promised that "his voice and vote shall be used in [blacks'] defense on all seasonable occasions." Although Embry would have preferred an African American congressional advocate concerning blacks, he conceded that Senator Bruce was a poor speaker; he assured his readers that based on his frequent discussions with Bruce, he believed the senator a man of great intelligence and capacity, with standing and influence in Congress.[24]

Many blacks besides Banks rejected the "Embry Plan." Cyrus D. Bell, a resident of Omaha and occasional correspondent to the *Citizen*, opposed Windom's resolution. Bell maintained that it "would have the Government to take the initiative in removing *citizens* from one part of its dominion to another, because they cannot exercise their rights as citizens in their present home." Bell argued that it would be an admission that the government could not or would not protect such citizens in their present location and noted that their removal would throw that responsibility onto other states and territories. He abhorred the idea of "locating thousands and thousands of un-acclimated, unprepared men, women and children in any Territory set apart exclusively for them." This would set emigrants up for outrages that would surpass southern atrocities, Bell wrote.[25]

Embry, it turned out, was furious after Senator Windom introduced the "Windom Resolution" and took credit for what was, Embry wrote in the *Colored Citizen*, "in fact, and emphatically the 'Embry

Senator William Windom (R-MN). Courtesy of Library of Congress, Prints & Photographs Division.

Plan.'" Embry complained that the "scheme was never heard of here until I came and wrote an article on it." Outraged, he listed the names of all the members of Congress he had lobbied during the past year. He also castigated Senator Ingalls for believing that blacks were "a dependent race" who would not "go out and build cities, found new communities and turn the desert into fields," but were only "willing to follow where the white man leads the way."[26] In a subsequent letter Embry directed *Citizen* readers to the March 1879 issue of the *North American Review*, in which they could read the opinions of "an array of the brightest intellect our country affords, engaged in an earnest, thoughtful wrestle with the problem of negro suffrage and citizenship."[27]

Cyrus Bell again took exception to the "Embry Plan" of governmental removal of blacks from the South, accusing Embry of bullying. "The presumptuous author . . . considers himself infallible," Bell wrote to the *Citizen*. "He may yet learn that making faces[,] and throwing mud at those with whom he may disagree, will not always harmonize them to his opinions."[28] Bell then endorsed some of Ingalls's observations about the "inherent moral and intellectual weakness that is so characteristic of us" and concluded with another attack on Embry.

The emigration debate was causing divisions to widen between Kansas African American politicians. In an attempt to mend them, in early 1879 the *Citizen* endorsed the idea of a national convention of "colored men." W. B. Townsend heartily endorsed the idea and wanted the gathering to focus on forcing the Republican Party to protect the rights and property of blacks in the South.[29] However, Leavenworth lawyer John S. Waller proposed that such a convention be confined to the state of Kansas and suggested that "there be one representative sent for every one hundred colored people in the State sent from each place, and that the purpose of said convention shall be to adopt measures relative to the reception and location, and rendering any other needed assistance to the migration of our people from the South."[30] The *Citizen* called for debate on Waller's proposal.

Kansas blacks seem to have immediately shifted their focus from migration to quarreling over the advisability of a "colored convention" versus a "colored conference." The former would comprise elected delegates, while a conference would be attended by "leading men of the race." Eagleson defended conventions over conferences, as he doubted the "character, ability, and standing" of self-appointed leading men. He suspected they would have "but little weight or influence with the American people, because the question as to what amount of blackness they had would be an open one." He added that "in almost every community about every other man you meet considers himself a *leading* man, and just as soon as the invitation for leading men to meet in conference should be issued, each of these would be ready to swear that he was the man intended."[31] Although Cyrus Bell agreed with Eagleson that conventions were preferable to conferences, he complained about the lack of progress made by those he had attended in the past that "never achieved a single act which resulted in the least benefit to those who have sent them." However, if the object was to "provide ways and means for advancing the political, moral and intellectual interests of this whole people, then we are ready to vote 'aye' upon the proposition of properly elected delegates."[32]

The debate over convention versus conference became more acidic than the emigration debate. On March 27, 1879, Eagleson attended a black political meeting in Topeka that reinforced his wariness of men who might proclaim themselves leaders. He reported remarks that would incite "ridicule and contempt in the minds of intelligent men" and would bring "disgrace on our efforts, and spread discontent and humiliation among the thinking portion of our people."[33] There were many anonymous letters to the *Citizen*, letters said by Eagleson to be too improper for publication, letters from newspaper editors outside Kansas, and letters from persons responding to things they had never read in the paper, only heard about.[34]

Finally Eagleson appealed to the two he called the "grand moguls" of western Kansas, saying, "Let us hear from McCabe and Hall on the all-important subject."[35] But apparently neither one commented publicly on the debate over convention versus conference, possibly because plans were now under way for the National Conference of Colored Men, to be held in Tennessee in May. Hall did wish to express his views on black migration, however, and his opinion was unusual for the time. He did not endorse any of the approaches advanced by eastern politicians or Kansas blacks. Viewing African Americans not as a group but as a collection of individuals, in July 1878 he urged them not to unite but to emulate Jews: "Scatter out as did the Jews in England, when under the law," Hall wrote. "Get all the intelligence, property, and money you can, and in the process of time with you, as with the Jews, will come a favorable solution to the race problem. The more the race unites the greater will be the pressure against it, and the more rapidly [it will] go to the wall. But scattered out, all over this vast country, each one doing the very best his circumstance allows, you will find the pressure gradually lessening for want of an object on which to concentrate, until it will finally disappear. Don't stop at one State, but take in the entire country." It was a prescient view, really, and the confident author signed off, "Yours for progress, A. T. Hall, Jr."[36]

Hall was not the only one who urged racial diffusion, though the opinion must have been unpopular at the time. In his testimony before the Voorhees Committee, Alabaman James Rapier stated, "I have visited Kansas: and I want to see the negroes scattered from the Atlantic to the Pacific, and not huddled together. This has been our weakness. We have always thought that banding together was our strength; but in this particular case it has been our weakness. We do not want to go in crowds that will excite the prejudices of the people; we do not want to go to any particular State or any particular Territory."[37]

The National Conference of Colored Men would begin on May 6, 1879, in Nashville. Prominent African Americans nationwide had called for serious discussions about issues challenging blacks, and the conference agenda would cover such topics as civil rights and legal justice, unity, morality and religion, black migration, beneficial associations, sanitary and social conditions, literary advancement, education, commerce and labor, and the influence of women.[38]

W. B. Townsend objected in the *Colored Citizen* to all conferences and conventions, whether national or sponsored by the state, insisting them a waste of time and money. In Kansas, the influx of poor blacks from the South was increasing. He wrote, "We don't want so much deliberation about feeding the hungry and administering to the sick; ... what we want to do is to exercise more practical benevolence coupled with the will to act."[39] Nevertheless, Kansas would send a delegate to

Nashville: T. W. Henderson, associate editor of the *Citizen* and pastor of St. John AME, in compliance with a resolution passed at meeting of the Kansas Freedmen's Relief Association.[40]

Henderson arrived in Nashville a day late, but he reported that when the chairman announced that a representative from Kansas was present,

> such shouts and applause I have but seldom heard. Men and women, old and young, shouted at the very top of their voices . . . the idea of Kansas, which to the colored man of America, is the grandest, greatest, and freest of all the States of the Union, being represented was too great a sign to them to be passed in silence. Let it be remembered that since the day that the name of Old John Brown become known as the very chief among the enemies of slavery . . . the very name of the State has become dear to the heart of every black man from one end of this country to the other, and hence, whenever the name of Kansas was pronounced in the conference room, applause at once began.[41]

From two to three thousands spectators attended each session, including the governor of Tennessee. Among the distinguished African American attendees were former governor P. B. S. Pinchback and former congressman John Roy Lynch, a U.S. representative from Louisiana. Henderson later wrote "There never was assembled, in this country since the days our fathers met to sever the Colonies from Brittan's rule by the adoption of a declaration of independence, a more serious, earnest and determined set of men than those who composed this meeting."[42] At the end of the conference, the all-important Committee on Migration submitted this resolution, which was unanimously passed by the convention:

> Whereas a further submission to the wrongs imposed, and a further acquiescence in the abrogation of our rights and privileges would prove us unfit for citizenship, devoid of manhood, and unworthy the respect of men; therefore
>
> *Resolved*, That it is the sense of this Conference that the great current of migration sweeping people, which has, for the

past few months, taken so many of our people from their homes in the South, and which is still carrying hundreds to the free and fertile West, should be encouraged and kept in motion until those who remain are accorded every right and privilege guaranteed by the Constitution and laws.[43]

The relative lull in politics and events that provided opportunity for thoughtful analysis and consideration of issues soon passed. Migration would go from a topic of debate to a deluge of actual refugees from the South. Discussion of control over educational opportunities would yield to the reality of de facto segregation, as African American emigrants settled in clusters, just as other migrant groups did. As of December 31, 1879, William Eagleson and his brother James ceased publication of the *Colored Citizen*. A joint stock company bought them out and started a new paper, the *Kansas Herald*, with Eagleson as co-editor. It was quickly renamed the *Herald of Kansas* to avoid a lawsuit. The *Herald* would only be published through June 1880. Then the African American *Topeka Tribune* followed, with a gap in publication between September 1881 to June 1883. During this brief golden age for black editors and publishers, these papers provided a forum for Kansas African Americans of the time to express divergent views on matters critical to the race—and they remain an important primary source for historians today.

Chapter 8
Give No Aid to the Sharks

Our number of refugees in this city fluctuates very much. Topeka, our headquarters is very much crowded, resulting in sickness and death. The aim of this association [Kansas Freedmen's Relief Association] is to provide necessary food, shelter, clothing, & c, for them to procure work and find homes in families.
                                    Testimony of M. Bosworth

IMMEDIATELY AFTER THE CIVIL WAR, a few African Americans in the South made modest gains. Some were elected to public office, and some acquired land and even prospered. But economic conditions throughout the country were harsh. Abraham Lincoln's successor as president, Andrew Johnson, restored land to a number of previous slave owners and granted amnesty to former Confederates who swore allegiance to the United States. Northerners, reeling from the cost of the Civil War, became indifferent to the plight of southerners, black and white. The U.S. financial crisis that came to be known as the Panic of 1873 led to a long period of depression, and Northern idealists mostly concentrated on protecting their own holdings. Meanwhile white southerners increased their violence against African Americans, blaming them for the annihilation of the southern economy but needing their labor. Whites conscripted blacks into chain gangs through trumped-up criminal charges (of vagrancy, for example). White rape and murder of blacks were on the rise. And economic conditions for black tenant farmers were hardly different from their conditions under slavery.

In Washington, the Voorhees Committee heard chilling reports of white retaliation against blacks determined to escape the South. One of the most persuasive witnesses to document white violence was Charlton H. Tandy of St. Louis. An effective and persistent champion for black rights, Tandy had helped establish the Lincoln Institute, said to be the first school of higher education for blacks in Missouri. Born to free black parents in Kentucky, Tandy was a captain in the Civil War and served in a variety of local, state, and federal government positions afterward. Nell Painter wrote that Tandy, along with John Turner and Reverend Moses Dickson organized the Colored Refugee Relief Board at the St. Paul's African Methodist Episcopal Church in St. Louis, March 1879 and "[f]or the next two years the group fed, clothed, housed, and bought passage to Kansas for approximately 10,000 migrants."[1]

As historian Bryan M. Jack noted, these Exodusters "bore little resemblance to the relatively well-equipped, well-organized earlier migrants."[2] In St. Louis, the arrival of destitute refugees presented an excruciating dilemma for African Americans who had established middle-class communities, just as it would in Kansas. Abstract debate on the plight of southern blacks had been one thing, but confronting the physical reality of diseased, impoverished, and terrified humans was quite another.

Those Exodusters who did make it to Kansas found that social services there were overwhelmed. White and black Kansans needed to figure out how to absorb the teeming masses that had landed in the state, and race relations were tested. James N. Leiker wrote that the influx of Exodusters brought all the contradictions to the surface. In the West, blacks enjoyed high degrees of physical and economic autonomy" but "on the other hand, Kansans and other westerners generally frown on 'artificial' efforts of government to assist disadvantaged groups, or to establish policies of racial integration that interfere with an individual's right to associate with whom he or she pleases."[3] By late March 1879, the *Colored Citizen* began weighing in on the practicalities of blacks moving from the South to Kansas. Editor Eagleson castigated the "white Republican papers of Kansas" that had supported freeing the slaves but afterward objected to the mass migration from the South. The *Citizen* urged immigrants to "come on. If they come here and starve and die as well, it is better to starve to death in Kansas than to be shot and killed in the South."[4]

In early April, the *Leavenworth Times* objected to national reports that Kansas wanted to turn blacks away, asserting, "Kansas extends an invitation to men of all races and nationalities to come and make their homes with her; we invite white men, black men, yellow men, and men of every other color, only asking that they shall come prepared to take care of themselves.... The objection that has been raised to the multitude now coming from the South is not that they are black or humble, but that a large proportion of them are destitute and helpless, and immediately upon their arrival here would become a charge upon the public."[5]

By May, the *Colored Citizen* was becoming alarmed at the condition of refugees. Eagleson cautioned immigrants that homestead land "could only be acquired by hard work." He advised southern blacks "never to leave home for Kansas" without having money and definite plans for what to do after arriving. And he again reminded those thinking of making the journey that "in Kansas everybody must work or starve." Additionally, Eagleson was distressed over the large of number of old persons arriving in the state. Vigorous young men and women could earn a living, he said, but the elderly would not.[6]

The National Conference of Colored Men that met in May 1879 in Nashville unanimously adopted the resolutions of the Committee on Migration endorsing the right of blacks to emigrate.[7] Although the committee lamented the conditions forcing African Americans to leave the South, members were entirely sympathetic with their determination to seek real freedom. By the end of May, many northern newspapers were paying attention to the situation. Eagleson rejoiced that the "North is getting aroused, which means salvation to the black man of America."[8]

In July, the prestigious New York publication *Harper's Weekly* published three illustrations representing "The Colored Exodus—Scenes at Topeka, Kansas."[9] This was in keeping with the magazine's early interest in all things Kansas, which it regarded as the wildest state in the Union. The accompanying editorial commented that southern whites were alarmed, with planters curtailing agricultural plans because of the scarcity of labor. Southern editors printed accounts of the dire conditions of refugees who had viewed Kansas as the Promised Land. The *Daily Democrat*, a New Orleans paper, gloated that the town of Wyandotte, Kansas, had decided that "no more paupers shall be landed at that point."[10] J. S. Stockton, the mayor of Wyandotte, the paper reported, had issued a proclamation to owners of steamboats and transportation companies, stating that "all boats, officers, and agents disobeying the proclamation would be held legally responsible." This involved a hefty fine, with boats seized until the fine was paid. The town's citizens, the *Daily Democrat* said, prevented boats from landing for "self-protection."[11]

Stockton pleaded in a letter published in Topeka's *Commonwealth*: "Our city is filled with colored refugees, utterly destitute. Large numbers have died and many are now sick. This city has struggled to stem this terrible tide of pauperism, hoping to open up a way for forwarding these destitute emigrants to western homes. . . . Surrounded by the present hordes of sick, dying and destitute men, women and children that must starve unless the generous-hearted people of the United States will respond to our call for aid."[12] Stockton wrote that Wyandotte's normal commerce had largely been suspended, as the focus was on immigrant families arriving barefoot, in rags, hungry, with broods of children, and sick and diseased. Many migrants were forced to camp in the woods, and a relief agent in Independence, Missouri, reported that a single family had lost five sons "who were frozen to death coming through."[13] Caroline De Green of Topeka later testified before the Voorhees Committee that the barracks there "were crowded to their utmost capacity" with Exodusters.[14] And a reporter for the *St. Louis Globe Democrat* who interviewed migrants there wrote that passengers waiting to board a steamer for Kansas were "living moving rags, animated rag bags."[15]

In the South, commentary was scornful. The *Vicksburg Herald* asserted that only the most "ignorant of the plantation negroes are moving away" and that the "sharp, shrewd darkies know better."[16] According to the paper, some refugees believed they would receive free land and money to get a fresh start in Kansas and that only blacks would be allowed to vote. The *Herald* scoffed at a circular exalting conditions in Kansas: it was said to picture a newly arrived black family living in a gabled house with dormered French windows, the father leisurely reading a newspaper while his wife directed servants.[17] In Topeka the *Commonwealth* warned blacks anticipating a glorious new start in Kansas that "they are not needed here. There is nothing before them but hardship, privation and beggary."[18]

Some letters to editors were vicious. The *North Topeka Times* published a letter from someone who claimed to have a cargo of "emancipated slaves ready for shipment—cheap, very cheap indeed—consignee to pay freight." The author of the letter hoped the editor, a former friend, would "open [his] heart and except [sic] this cargo, pay charges thereon, and distribute them about your Black Republicans, about which your state is so proud." The embittered writer continued, "They have once been the lawful property of the South, they have been a valuable possession of a great and noble people, but now since they are worthless, yea, an oppression to our county, have them, have the[m] all, and if we can not get along without a nuisance, let us have the Chinamen; he is a least industrious and has his wants easily satisfied.[19]

On April 28, 1879, the African American citizens of Topeka formed a permanent organization, the Kansas Colored State Immigration Bureau (Central Committee) to determine the needs of the Exodusters arriving in Kansas and to form a strategy for rendering aid.[20] One of its first steps was to prepare and distribute a circular in the southern states that would prepare blacks for conditions in Kansas. The organization was headquartered at the *Colored Citizen*'s office and readers were instructed to send donations there. The committee "hoped that local organizations among the colored people will be formed in every town in Kansas."[21] The similarity of names for the various organizations and proliferation of local organizations in eastern Kansas would soon cause confusion among the donors.

The Kansas Freedmen's Relief Association (KFRA) was incorporated May 8, 1879. This organization was the largest and most successful of the relief agencies and was the creation of the crusading governor of Kansas, John Pierce St. John, who served as its president. There were fifteen men on the board of directors.[22] Nine of the directors were from Topeka and the other six were from the Kansas towns of Atchison, Iola, Seneca, Marysville, Independence, and Winfield. One of the directors, John Milton Brown, an African American, helped draft the by-laws and constitutions of both the Kansas Freedmen's Relief Association and the Kansas Colored State Immigration Bureau formed the previous month.[23] Brown would become the superintendent of the KFRA.

Nationwide the plight of the Exodusters was attracting sympathy. Senator John J. Ingalls reported that he had referred a bill to the Committee on Appropriations authorizing the secretary of war to issue rations and clothing to "destitute refugees."[24] President Hayes maintained publicly it was the "right of the negro to emigrate whenever he saw fit to do so" and that their interests were served best by "their scattering throughout the western states, instead of crowding into any one of them."[25]

In June, the *Commonwealth* published a long letter from Governor St. John to a Louisianan who had written to inquire about conditions in Kansas. The beleaguered governor described the conditions for homesteading and stated that although the land was of good quality, it was unimproved and required "bone, muscle and energy, a free will to use it, coupled with sufficient money to buy a plow and a team." St. John warned future emigrants that the vision of forty acres and a mule was a myth intended to "mislead, deceive and wrong the colored people."[26]

The trickle of African American emigrants that began in March 1879 was becoming a deluge, and cracks began to show in the united front previously maintained by Kansas African Americans regarding aid. How much help did the newcomers need? Were they entitled to assistance? How much support could well-to-do blacks give without risking their hard-won status? Thomas Cox wrote that "the migrants seemed to contradict the ideal of self-reliance, an ethos endorsed by white and Negro Topekans."[27] For black Kansans, the issue of aid—assistance in the form of money, supplies, services, employment—was a divisive topic that starkly illuminated philosophical differences. On June 19, the *Topeka Capital* published an appeal under the heading "The Colored People." It gave a brief history of black suffering and then asked for contributions: "Having been kept in a penniless condition by our oppressors of the South, we appeal to the humane people of America for their sympathies and assistance in helping us to a land where peace, if not prosperity reigns. All donations sent to the Kansas Freedmen's Relief Association, to Topeka, will be thankfully received." Among the signers were Benjamin Singleton, instigator of the colonization movement into Kansas, and his agent and secretary of the association, Alonzo D. DeFrantz. However, Major J. K. Hudson, the white editor of the *Capital*, made a point of issuing a disclaimer below the appeal: "The above address was not authorized or approved by the Kansas Freedmen's Relief Association." Hudson insisted that the appeal was not "warranted by the condition of refuges [sic] in Kansas and . . . not supported or believed necessary by the intelligent hardworking colored people of Topeka." The *Capital* asserted that Kansas was not the best place for immigrants and that "Ohio, Illinois, Pennsylvania, Michigan, and Indiana present better fields today for the settlement of thousands of penniless refugees."[28]

White Americans nationwide joined the debate. The citizens of Worcester, Massachusetts, held a public meeting to interest people in raising funds to transport blacks from the South. Indiana volunteered to receive 5,000; Illinois 2,100 (and an additional 20,000 to its farms); and Pennsylvania 1,200. There was no mention of communicating with blacks regarding this magnanimity.[29]

Some predominately white Kansas towns took steps to prevent blacks from joining their communities. After the Kansas Freedmen's Relief Association sent ten healthy young adults and four children to Wichita at their own request, because some had acquaintances there, the Wichita city council met to raise money to send the refuges back. Acting mayor A. Wiegand notified the association that he intended to use his quarantine powers to prevent more Exodusters from entering the city. Under Kansas law he could do this, but his threats only applied to black immigrants, not whites.[30] The *Commonwealth* asked, "Quarantine against what?" The paper said that it was ridiculous to be frightened by the entry of "fourteen negroes, who asked nothing of them, who were in good health, able-bodied, and willing to work."[31]

When the Relief Association heard that Salina, Kansas, could provide work, twelve blacks went there. The *Saline Journal* referred to this small number of work-seeking newcomers as a major incursion, adding, "We do not blame the Topeka people for desiring to rid themselves of these troublesome charges, but we do find fault with a self-appointed committee that takes it upon themselves to cast a burden upon towns that do not desire such a burden."[32] And by the end of

July the *Weekly Clarion* in Jackson, Mississippi, quoted St. John as saying that "the funds of the association are about exhausted, and to send more of them here in addition to the number that are already here and must be provided for, would be a cruel outrage upon the black man."[33]

After the Kansas Freedmen's Relief Association was officially incorporated on May 8, 1879, Governor St. John put Elizabeth Comstock, born in England in 1815, in charge of the organization. She was a Chicago-based member of the Society of Friends (Quakers) and greatly admired by St. John for her selfless charity work. Comstock traveled to Kansas, where a *Commonwealth* reporter described her as a "gray-haired, bright-eyed lady well on in years," who dressed in "the picturesque Quaker costume" and used "the Scriptural 'thee' and 'thou' in lieu of the more modern personal pronouns." Comstock solicited funds for the constructions of barracks to help accommodate the Exodusters, and some were built in the north side of Topeka. A reporter for the *Daily Capital* wrote that these "afforded little shelter from the storms," however, and said that a room used as temporary hospital was "in filthy condition," and asserted that the immigrants "should be compelled to do their duty toward keeping the place clean."[34]

Laura S. Haviland, a resident of Michigan and also a member of the Society of Friends, joined Comstock in Kansas and became the secretary of the Freedmen's Relief Association. Haviland had been a fearless champion of civil rights for blacks since before the Civil War and established Michigan's first stop on the Underground Railroad. At times she had even personally escorted slaves to Canada. Despite threats against her life, Haviland never relented in her efforts to secure freedom for blacks. In her autobiography she wrote, "I would not for my right hand become instrumental in returning one escaped slave to bondage. I firmly believe in our Declaration of Independence, that all men are created free and equal, and that no human being has a right to make merchandise of others born in humbler stations, and place them on a level with horses, cattle, and sheep, knocking them off the auction-block to the highest bidder, sundering family ties, and outraging the purest and tenderest feelings of human nature."[35]

Elizabeth Leslie Comstock and Laura Smith Haviland. Courtesy of Library of Congress, Manuscript Division, Records of the National Woman's Party.

The two women made formidable partners and on December 31, 1879, opened a warehouse and distributing center for the Kansas Freedmen's Relief Association in North Topeka. The building was forty feet long and twenty feet wide. From then until March 1880 the organization received 1,880 packages. Each one—box, bale, or barrel—was numbered and labeled, with the number registered in a ledger along with names and locations of donors. Goods such as men's coats, pants, vests, and bedding were kept in separate piles.[36] Despite the efforts of the KFRA, the number of blacks arriving daily in eastern Kansas depleted the cache of contributions, and political controversy accelerated. Comstock and Haviland would deny allegations by Voorhees hearing witnesses in 1880 that they were in the work for the money, and Comstock would point out that the twenty workers for the Relief Association had altogether received a mere $551.60 for six months.

Residents of western Kansas, both black and white, were also embroiled in the aid argument. Despite the role he had played in securing supplies for the Nicodemus colonists, A. T. Hall was opposed to black immigrants receiving additional aid. In a scathing letter to the *Stockton News* in March 1879, Hall accused Reverend S. P. Roundtree, one of the founders of the Nicodemus, and Reverend Silas Lee, a highly respected minister, of keeping collected aid for themselves, and he accused John Niles of reselling donated items and keeping the money. Claiming that the three men had solicited in the name of the Nicodemus colonists, Hall called for a meeting to formally disband the colony and in the meantime asked the "generous public" to "give no aid to the sharks who are begging it, as they represent no persons but themselves."[37] Following this March 27 meeting, the *Colored Citizen* published the following communication from Nicodemus:

> Editor Colored Citizen—Sir you will please publish the following resolutions which were unanimously passed at meeting held by the Nicodemus Colony today....
>
> WHEREAS,—After 18 months residence in the State of Kansas and County of Graham, amid hardships innumerable. And

whereas our condition, hard at best, has gradually improved during the term of our residence here. And Whereas, we feel ourselves now to be in a condition to stand alone.

THEREFORE be it resolved,—That this community now known as the Nicodemus Graham County Colony, be, on and after this date dissolved its officers and members to become citizens of Graham County in common with all others.

RESOLVED—That a vote of thanks be extended to the generous public of this and other States for the assistance rendered us, and the officers of the K.P.R.R. [Kansas Pacific Railway] Co. for the favors they have shown us and to the officers of our colony, for the zeal and interest which they have manifested in getting us established.

RESOLVED—That any person or persons who may hereafter solicit aid in the name of the Nicodemus Graham Co., Colony, be prosecuted to the full extent of the law.

RESOLVED—That the Public Press through-out the country be requested to publish these resolutions.[38]

The resolutions were signed: "J. W. Niles, President; E. P. McCabe, Secretary."

It was a stunning move. No doubt, part of the colonists' motive was to dissociate from the plight of the needy Exodusters. However, Hall's forceful arguments in favor of these resolutions also protected his own interests. His and McCabe's thriving land business would be harmed if the perception of Graham County was that of an undesirable area for settlement where people could not make a living. Additionally, as a highly moral and religious man, Hall would have regarded those who did not work and received unneeded assistance as unethical persons. He would have been outraged by any fraudulent solicitation by members of the community.

Times were hard, and even a great number of white settlers in Graham County were asking for aid. Governor St. John was inundated with letters in 1880. A Graham County man, James Himes, asked that his name be kept secret "for it greives [sic] me to have to ask for aid." His horse had died, he wrote, and he had to hire a man to break the sod, and he was a "stranger among strangers." He went on to say that "grasshoppers took what corn I had planted." He only asked for money to buy food to see him through the winter. Some were even abandoning the state. "A number of good men have sold their claims at ruinous prices to get back east," wrote A. J. R. Smith from nearby Grainfield, Kansas.[39]

Hall's apparent dismissal of the needs of immigrant African Americans did not meet well with W. B. Townsend, the prominent black leader with whom Hall had clashed previously. In March 1880 Townsend wrote a column in the *Herald of Kansas* accusing politicians in Graham County of "misrepresenting the condition of those poor people to the public by saying that there is no suffering there, simply for political purposes." He reminded readers that Graham County was about to be organized, and each locality aspiring for the county seat "is striving to show that it and its people are the most prosperous and above want."[40]

At a meeting in Hill City, a committee investigating the need for aid formed the Graham County Aid Association, but Benjamin B. F. Graves, editor of the *Millbrook Times*, ranted that the association "gave rise to stories of want, suffering and destitution" and encouraged idleness in "men always howling about hard times," and "always eagerly looking for work and praying they might not find it." He especially objected to "begging committees" that did the work for individuals "either ashamed or too lazy to beg for themselves." Graves protested that it would have a damaging effect on the immigration into Graham County.[41]

All the Graham County newspapers feuded over the aid issue. The *Western Star*, based in Hill City, angrily responded to the following exert from the *Millbrook Times*: "Be it understood the Graham county is not reduced to beggary and the so-called Graham County Aid Association was manufactured in Hill City without consulting the county at large, and it in no wise represents the condition or desire of the people of this county."[42] *Western Star* editor Thomas Beaumont retorted that the first application to the committee was from Millbrook and added,

"How contemptible it is for a paper to put such a 'nice' face on things about its town and cast reflection upon other when in reality they are in the same fix as their neighbors."[43]

A good friend of the governor, John Inlow, had been appointed by the Graham County Aid Association to go to eastern Kansas and solicit assistance. Inlow wrote to St. John about what he saw to be the perilous condition of Graham County residents, referred to his own poor health, and said he was taking St. John's advice to "live a Christian life."[44] Meanwhile, things were looking up. On December 29, 1879, St. John had appealed for help to Jay Gould, the New York railroad magnate who in 1880 controlled ten thousand miles of railway, about one-ninth of the railway mileage of the United States. J. A. Keeney of Trego County called on Gould personally on behalf of St. John. On January 10, Keeney happily reported that St. John had Gould's permission to draw $85,000 to help Kansans in distress "along the line of the Kansas Pacific Railway." The railroad magnate had a reputation as ruthless, but Keeney reported to St. John that "Gould has a big heart," calling him a "much better man than many who are very pretentious."[45] Gould immediately telegraphed St. John the authority to "draw on me at sight for the requisite funds to buy food and clothing," and he affirmed this donation in a letter to St. John dated January 12, 1880, in which he urged the Kansas governor to determine the recipients personally and quickly before the press could "greatly exaggerate" conditions and thwart migration into the state."[46] Gould gave St. John full discretion over the matter with no restrictions. Naturally, Gould was eager to promote immigration into the plains states, as settlers then used his vast railroad complex to move grain.

Elated over the news about the "liberal donations" from "Honorable Jay Gould," McCabe wrote to St. John on January 26 and reported that "there were "twenty families white and colored, who were in absolute need and the balance will pull through all right."[47] St. John immediately replied that he now had provisions at Buffalo Park (now Park, Kansas) and WaKeeney but was distressed over conflicting accounts in all the papers, with some reporting that the "whole cry about destitution is a fraud." The governor wrote to McCabe and that "under such circumstances it is very difficult to determine just what I ought to do."⁴⁸ He advised McCabe that it would be necessary for the heads of household to apply for aid in person because of the necessity of filing affidavits.

Confusion continued. St. John soon afterward received a letter from the Graham County Aid Association—written by A. R. George and addressed to "His Excellency"—requesting free transportation of goods into the county rather than requiring recipients to travel to a more distant distribution site. St. John's agent, R. D. Caldren, selected the governor's friend John Inlow to distribute goods in Graham County at Hill City on February 14.⁴⁹

On February 21, St. John received an angry letter from McCabe, who informed the governor that his request for aid had been rejected:

> I sent the enclosed affidavits to Hill City for the Aid so kindly tendered by Jay Gould and the same are returned because of their invalidity. Now I desire to know if any affidavit emanating from a Notary Public in the State is valid. I want it plainly understood that I am not asking aid personally, from Jay Gould with his untold millions nor any other gentleman, but it was at the urgent request of some few who (<u>unfortunately are black</u>) desired Assistance, that I made the appeal at all. I am sorry, but I shall never be guilty of a similar offense. Be kind enough if you will, to let me know as to the validity of my notorial signature and seal. Enclosed please find the notice ad published upon which in conjunction with your personal letter, I acted.
>
> Very Respectfully
> E. P. McCabe⁵⁰

This was clearly the last straw for the long-suffering, frequently vilified, exhausted St. John. He replied to McCabe that he had ordered the agent in charge to print special forms for the affidavits and said, "I suppose that he, in refusing to recognize any other affidavit, did what he believed at the time to be his duty." St. John went on: "It is unnecessary for you to underscore with double lines the word "black," in

Edward Preston McCabe. Courtesy of Kansas Historical Society.

writing to me. I think that I have exhibited during my life as much respect for men of that color as almost any other person, and certainly, in my dealings with mankind, have not made any distinction on account of the color of a man's skin." The governor explained that the formal affidavits were duplicates, with one "to be filed in this department" and the other sent to Jay Gould. He defended his agent, saying: "It is a very unpleasant job for anyone to undertake, to distribute aid. I find, as a rule, that it is met with a great many more curses then thanks, for it is impossible to satisfy everyone."[51]

Although St. John took umbrage at McCabe's "underscoring with double lines the word 'black,'" in fact, McCabe habitually underlined words in most of the letters he wrote. McCabe had a reputation for sarcasm, which was certainly evident in the tone of the letter, but he may have been unaware that St. John would be angered by the heavy emphasis on the word "black."

According to the Hill City *Western Star*, the governor obtained from Jay Gould for Graham County 1,000 pounds of flour, 1,800 pounds of cornmeal, 1,323 pounds of bacon, 400 pounds of beef, and one box of baking powder.[52] In a letter to the *Millbrook Times*, R. W. McFarland suggested that the box of baking power was "doubtless intended to show the people that it was not provisions they needed but something to raise or lighten their spirits."[53] The *Graham County Lever*, on the other hand, scoffed at the "deadbeats who were in their glory as they lugged away provisions enough to last them in idleness until the next day of distribution" and referred to the recipients as "human vampires."[54] The *Leavenworth Times* stated that "if any one has any idea or can tell in figures anywhere near the exact number of people in the western part of Kansas who are starving he will do the state a great favor."[55]

Kansans were quite vexed over the nationwide jeering regarding aid. In fact, Americans outside the state had regarded Kansas as peculiar since territorial organization, when the U.S. Congress was presented with four separate Kansas constitutions authored by warring political factions vying for legitimacy. The state had drawn unwelcome attention during the bloody border wars with Missouri, which escalated into violent conflicts over Kansas entering the Union as a pro-slavery or free state. The *Harper's Weekly* reporter who had begun a trip on the newly created stage company the Butterfield Overland Despatch Express to write about the flora and fauna but ended up describing massacres at every stage station added to Kansas's reputation as being dangerous and unpredictable. Noble Prentiss, a lifelong Kansas journalist, noted in 1891, according to historian Craig Miner, that "hysterical historians" in the media showed a "disposition to see something extraordinary, striking and unheard-of" in everything about Kansas.[56]

The editor of the Huntington, West Virginia, *Advertiser*, who had read of that "subscriptions are asked for from North Topeka, Kansas for the colored people who are suffering," wrote, "It is a mighty peculiar month in the year when there is not something the matter in Kansas. . . . If they would not cry for charity for a whole year it would be good for the State."[57] George Irwin, the editor of the *Topeka Weekly Times*, reprinted these comments and was livid. Such items, he rejoined, "are appearing constantly in the Eastern Press" and were the logical outcome of "the refugee business." Irwin did not blame eastern editors or even "the good people of Kansas," but the "carpet baggers from the East, who set up 'begging shops' . . . with headquarters in Topeka; and sent agents East on soliciting tours; flooded the country with pathetic appeals, and gathered in the Shekels by the barrel." Irwin asserted,

> [Kansas] has no call for aid:
>
> Does not want aid.
>
> The people are nearly all able to take care of themselves, and those who are not will be taken care of by Kansans; and the good people of the East are notified that all persons begging the East for Kansas sufferers—
>
> Are frauds.
>
> There is no suffering in Kansas that our own people cannot remedy.[58]

Despite protests to the contrary, the reality of thousands of Exodusters converging on the state challenged Kansans morally, philosophically, and financially. The need to provide for impoverished and often frightened immigrants sharpened the debate among African Americans in both eastern and western Kansas regarding assistance in any form. Abram Hall certainly did not abandon his stance that blacks were as capable as whites in every aspect and needed little help. E. P. McCabe hardened his view that blacks needed powerful advocates in political office to ensure they received their rightful share of the country's bounty. And John Niles continued to believe that the white race owed blacks for the time they spent in slavery, and he expounded on this at every opportunity.

Chapter 9
The Colored People Hold the Key

It was said by men who have opposed our progress, as well as our liberty, that when we were free that we would conduct ourselves in the most unbecoming manner, that we would be guilty of all enormous outrages; but time has proved that such fears or hopes, as the case may be, were founded in error, and today we stand before the world, for uprightness, industry, and, thrift, the peers of any similar class on the face of the globe, and challenge the admiration of fair-minded men everywhere.
    Testimony of John Henri Burch

IN AN UNEXPECTED AND AUDACIOUS MOVE, in 1879 Abram Hall spearheaded a campaign to organize Graham County. All the counties in Kansas were named and the boundaries set by the state legislature in 1868. The "unorganized county of Graham" was attached to Rooks County for judicial purposes. An unorganized county lacked law enforcement and did not have an official legal structure. Counties could not be organized until they had attained a population of 1,500 inhabitants and 250 households.[1] Even then, someone had to formally instigate organization. Moreover, Hall did it during the volatile period in Kansas history when the state was quarreling over the Exodusters. Perhaps Hall was able to succeed in this move only *because* distracted Kansans were wrestling with the massive problems regarding the immigration of ex-slaves. Regardless, it is doubtful whether any other Kansas African American had the skills to successfully promote such a controversial agenda during this troubled period. There were several reasons why some in the county did not want the formal organization of Graham County at that time. The white population wanted to delay the issue until more whites were in the county and were worried about blacks determining the location of the county seat. Others wanted to avoid coming under state tax obligations or risk being forced to vote bonds for railroad construction or acquire the burden of financing formal public education. Brawls over county organization and county seat locations would soon embroil half of the state's nascent counties, conflicts that were sometimes lethal.[2]

Hall had a remarkable ability to deal with difficult political situations. Not an assimilationist, he assumed that whites would recognize his equality and expected people to measure his worth by how he conducted himself. He was a powerful advocate for equal rights for African Americans, and he lived his life and dealt with others in accordance with his belief that an educated black man need not defer to whites. He often ignored race and simply focused on issues critical to western Kansas: roads, schools, law enforcement, commerce, and housing. Hall did not hesitate to make decisions for the "good of the commonwealth" that other blacks might consider ill-advised for the good of the race.

During 1878, Hall had been neutral regarding county organization. In a December letter to the *Stockton News* he wrote, "There are a class of men in this county who are bent on organizing the county in some one or the other manner," but he predicted that "nothing will grow out of it, save bad blood and heartache." "The colored people hold the key to the situation and will no doubt use their advantage," he said. The key lay in the strength of Nicodemus's unified voting block, because the white vote was split among a number of towns. In a letter to the *Atchison Champion* the same month, Hall noted that there were "myriads of aspirants for county honors" but that "public opinion and comment should be held in abeyance" until slates were known.[3]

By the end of 1878, however, Hall seems to have become more concerned about the county seat issue, writing, "Nicodemus has hopes of proving to be the dark, yet winning, town in the race. She will certainly command the entire Negro vote of the county, and the white vote in her immediate vicinity, which is about double the vote which any of the other five points can bring to bear." He did not name the five points in the *Stockton News*, but mentioned the town of Victor, which only existed on paper "and in the minds of the expectant ones up Spring Creek."[4] Later that month in a letter to the *Atchison Champion* he stated that the "fight for the county seat has narrowed down to Gettysburg and Hill City." One of the eventual contenders, Roscoe, did not exist yet. He was aware that some of the settlers living on Bow Creek favored municipal (township) organization but believed "the mass of Grahamites prefer county organization, as the lesser evil."[5] In a February letter to the *Stockton News*, Hall observed that although "Stevensville is the latest aspirant for the county seat, Nicodemus is still in the field, and it has been well said that 'the colored troops fight nobly.'"[6]

Hall's letters and columns published in papers outside Graham County, and his correspondence with new elected governor St. John, reveal the brewing controversy. Hall and McCabe met with the governor shortly after his January 13, 1879, inauguration. They asked him to designate Nicodemus as the temporary county seat, and they later referred to this meeting in a letter sent April 11, 1879.[7]

> We desire to refresh your memory relative to your promise to us, at an interview held with you at your office, during the month of January. The promise was that, when Graham County applied for organization, if in any manner consistent with your position you could further the interests of Nicodemus you would do so. Memorials to your Excellency praying for organization are now circulating throughout the county and are receiving many signatures of bona fide residents and householders.... What we ask of you is, to use your option, thus given you by the signers, and declare Nicodemus as temporary County Seat. We trust that you will find it within the scope of your jurisdiction to favor us, for our sole purpose in desiring it is the upbuilding of Nicodemus, and our people are the first settlers and desire it only temporary. Please favor us with an early reply.[8]

St. John replied April 17, 1879: "I must be governed, as I stated to you when you were here, by a petition of citizens." He assured them that "it will afford me pleasure to do anything I can consistent with my duty to favor your people and locality," and he advised them to get up a petition.[9] However, Hall was undoubtedly shrewd enough to realize that a petition for Nicodemus would fail as the whites would unite against the blacks.

In a May 7 letter to the *Stockton News*, Hall demonstrated that community issues often transcended racial agendas. Whites and blacks alike could be equally victimized by careless legislation, and as an attorney Hall was qualified to assess this. In this letter he criticized "the grave and reverend solons who misrepresented their constituency so ably"—referring to the state legislature approval on March 12 of an act altering boundaries of Sheridan County, a change that encroached on Graham County's territory and eliminated four townships along with proposed county seat locations. Hall and McCabe wrote to the state's attorney general, Willard Davis, asking for an official opinion as to the validity of the legislation, and Davis assured them that the previously established boundary of Graham County would not be affected, although "what the Legislature intended cannot be determined . . . and must remain in uncertainty till that body again meets and settles it."[10] In the meantime, this confusion fueled further discussion and debate over the formal organization of Graham County.[11] Farmer Fred Harris made the point that "We are surrounded on three sides by organized counties, which are ready to possess themselves of a portion of our territory, and unless we organize we are powerless to prevent it. Our county is none too large now; shall we allow our more enterprising neighbors to gobble a tier of townships from each side?"[12]

It may have been concern over the vulnerability of Graham County that prompted Hall to organize Nicodemus Township, though he clearly preferred county organization. Graham County was then attached to Rooks County for judicial purposes, and, as long as Graham County was unorganized, its residents were required to conduct all municipal business and file all legal papers—even affidavits—at Stockton, the Rooks County seat. Trips to Stockton were difficult even when the weather was mild. And although a justice of the peace could attend to some matters, and as a notary public McCabe attested to the validity of a number of signatures, this authority was through his commission in Rooks County. The successful organization of Nicodemus Township, then, was financially and logistically advantageous for Hall and McCabe.

There are two legal definitions of townships. One is the relatively noncontroversial thirty-six-square-mile division of land determined by surveying, a legal description that appears in deeds assigning public domain. The second kind, municipal townships, are corporate bodies with the power to make contracts, hold elections, levy taxes, and raise militias. Municipal townships can authorize roads and bridges and issue bonds for their construction and maintenance. In the case of Nicodemus, organizing a municipal township in the unorganized county of Graham would transfer municipal authority from Rooks County to the new township itself.[13]

On July 7, 1879, twenty-five African Americans from Nicodemus presented a petition for the organization of Nicodemus Township to Rooks County commissioners J. S. McComb, R. S. Shorthill, and Eli Sherman. Nicodemus was "fixed as the place holding the election," and the commissioners met again on July 29 in a special session to formalize election proceedings. At that session Rooks County sheriff John Shaw interrupted the board with an injunction restraining the commissioners from ordering the election, but the injunction was in vain. By law, whenever "twenty-five electors in any such unorganized county" petitioned authorized country commissioners (such as those in Rooks County) for municipal organization at the place they dictated as "convenient," the commissioners were compelled to act.[14] The white population of Graham County was too late to deflect the bold move that would force them to vote and conduct their official municipal business in a black town.[15]

During turbulent July 1879, Benjamin B. F. Graves, launched the *Millbrook Times*, a Greenbacker paper in a Democratic stronghold. Graves was from New York and thirty-two years old when he came to Graham County. There is no extant information as to what drew him there in the first place. In his initial political statement, he promised to "call no man a fool because he is a Republican, and an idiot because he is a Democrat or an imbecile because he is a Greenbacker."[16]

In the first issue, published July 11, Graves established a neutral stance toward race, saying he had "no sentimentality in the matter." He claimed to "regard the white and black man as equals" and insisted that "if their conduct is equally good, we shall not profess any inordinate love for the colored man, nor extol him above the clouds, with a view to securing his support when elections are held; . . . for our colored people are too intelligent to be deceived with such chaff."[17] Hall was pleased and sent the editor a letter that was printed in the second edition of the *Times*, a week later: "We respect your sentiments regarding colored people. We do not wish to be put above our white neighbors, and when we see one of them professing to elevate us to that position we very naturally question his motives. All we wish is those equal rights which the law guarantees to us, and this we are satisfied you are willing to grant us. If the *Millbrook Times* speaks the sentiments of the Millbrook people we are all Millbrook men."[18]

Hall, a staunch Republican, would maintain a mutually respectful relationship with Graves despite political differences. But at this time, in July 1879, Graves had learned of the petition to organize Nicodemus Township, and in the same issue of the *Times* containing Hall's letter he wrote,

> We must protest against a law which makes two thousand citizens of this county subject to the will or caprice of any twenty-five men, without giving the great mass of people a chance to speak a word in their own behalf. It matters not if every man in the county is opposed to the thing, saye [sic] twenty-five, for these twenty-five are the sole dictators in the matter. . . .
>
> We don't object to what has been done because of the race of those who have done it, nor because of the location of township headquarters at Nicodemus, but we do most emphatically denounce the law which enables any twenty-five men to defy the wishes of every other man in the county.[19]

Hall's response to this was published in the next edition of the *Times*, a week later: "We were not prepared for quite so general a disapproval of the township organization. . . . Wishing to organize the county . . . and meeting with ill success we took the step . . . as a last resort. We should have been satisfied had the same thing been done by any other place in the county, but having no hopes of their doing it we did it ourselves."[20] The only recourse for the white population to avoid conducting their official business in a black town indefinitely was to organize the county and force Governor St. John to appoint a temporary county seat until the official election of the permanent site.

Graves wrote to the governor asking "what rule, if any, is adhered to in designating the temporary county seat of an unorganized county where there are two or more aspirants for the position?" St. John replied that he was required to locate the temporary county seat wherever the majority of "legal voters" indicated by their signatures on a petition. "The law is plain and leaves no discretionary power in the matter."[21]

Furious over the petition emanating from Nicodemus, Gettysburg residents entered the fray. F. E. Bowers, a carpenter and Gettysburg's deputy superintendent of public instruction, wrote to the governor complaining about the township organization by the "colored portion of the county aided by a few white men whose record for honesty is not the best, without knowledge or consent of the better portion and majority of the people of the county." Bowers insisted that the motive behind the Nicodemus petition was the $10,000 in bonds that would be given to the new county seat. He concluded that, despite the financial hardships, county organization would be preferable and asked St. John to consider the matter.[22]

On October 11, St. John received a petition initiated and circulated by N. C. Terrell, a wealthy businessman residing in Millbrook. The petitioners requested the "speedy organization" of Graham County, asked that Millbrook be established as county seat, and that Abram Hall be appointed census taker for a one-time census, validating fifteen hundred bona fide inhabitants of an unorganized county, as required by law for formal organization. This census would be separate from the federal census mandated by the U.S. Constitution that would also take place in 1880. The position of census taker was viewed as a political plum, and it was quite lucrative. The job paid three dollars a day and six cents a mile "for each mile necessarily and actually employed in making the return to the governor." A Millbrook family of attorneys who were friends of St. John—Charles, T. T., and Ida Tillotson—supported Terrell.[23]

When by early November no action had yet been taken on Terrell's petition, Hall wrote to St. John urging him to act:

> More than three weeks have passed away since I conferred with you relative to granting a petition from the citizens of Graham County, asking you to appoint me as census-taker. The objection which you raised to the affidavit of the three free-holders, was met immediately after I returned to this county, and a new

affidavit such an one as you had approved, was made out and subscribed and sworn to by the free-holders, and forwarded without delay to you. Since [then] we have patiently waited to receive the appointment asked, or to learn . . . why it was withheld. . . . Meanwhile the other points that are desirous of catching the plumb of temporary county-seat, encouraged by your silence, are using every endeavor, both *fair and foul* to change the current of public sentiment in their favor.[24]

As evidence of foul means, Hall enclosed four affidavits by Nicodemus residents claiming they had been tricked into signing petitions for Gettysburg when they were actually in favor of Millbrook for county seat. Two of the men declared that the bearers of the petition had said that the "colored leaders" of Nicodemus, naming Hall and McCabe, had sold their people out. St. John replied to Hall with a letter dated November 6, saying that "under the law (with which you I suppose are familiar) when my attention is called to alleged fraud connected with the memorial asking the appointment of a census taker, it becomes my duty to investigate."[25] He later found the accusations against Hall to be unfounded.

The same day he wrote Hall, the governor received a petition from Gettysburg. Commercially printed, with an elaborately scripted heading, the petition asked for a specific slate of county officers, with Robert Richmond as census taker. Richmond was not the only contender vying with Hall for the position. Another notable rival was Thomas Beaumont, an attorney and editor of the Hill City paper, the *Western Star*. His copublisher, T. H. McGill, also desired the position but said he was willing to be named "assistant when the time is ripe." McGill thought Beaumont's appointment "would be satisfactory to the people here."[26]

John Henry, a Baptist minister whose territory included Nicodemus, warned St. John that Hall's appointment was risky and that "the feeling against the first office of the Co[unty] being given to a Col[ored] man is intense." He believed "Hall could more easily fill any other office than the one to which he aspires: the one that would bring him in contact with every excited man in the Co[unty]." Henry's concern was

Kansas governor John Pierce St. John. Courtesy of Kansas Historical Society.

well founded, as John Landis, the man who originally surveyed land for the colonists, had repeatedly been threatened and was eventually murdered. Daniel Hickman, one of the original settlers, and other blacks, believed Landis was killed because there was opposition by whites to a settlement of African Americans. The *Western Star* referred to the killing as "a ku-klux measure."[27]

Hall's courage during this volatile era was matched by St. John's commitment to equal treatment of humans irrespective of race. Hall's request to be appointed census taker came during a particularly difficult time for the governor, as blacks from the South swept into the state. At one point, an early-twentieth-century historian wrote, St. John was even asked to issue a proclamation and "arrest this disastrous flood of Negro paupers in its flow to Kansas."[28] In January 1880, when the U.S. Senate began investigating the black exodus from the South, St. John was accused of luring blacks to his state. However, G. W. Carey, vice president of the Emigrants Relief Board (based in Topeka), introduced correspondence from St. John during the Voorhees Committee hearings and presented the governor as an able crusader for equal—rather than preferential—treatment of African Americans. Carey entered into testimony St. John's widely printed letter denying that he had offered special inducements to blacks.[29]

In accordance with his racial neutrality, St. John acknowledged Hall's superior qualifications and appointed him census taker on November 10, 1879. Despite its benefits, it was not an easy job. As always census takers were considered intrusive under the best of circumstances. With Hall serving in the position, whites living in Graham County—some of whom were allegedly former "bushwhackers" (participants in savage guerrilla warfare) from Missouri—were confronted with a highly educated, Shakespeare-quoting, Latin-spouting, French-speaking African American asking them if they could read and write.[30]

St. John wrote to Hall on November 21, 1879, that "during the time you are engaged in your official duties as census taker, you shall in no manner electioneer, or use your influence in favor or against any place aspiring to become the temporary county seat."[31] However, Hall could still participate in the "township convention" held at Nicodemus on November 22, 1879, to elect candidates for township officers. Hall was elected convention chairman, and editor Graves was elected secretary. An "Equal Rights Ticket" was formed from a multiracial, nonpartisan alliance of blacks, whites, Democrats, Greenbackers, and Republicans from Millbrook and Nicodemus. Citizens of Roscoe partially adopted this ticket, though they added three candidates from their own town. Gettysburg, however, nominated the "People's Township Organization Ticket," which was composed entirely of white men. At the December 3, 1879, township election, the "Equal Rights Ticket" handily won all of the positions except that of one constable.[32]

Township officers were elected for a one-year term on a schedule determined by state law. The township officers elected at Nicodemus in December would serve only two months before the mandatory state election. If the county was not organized and the temporary county seat designated before that time, the citizens of Graham County would be forced to bear the expense of a second township election and to conduct their business in a black town. This made Hall's work as census taker all the more important. He began taking the census on November 24, 1879. Three weeks later, however, he "postponed operations" and with the permission of St. John went to Chicago to visit his family. He resumed work January 8, 1880. This interruption prompted several outraged letters and editorials. Moreover, the novelty of a black man serving as census taker provoked a great deal of comment, pro and con. The *Ness County Pioneer* noted that Graham County had a "colored census taker," which "doesn't seem to suit some of the white trash pretty well." The *Western Star* accused Hall of taking money, and the *Graham County Lever*, located in Gettysburg, denied the rumor that the town would meet Hall "with violent opposition in the discharge of his duties on account of his color."[33]

In January 1880, Graves's *Millbrook Times* praised Hall:

> Some of our people have been heard to exclaim "what manner of man is this of whom we have heard so much?" What must be their surprise when our worthy census taker drops in on them with a quiet good morning, and with book and pencil in hand immediately proceed[s] to ask the necessary questions and book them accordingly. When he arises, to go about his "master's work" he leaves friends where perhaps he had enemies; he has the rare faculty of combining pleasure with business; and can gently talk the old folks to sleep on topics of general conversation and then he can entertain the young folks with choice music and good jokes; and after all have a few kind words left for the dog.[34]

Not all citizens shared editor Graves's kindly assessment of Hall, but while compiling the census Hall strictly adhered to St. John's prohibition against campaigning while so engaged. Consequently, the governor received affidavits from persons saying that they had questioned the census taker about the shape of various petitions and that Hall would not respond.[35]

Hall completed his census March 6, 1880, and went to Topeka where he presented the information to St. John. His report included a newsy summary with his cheerful overview that Graham County showed "a degree of settlement and improvement wholly without a parallel in the annuals [sic] of the state."[36] Jubilant over the successful census, each of the towns contending for St. John's appointment as temporary county seat—Hill City, Millbrook, Gettysburg, and Roscoe—rushed to gather the greatest number of signatures on a "memorial" (petition). That month the governor was bombarded with petitions, affidavits, letters, accusations of fraud, personal visits, conflicting reports, threats, appeals to his zeal for temperance, pleas for racial advocacy, and, in the case of the Tillotson family, blatant attempts to exploit friendship.

One of the first petitions came from Hill City. It contained 596 signatures. Hall wrote the heading, acknowledging that many of the names would appear on other petitions "under the stress of various misrepresentations." Its first signatures, in a bold hand, were those of Hall and E. P. McCabe. The next day St. John received a petition with 704 signatures requesting that Millbrook be named the temporary county seat. Remarkably, it too contained the signatures of Hall and McCabe. McCabe's signature was on line 424 and Hall's on line 101. McCabe declared in a personal letter to St. John, received March 3, 1880, that his signature on the Millbrook petition had been placed there "without his consent and for no other purpose than as an inducement or bid for the support of the Colored Element," and he said that he refused "to touch or handle the unclean thing." However, McCabe's personal signature was quite distinctive, and almost certainly was legitimate, not forged, on this petition.[37]

Hall and McCabe's signatures were also on a petition for the town of Roscoe, where they would consistently advertise their legal services once the town acquired a paper in June 1880.[38] Neither of the men's signatures ever appeared on Gettysburg petitions. Hall did not contribute correspondence or columns to the Gettysburg-based *Graham County Lever*, nor did he and McCabe advertise in the publication. Its original editor, H. S. Hogue, was quite disdainful of African Americans.

A number of the petitions were undated and contained scratched out names. Persons also wrote St. John asking him to remove their name from one petition and place it on another. L. P. Boyd, a Gettysburg man, summed up fraudulent methods used by all the towns in a letter castigating Millbrook: signatures in excess of the number of petitioners on the census return; signatures of non-residents and non-voters; signatures of persons who had been in the county less than four months; fraudulent, illegal, or minor signatures; and unverified signatures. Some petitions lacked the oath that their signatures were genuine.[39]

There was no question that fraud was rampant. Three cowboys from Sheridan County even swore out an affidavit that "while sojourning in [the] town of Gettysburg," they had been asked to sign a paper asking Congress to pass a bill loaning settlers money at a reasonable rate of interest. They signed, they said, but later learned their names had been torn off the paper and attached to a petition for Gettysburg as county seat. Rooks County meanwhile was inundated by a cascade of affidavits and endured the constant hullabaloo of its neighbor. The editor of the *Stockton News* wrote: "Rooks County is glad to get rid of the many malicious and trifling law suits which are constantly arising in Graham County. Yes, go! We bid you God speed. What will you give on the dollar for the fees Graham County owes the officers of Rooks County?"[40]

Bewildered by the whole fiasco, St. John replied to an irate Thomas Beaumont, editor of the *Western Star*, regarding rumors that Hill City had been eliminated from the race, that the town's "petition is in very bad shape, so much as to render it out of the question for consideration." The governor noted that although he was in personal contact with his census taker, Hall "seemed to be unable to straighten out the matter." However, while he had disqualified the tattered and mutilated Hill City petition, St. John was not "throwing Hill City out of the race."[41]

On March 30, St. John received a brief, in Hall's handwriting, filed on behalf of Roscoe by the firm of Hall and McCabe. At last Hall and McCabe revealed their final choice for the temporary county seat. They were "Roscoe men." They argued that, out of all the towns in the county, Roscoe could claim the greatest number of electors and residents. To support their case, they called into question the results of the 1880 U.S. census, noting that up to 150 people living in "a portion of the state not embraced within the legal boundaries of Graham County" had been counted as living there. The mistake had been made, they said, because although the state legislature had never repealed the act that changed the border between Sheridan and Graham Counties, the census had been conducted as if the law had been rescinded.[42]

Hall and McCabe went on to accuse both Gettysburg and Millbrook of fraud and reasoned that the land north of the Solomon River, which divided the county, was more attractive for settlement and contained the "most numerous populated townships in Graham County," while the land south of the river "is all or nearly all of it within the limits of the U.S. land grant to the Kansas Pacific railroad company." The long "brief" concluded: "The petitions emanating from and for Roscoe, have been presented just as they were circulated, each one certified to before a proper officer as containing none other than genuine signatures of bonafide householders, and legal electors of Graham County. If the exigencies of this contest demand any better or stronger evidence of clear memorials than are they, then we pronounce it rigor and not law. This is our case, and here we rest it." They signed themselves "Hall and McCabe / Atty's for Roscoe."[43]

Earlier that month St. John had written Attorney General Davis regarding the issue of the legal boundaries eloquently delineated by Hall. Davis replied on March 18 that the territories of Kansas counties had been defined in 1868 and that the "inconsistencies and absurdities of said act" of the recent sessions of the legislature "seem so glaring and irreconcilable, that it seems to be void for uncertainty," saying he would "forbid its recognition as a valid statute."[44] At the time that he composed the Roscoe brief, Hall would not have been privy to Davis's opinion.

On April 1, 1880, the governor issued a proclamation announcing the official organization of Graham County, naming Millbrook as the temporary county seat. In this document he appointed John Inlow, A. E. Moses, and O. J. Nevens as county commissioners, and E. P. McCabe as county clerk.[45] The newly appointed county officials met on April 13 at the Maulsby Building in Millbrook, and the official election for the county seat was set for June 1, 1880. There were four separate county seat elections. The results in the first contest: Gettysburg, 345; Millbrook, 332; Roscoe, 332; Hill City, 90; Nicodemus, 52.[46] Millbrook immediately accused Gettysburg of fraud, and Gettysburg accused Millbrook of fraud. F. P. Kellogg, the editor of the *Roscoe Tribune*, claimed Millbrook kept all the county records in a "small box, labelled all over with 'Arm & Hammer Saleratus' that answers to the purpose of a safe. Township officer's bonds filed, commissioner's proceedings and county clerk's business all in the same box. When a document is needed, the clerk shuts his eyes and reaches in the box." Despite having received the most votes, Gettysburg did not receive a majority and Millbrook remained the temporary county seat.[47]

The next county seat vote was the same year, November 2, 1880, during the state and federal elections. Predictably, the county went solidly Republican, as did the nation, and James Garfield was elected president by a large majority. But once again the county seat vote did not produce a permanent result. Gettysburg received 114 votes, Millbrook 209, Hill City 186, Roscoe 132, and a new contender labeled "Center of the County" received 30 votes.[48] Of course there was no town named "Center of the County," but one could be created in a short time. The distance to the county seat had always been an issue.

The lack of a majority and the absence of a courthouse left Millbrook vulnerable to a challenge a year later. On June 7, 1881, A. Mort, chairman of the Graham County commissioners at the request of the other two commissioners, Hiram Cooper and R. W. McGraw, called a special meeting to consider a petition bearing the names of 741 persons.[49] Citing chapter twenty-six of *Compiled Laws of Kansas*, they demanded a special election because a vote of the legal electors had not determined the permanent location of the county seat. Furthermore, Millbrook had not erected the required "county buildings at a cost of one thousand dollars." A special election was indeed scheduled—and it was held on July 12. This time, 878 votes were cast, with Gettysburg receiving 281, Millbrook 247, Roscoe 221, and Hill City 129.[50] As before, neither Millbrook nor Gettysburg had received a majority. Since this had been a special election Kansas law mandated that a runoff election had to be held the second Tuesday after the preceding vote, with only the two towns receiving the highest votes on the ballot.[51] A runoff between the two towns (Gettysburg and Millbrook) was held on July 26, This time Millbrook received 473 votes, Gettysburg 348—and so Millbrook was finally declared the permanent county seat of Graham County. Editor T. H. McGill suggested that "Gettysburg should go out behind a hay-stack and hate itself to death."[52]

Abram Hall left Graham County for good in October 1880 before the second county seat vote. A number of local papers and the *Atchison Champion* speculated that he intended to get married and said that his "heart was in Topeka."[53] However, by the time he would marry, in 1883, he would be living outside the state of Kansas. Many years later, in a letter to Kathyrne Henri, organizer of the sixtieth anniversary celebration of Nicodemus, Hall indicated that he had left Nicodemus to assume a St. Louis editorship of the Washington-based *National Tribune*. Upon his departure, the *Roscoe Tribune* printed this tribute: "Mr. Hall honorably distinguished himself in the early days of the Nicodemus colony, and was connected with it while the colonial organization lasted. Should the result of the Nicodemus experiment be to prove that the colored people from the South can settle and permanently succeed on the public lands in the West, Mr. Hall's name will be preserved as one of the benefactors of his race."[54]

By 1882 Hall was back at his old job as city editor of the *Chicago Conservator*, where he demonstrated the durability of the relationships he had formed in Kansas. In the December 16, 1882, *Conservator* he reported that N. C. Terrell, "the founder and principal business man" of Millbrook, Kansas, had "honored our sanctum with a call and told us quite a batch of news concerning our frontier friends."[55] The *Conservator* would also publish a write-up of his marriage, to Mary E. (Minnie) Robinson, an event that took place September 6, 1883, at the Wylie Avenue African Methodist Episcopal Church in Pittsburgh,

Pennsylvania.[56] Minnie Robinson had been the first African American girl to pass the tests for admission to the Central High School and was the soprano soloist at the Bethel African Methodist Episcopal Church in Pittsburgh. Her girlhood home was said to have been "the center of the literary social life of ambitious race young men and women," and she had toured with several well-known concert companies. The paper emphasized her exemplary scholarship and the benefits of her "very extensive travel."[57] The *Conservator* then praised Hall's abilities: "The groom is as well-known as any other young man of his age. Having a natural ability for literary work, and a laudable ambition to excel, he has made a bright record by the use of his facile and trenchant pen. He is one of the pioneers in the colored journalism, and deserves the recognition he has received."[58]

The Halls lived in Chicago seven years, then moved to Pittsburgh, where Hall continued his career in journalism and extended his congenial relationships with whites. He wrote the "Afro-American Notes" column for the white-owned *Pittsburgh Press* for thirty-two years and contributed similar columns to the *Chicago Tribune*. At the same time Hall maintained a thirty-two-year career as a clerk in the Allegheny County treasurer's office. His employment in this position usually held by a white man was as noteworthy as when he had been census taker in Graham County. Hall was also employed for a time in the Federal Writers' Project for the Works Progress Administration (part of a 2 percent black minority there) and contributed chapters to *The WPA History of the Negro in Pittsburgh*, which would go unpublished until 2004.

Abram and Minnie Hall lived in Pittsburgh's Hill District, which is said to have been considered one of the most elite African American communities in America, and there they raised five children. A profile of Hall that appeared in the *Pittsburgh Post-Gazette* in 2010 said that he was "one of the twenty-five founding members of F.R.O.G.S, an organization whose purpose was simply to have fun" and noted that Hall "gained a reputation for throwing *the* social events in black society." This was apparently the light-skinned elite of black society: a number of the men "could have passed for white if they [had so chosen]."[59] The Halls were active in the Holy Cross AME Church, where Abram

Abram Thompson Hall, age ninety-two. Courtesy of Graham County Historical Society.

served on the vestry for a number of years, and Minnie was one of the original members of the Aurora Reading Club, an African American women's self-improvement organization, whose motto was "Lifting as we climb." The Halls had five children. Mary (Minnie) died October 26, 1920, and in 1924 Hall married Louise Chaplin Kerr, in Buffalo, New

York. They lived in Pittsburgh. Louise died January 9, 1947, from injuries suffered when her clothing caught fire from a cook stove.[60]

In addition to editorials, Hall's prose and poetry appeared in a number of magazines, and he also published a book of poetry. He died January 7, 1951, at the age of ninety-nine, at the home of his son Orrington Hall, four months short of his goal of one hundred. It was front-page news, as the *Pittsburgh Press* reported the demise of "one of Pittsburgh's oldest, most respected and beloved citizens."[61]

Throughout his long life Hall was referred to as "genial" and admired for his insight on racial issues, and he was undoubtedly atypical in his educational level and abilities. His contribution to Kansas and black history was as a forerunner for intelligent interracial compromise. Although deeply committed to "uplifting the race," Hall was not isolated within a racial enclave. Instead he forged political alliances with whites to cope with problems challenging all communities of settlers in the American West, and other African Americans moving west would follow his lead. Like Hall, they would run for office on multiracial slates, seek political appointments, lobby for causes, and write letters and articles.

Hall's publications and correspondence, and the subsequent response of the white communities, prove that he forced the organization of Graham County at a time when the white population preferred to delay this. As Benjamin Graves pointed out, when Hall organized Nicodemus Township, he subjected the entire white population of Graham County to the "will of . . . twenty-five men," black men, at that. Given the violence that often characterized county seat wars in western Kansas in his day, Hall's nonviolent political maneuvers in the organization of Graham County were all the more remarkable.[62]

Chapter 10
One Tree Bore Bread, Another Bore Lard

He got it into the minds of the people there that they could go to Liberia; that there was one tree there that bore the bread and another tree that bore the lard, and they had nothing at all to do but to go to one tree and dry the fruit . . . that gave the bread, and to the other tree and cut it and set a bucket under and catch the lard. . . . I looked at the man and I didn't like his face. . . . I said to the boys, "Boys, you had better let that man alone; he is a swindler."
                                                      Testimony of Louis Stubblefield

WITNESSES TESTIFYING BEFORE the Voorhees Committee reported rampant fraud in connection with the African American migration. Blacks swindled other blacks as well as whites, and whites swindled other whites as well as blacks. Swindles promising trees that bore bread and lard were unusually transparent. However, for sheer gall, it would be difficult to match the audacious schemes of one of the founders of Nicodemus, John W. Niles. No other resident of the colony was more controversial.

Born into slavery in 1842 to a European father and a black mother, Niles served time in Tennessee in 1869 for killing a man but was later pardoned. After his release and subsequent migration to Lexington, Kentucky, he became involved in W. R. Hill's colonization organization and was one of the founders and secretary of the Nicodemus Graham County Colony. Lulu Craig referred to Niles as "genteel, neat, and a ready speaker," saying that his "convincing eloquent manner" drew immediate sympathy for the colonists and their plight when he solicited aid on their behalf. She clearly supported Niles and viewed him as a hero rather than a huckster: "What small sums of money were given to Mr. Niles by the donators in the various places were used by him to defray his current expenses and those who had opposed his selection as a solicitor, although sharing in the bounty of what he shipped in at frequent intervals made a printed protest in the newspapers of the state against any and all of Niles' operations."[1] Likewise Daniel Hickman stated that Niles would "always be remembered with veneration by the older members of the colony" because he had secured supplies for them.[2]

Outsiders saw him differently. A reporter from the *New York Herald* in 1882 described Niles as a "cinnamon-colored negro of about forty-five years," and wrote: "He is heavy set, [weighs] about one hundred and ninety pounds and is about five feet ten inches in height. His eyes are small, are sunken deep in his head and are very wide apart. His movements are quiet, cautious and snakelike. In his speech he shows an effort at eloquence, but his great ignorance is exposed in the first sentence. There is absolutely no argument or logic in his harangue, which is made up entirely from threadbare quotations of stump speakers twenty years ago. The whole make-up of the man shows him to be a cunning ignoramus."[3]

Unlike Craig and Hickman, some of the Nicodemus colonists also sensed cunning and suspected that Niles's efforts were self-serving. Hall reversed his original support of Niles and publicly denounced his solicitation of aid as early as March 1879, warning that Niles was selling a portion of the goods and keeping the money for himself.[4] W. L. Chambers's biography presents Niles as an accomplished con artist who fraudulently mortgaged a corn crop he did not own and later "fleeced many colored people out of first payments on tracts of land he had no authority to sell."[5] He describes Niles as having a very "aggressive, energetic, and dominating personality . . . [with] an everlasting flow of conversation."[6]

Niles was involved in the first lawsuit in Graham County. Until that time the colonists had been "too busy digging in to waste time setting around a Justice of the Peace's office on some tiny cause," Hall wrote Craig. This suit, he said, was a "trumped up assault and battery case instituted by one William Smith vs. J. W. Niles," and "nearly the whole colony trekked to Stockton for the hearing before Squire Kent." As for the alleged assault, it seems that Smith had butted in on a conversation, persisted in talking, and then been "tapped several times with a willow switch that Mr. Niles had been dusting his trousers with." Although the case was dismissed, Niles was fined five dollars and court costs. Niles, having passed his money to a friend, showed Kent non-transferable registered government bonds, which were of no use to the court. The squire then demanded Niles's flashy watch.[7]

Historian Kenneth Hamilton wrote that Niles "did not have the literacy of some of the immigrants."[8] He was a forceful speaker, but his verbal communication skills far exceeded his writing ability. Niles served as deputy county clerk under McCabe in 1880, and then John DePrad, who succeeded McCabe, also appointed him to that position.[9] One might infer from the ample evidence in county records and newspapers that Niles wrote quite well. He not only recorded official business but also regularly lambasted in print the opinions of white editors and their contributors. Nevertheless, his letters to Governor St. John in his own handwriting are inferior to the literate phrasing that appeared in print. One of his appeals to St. John asking for personal assistance to get his family from Kentucky to Kansas contained well-reasoned arguments expressed with misspellings and peculiar punctuation. Niles was typical of ex-slaves with high intelligence who lacked the opportunity for formal education. Niles may have dictated his columns, legal notices, and letters to other blacks in the community, or editors may have cleaned up his grammar and spelling before printing his material.

With the money he earned as a deputy clerk and gains made as a "private banker and commodities trader for the blacks of Graham County," Niles began to display a flamboyant taste for "clothes, carriages, and women."[10] From 1877 to 1880 Niles exerted influence at the county level, while Hall and McCabe were the only western Kansas blacks well known at the state level. No doubt Niles lacked the money for the trips to Topeka enjoyed by his two friends.

Quarrels over the influx of the Exodusters had left Kansas African Americans in disarray. These divisions were exacerbated by the lack of black representation in the ranks of state Republicans. They felt validity gained during the 1879 political campaign was slipping away. In April 1880 the *Kansas Herald*, which succeeded the *Colored Citizen*, deplored the lack of unity and urged blacks to take steps at the upcoming statewide Convention of Colored Men to achieve more representation for the race at the state level than was usually accorded "hewers of wood and drawers of water."[11]

McCabe was the official delegate from Graham County to the state Republican convention in April 1880. Those present at the sparsely attended March organizational meeting of the Graham County Republican Party had paid more attention "to the game of ball outside" than to electing a delegate. Nevertheless, since there were several influential white men at the meeting, McCabe's election demonstrates the early biracial political interaction in the newly organized county. Both McCabe and Hall went to Topeka in April and worked to secure the election of W. B. Townsend as a delegate to the Republican National Convention. McCabe claimed the honor of presenting Townsend's credentials.[12] Ironically, just a week before, Townsend had jabbed at politicians who played down the suffering of the Nicodemus colony. Undoubtedly referring to Hall, Townsend's "Leavenworth Items" column in the *Kansas Herald* showed that he still chafed from his initial encounter with the northern journalist over aid to the colonists.[13]

Townsend was not elected delegate to party's national convention, and afterward he asserted that the redistricting of caucuses had separated him from his strongest supporters. He was offered the position as an alternate but declined. He later argued that agreeing to serve as an alternate would have invalidated the work done by the caucuses. Nevertheless, a number of Kansas African Americans felt that Townsend was betraying the trust of other blacks, who had worked so hard to secure a nomination, and had declined just because the position was inferior to what was originally intended.[14] The Reverend L. Fulbright, chairman of the upcoming Convention of Colored Men indicted McCabe too, implying that McCabe had not worked hard enough and charging that the "claims of 25,000 colored people were ignored." McCabe immediately sent a letter to the *Herald* claiming that Fulbright's attack had emanated from "envy or spleen." He characterized Fulbright as one of the "crabbed dyspeptic individuals . . . wholly unfit to take the lead themselves . . . [but] jealous of the other and better men going to the front."[15]

The Kansas Convention of Colored Men was held April 12, 1880, right on the heels of the predominantly white state Republican convention. The Graham County delegates, Hall, McCabe, Z. T. Fletcher, and Granville Lewis, were unable to attend but requested that their letter be read at the convention, then published in the *Herald*. They sent regrets due to the "press of business" but assured the delegates of their support for the "laudable purpose" for which the convention had convened. These western Kansas men joined their eastern counterparts, they said, in expressing impatience with the Republican Party and blacks' willingness to follow "a route which has been marked out for us by men not interested in either the election or equality of races."[16] Despite his absence, Hall was appointed to the permanent "State Executive Committee" of African Americans at this convention.[17] The *Millbrook Times* reported that the "State Central Committee of colored men" had endorsed Charles H. Langston for a place on the Republican ticket and waited to see if the white members of the Republican Party would honor their desire to see an African American man on the state ticket.[18]

Meanwhile, organization of the Graham County Republicans began poorly. Divisions over the placement of the county seat had led to much animosity, and the whites of Millbrook and Gettysburg began quarreling immediately over the legitimacy of meetings held in their respective towns.[19] Hill City leaders entered the fray and called for a convention, and Millbrook concluded that this was "dubbed 'republican' simply as a means of capturing unsuspecting people." The Nicodemus Township party members met in August and elected Niles chairman. *Millbrook Times* editor Benjamin Graves, as a staunch Greenbacker, later suggested that if the county Republicans had another convention "it would be impossible to get along with two tickets . . . they would have to have at least four."[20]

By August, there were two distinct camps of Republicans in the county and *Graham County Lever* editor Hogue described the Hill City convention as the "most contemptible rabble of politi-shysters, fence riders and copperheads who had the cheek to assemble in the name of the Republican Party." The *Lever* wrote that following the adjournment of the "mongrel convention," Niles was seen going down the street at Hill City, afoot, hat off and arms swinging, swearing eternal vengeance against "Commissioner Morehouse," whom Niles accused of withdrawing support for county clerk DePrad's bond. As Niles was DePrad's deputy, the denial of DePrad's bond directly affected his employment."[21]

In fact, DePrad was widely regarded as incompetent and would be soundly defeated in the subsequent election. McCabe would enter the fray, saying he had learned through Niles that "Mr. Knowlton," a Gettysburg man, had accused him of depriving DePrad of the opportunity to file his official bond. Denying that he coveted the position for himself, McCabe would write that the statement was a "malicious lie," insist that he was not a candidate, and challenge those circulating the statement to "come to the surface and defend him or themselves."[22]

In July 1880, with the following letter to the *Millbrook Times*, Niles progressed from county agitation to attracting statewide and eventually national attention:

> Allow me space in your columns to suggest an idea to the colored people throughout the United States, beginning in the State of Kansas, where the first precautionary step was taken regarding the rights of the down-trodden race, which right has never been secured and never will be without a concert of action. That action must consist in bringing suit against the U.S. government for damages to life, person and property, which according to the constitution and laws can be collected. The damage claimed is for the incarceration of slavery upon the whole race, for all of which the government owes us a compensation and must pay it or the constitution and laws will be disregarded and damned forever in the future.
>
> Therefore I, John W. Niles, as one of the aggrieved do assume the authority to call a state mass convention to be held at Nicodemus, Graham county, on Sept. 17th. Come one come all. It is hoped that all the friends of the race will be present. You are all respectfully invited to meet us on the occasion to hear and help us investigate the matter. More anon.[23]

Niles had held a first meeting on June 17, 1880, "to take in the best mode of which to petition the government for redress of grievances." In response, editor Graves struck a blow for his Greenbackers and asserted that "colored toilers must unite with the down-trodden white laborers and cut loose from the old parties who wish simply to use them as voting machines."[24]

Niles would subsequently use every opportunity to promote his belief that whites owed blacks restitution for time spent in slavery. The *Millbrook Times* reported that Niles had delivered the speech at an annual Fourth of July celebration, saying that Niles "with his usual patriotism got on his high horse when referring to various issues by which him and his race have been wronged."[25] In support of Niles's stance an anonymous Exoduster whose letter to the *Millbrook Times* was published on July 23, 1880:

> Another Exoduster, being one of the aggrieved . . . I, for one[,] highly endorse Niles' unique idea and hope he will be successful in his masterly undertaking. It is true the way in which we were set at liberty without a single dollar or farming utensil to commence with, and it was better for us to have remained in slavery where we were looked after as other brutes; but since emancipation we were forced to steal our neighbor's bread to save our lives and have thereby been made too dissipated and worthless to inhabit the earth. I wish Niles success. My sympathies are with him.[26]

The *Times* jabbed at the "famed orator," commenting, "We hear that there was a slight overflowing of the Niles at the greenback meeting in Nicodemus, but without any serious consequences." Graves's frequent comments about Niles veered between sarcasm and amazement. After Niles "retired" from his office of deputy county clerk and opened a livery stable late that year, Graves would take a poke at Niles's womanizing. The ex-clerk, Graves wrote, had "retired to private life and will hereafter devote his attention to agriculture and the study of anatomy."[27]

During this time of charged political activity, Niles antagonized whites and blacks with his campaign for reparations. In a blistering letter to *Rooks County Record* editor Tom McBreen, published in the *Stockton News*, Niles accused McBreen of waging "personal warfare" regarding Niles's views. He further accused the editor of "sailing under the banner of Republicanism, while in fact his ear lops the solid Democratic lop," and he depicted McBreen as "an enemy of the colored race."[28] The *Record*—McBreen—retorted, according to Chambers in *Niles of Nicodemus*, that Niles was a "fat mass of black ignorance and conceit, carrying 250 pounds of odoriferous averdupois and less than an ounce of brains and common sense."[29]

Smoothly exploiting other towns' outrage, the *Millbrook Times* continued its blatant courtship of black voters. Editor Graves referred to Niles as "the Honorable John Niles" and, after James Garfield was elected U.S. president in November, would suggest that he was worthy of a place in Garfield's cabinet.[30] Meanwhile Graves hoped to persuade the black community to switch from the Republican Party to the Greenback Party, and his paper gave ample publicity to the appearance of John Davis, a candidate for U.S. Congress who spoke at a Greenback rally in Nicodemus on September 6. Graves's headlines proclaimed that Davis "should be heard by every colored man who values his freedom."[31]

The Greenbackers held their first nominating convention in Graham County in September. The party was gaining a foothold in Kansas, reflecting blacks' disillusionment with the Republican Party. Graves predicted that African Americans would soon tire of Republicans using them as a voting machine and come over in a body to the Greenback Party, "the only party of equal rights and justice to all."[32] By 1881, African Americans across the country were angry over their inability to achieve political gains. Graves published a letter from Abram Hall, then the city editor at the *Chicago Conservator*, that bore testament to Hall's disillusionment with Republicans and his own disappointment with the easily misled black voter: "White politicians bamboozle him by shouting republicanism until he is such a thorough and irredeemable dupe that he believes it a positive sin to vote to anything else but a straight ticket. He honestly believes that the perpetuation of his right as a freeman depends upon his unquestioning support of every scoundrel and scalawag that proclaim[s] himself a republican. The colored voter is an arch dupe of American politics."³³ However, although Niles attended a number of Greenback meetings, he remained a Republican, as did Hall and McCabe. Niles was elected chairman of the Nicodemus Township Republican committee in August 1880.³⁴

Niles's next escapade in Graham County would involve the town of Roscoe, which Hall and McCabe had supported for the county seat. This time Niles would attract statewide attention. Platted in September 1879, Roscoe had been founded by a New Yorker, George E. Higinbotham. Located north and slightly west of Nicodemus on Spring Creek on firm bedrock, the town was more heavily timbered and had easier access to water than any other town in the county.³⁵ Roscoe grew steadily, although until June 1880 it lacked a newspaper to boom its merits. That year Higinbotham and his business partner, Barent Van Slyck, a fellow New Yorker, decided to construct a flour mill. Graham County historian Lowell Beecher wrote of this in 2009, "The expenditure of monies in support of the project, the sheer volume of labor demanded by all facets of the effort, the almost-incomprehensible economic and political implications attached to the edifice by its developers: each facet of the total undertaking remains impressive—even daunting—after the passage of well over a century."³⁶ Since a number of Nicodemus men were "mechanics"—highly skilled craftsmen of all types—some were employed to help build the four-story structure.

After Hall realized that Nicodemus would not have the requisite support to become the county seat but realized that African Americans would determine the outcome, he eventually endorsed Roscoe because the town provided jobs for Nicodemus blacks. Moreover, the *Roscoe Tribune*, beginning publication June 23, 1880, often commented favorably on Nicodemus's activities and citizens. Hall and McCabe and other African American businessmen immediately began advertising in the paper. Interracial working relationships, however, did not extend to social events. Under the headline "A Disgraceful Riot," the December 31, 1880, *Roscoe Tribune* gave an account of this. It seems that carpenters who had constructed the mill had hosted a dance party. At about ten o'clock the building "was filled to its utmost capacity," the paper reported, when a "dark cloud was seen approaching," and Niles and "twenty-five of his dusky followers" entered the building and proceeded to take seats formerly occupied by whites, forcing them to either stand all night or leave.[37] There are conflicting reports about what followed, but the *Roscoe Tribune* maintained that the managers of the mill merely asked these African Americans to defer to the ladies present and allow them to be seated. At this point, the paper said, Niles rose and announced that he and his entourage were "citizens of the highest magnitude" and that "death alone could put him out of the halls." The managers then closed the building, and the blacks left. However, the whites had merely ducked down into the basement, and after they assumed Niles and his followers had left, the managers opened the building again and resumed the dance. The blacks then returned, "and finding the doors closed, began stoning the building, and kept it up till the windows and sash were completely shattered." Then they shot into the building, and the whites returned the fire.

The Order of Mechanics called for Niles to settle for damages within ten days or face prosecution. The *Roscoe Tribune*'s local column in a subsequent edition read: "Wanted!—The name of the white girl who publicly kissed the negro at the late dance at the mill."[38] And the *Topeka Commonwealth* stated that as the blacks had withdrawn, the "stentorian voice of John W. Niles was heard to say: 'On with the dance. Let joy be unconfined.'"[39] The *Stockton News* also attributed this quote to John Niles.[40]

Appalled that the riot had attracted statewide attention, *Roscoe Tribune* editor Frank P. Kellogg upheld the right of the blacks to attend the dance but favored prosecuting them for damaging the mill site. Addressing men from Nicodemus, he wrote: "As regards your vote for county seat, we never received any from you, never expect any, neither do we want any."[41] And he printed a subsequent letter from an anonymous Nicodemus man without bothering to clean up the spelling and grammar. The correspondent was probably S. P. Roundtree, as he signed his letter "Friend & Secty. N.I.C.C" (Lula Craig listed Roundtree as secretary of one of the original organizations that founded Nicodemus), and Nell Painter in *Exodusters* quotes from a letter Roundtree wrote to Kansas governor Anthony, which used the same pattern of random capitalization and splitting multisyllabic words into one-syllable parts.[42] Regardless, this letter offers quite a different take on the circumstances of the riot. The author insisted that the whites—Norton outsiders in particular—started the trouble and "we the 'black clouds' finished it." The letter writer pointed out that the invitation had read "come one & all," alluded to the murder of John Landis by "gentlemen from Norton," and concluded with the statement that blacks intended to stay in Graham County.[43]

Millbrook Times editor Graves chose words very carefully when commenting on the riot. No matter what the circumstances, Millbrook still needed the black vote to secure the county seat. Graves gave a brief account of the event, simply stated that "the colored troops appeared and demanded equal rights with the whites," and added, "We have not learned the particulars."[44] However, on January 14, 1881, he printed a letter from H. L. Vanduvall, a black teacher, who castigated *Roscoe Tribune* editor Kellogg. Vanduvall pointed out that Kellogg praised "the dark clouds" when he wanted them to vote "the so-called Republican ticket" and accused Kellogg of opening the columns of the *Tribune* for "a revival of that damnable question of color which cost us a four years' war and millions of treasure." Vanduvall concluded by praising Niles: "Go it Uncle John we will stand by you."[45]

Prior to the Roscoe riot, editor H. S. Hogue of the *Graham County Lever*—no friend of blacks—had published an editorial lamenting the lack of a mill in Graham County, whereas the neighboring Decatur County had three. Hogue insisted that failure to resolve the county seat question had seriously retarded investment.[46] Immediately after the riot, Hogue published a brief neutral account of the event. As with Graves, the editor still was courting the blacks' vote to make Gettysburg the county seat and did not want to antagonize the men of Nicodemus. Then in a subsequent issue he seized the opportunity to promote Gettysburg as the best location for a mill, suggesting that the bank of Sand Creek was ideal in case the colonists no longer wanted to work in Roscoe.

By now Abram Hall was in St. Louis. Had he still been in Graham County, he would not have tried to breech social boundaries but would have served as a mediator. He understood the delicacy of racial interaction that was primarily limited to commerce, education, and politics. Niles probably understood the boundaries but fed on controversy and so introduced unnecessary racial division. There is no extant record of McCabe's reaction to the Roscoe riot.

Niles had been in the public eye before the riot, when he published a notice in the *Topeka Commonwealth* that he would address "the people of Kansas at the State House, in Topeka, on Saturday November 27, at 2 P.M. Subject—Law in regard to reimbursing the colored people for loss and damage sustained while in slavery." Two and a half months later, on February 14, 1881, James F. Legate, one of Kansas's most esteemed state legislators, offered House Concurrent Resolution No. 40, "relating to the compensation of the colored race of the United States for years of slavery, etc." The resolution was "laid over under the rules."[47] But on March 4, Legate urged the Kansas House of Representatives to adopt the resolution, and the motion passed.[48]

Legate was an active supporter of African American causes. A member of both the Kansas house and senate at various times, in 1881 he was chairman of the prestigious Ways and Means Committee of the house as well as serving on the committees for insurance and public land. Although the house *Journal* did not print the detailed wording of his resolution, the *Graham County Lever* reported that Legate asked the house to support "provision by Congress for paying slaves for labor before they were set free." In *Niles of Nicodemus*, Chambers writes that Legate asked Congress "to perform this act of restitution and justice."[49] In the meantime, Niles wrote articles protesting that he, not Jim Legate, was the "father of this scheme" and that he would not "permit another to seize the laurels that belong upon my immortal brow. I am to live always in the hearts of my countrymen."[50]

A few months later Niles was immortalized for criminal activities, not for his reparation efforts. He mortgaged a fictitious corn crop. Chambers writes with rueful admiration about Niles's abilities, saying that when Niles chose to represent himself at his trial the "ablest galaxy of legal stars in that part of the state" were arrayed against him. The *Graham County Lever* reported that "lightning could not have struck anywhere in that region without hitting an attorney." Prosecuting attorneys W. H. Barnes (who later became a successful lawyer in California), M. C. Reville (who became a federal judge), John C.

Denney, and Colonel D. J. Johnston were among the "terrible pack of legal wolves let loose on the offending darkey."[51]

The facts of the case were not in dispute. C. C. Woods managed the Rooks County Bank for his brother-in-law, the owner, Jay J. Smyth of Iowa. While Woods was away, Smyth was in charge of the bank. On March 1, 1881, Niles came into the bank and asked Smyth to loan him money on about fifteen hundred bushels of corn, which he said he had "piled up in a big shed," claiming he had bought the colonists' crop and was now short of cash. ("Corn was as good as gold to the Iowan," Chambers notes.) Smyth drew up a note and gave Niles the money. However, when Woods returned a couple of days later—and he knew Niles well—he informed Smyth that he had been stung, as the homesteaders had only raised a few nubbins. Law enforcement officials tracked Niles down despite his resourceful attempts to elude capture.[52]

Many years later, Chambers recalled a great deal of Niles's "eloquent and soulful" three-hour presentation at his trial. Niles had played on the jury's inherent hostility toward predatory bankers. Thirty-six to forty percent interest a year was not uncommon for bank loans at the time. Chattel notes usually listed every single pot and pan, fence posts, and even hand towels. Niles insisted that "if the good Lord didn't allow the colored people of Demus to raise a crop this year because he hadn't enough rain to spare, we couldn't help it. I mortgaged what should have been there." But his most persuasive argument encompassed his views on slave reparations:

> For a long long time we were happy and free until the white man came, loaded us with chains and brought us over to this land to be his slaves. For many years we have bent our backs in toil for him, He and his forefathers took away from us all we earned, making him rich, while all we got was a little food and a few clothes . . . many kicks, blows and the lash. He bought and sold us like cattle, tore our wives and children from us, robbed us, kept us ignorant, degraded . . . Now because I got a little money from a white man's bank and no money for security, I am to be punished. . . . They are going to deprive me of my liberty once more, without waiting to see if I will pay back the

money—because I am a member of that black race they stole from so long.[53]

After eight hours of deliberation, the jury voted eleven for conviction and one for acquittal. A hung jury astonished the county attorney, the assisting lawyers, and the bankers.[54] Editor Graves had been subpoenaed to testify at the trial and later wrote in the *Millbrook Times* that state's witnesses had sworn that Niles had never owned six hundred bushels of corn, but "the counsel for the state (Barnes) tried to "outvie Niles in ignorance." Not to be outdone, witnesses for the defense swore that Niles was commonly known as a dealer in corn. Graves pointed out that the poorly drawn contract read "600 bushels of corn in the crib and field at Nicodemus." He scoffed at the state's attorneys' failure to prove that Niles "had not the property in question."[55]

Judge D. C. Nellis criticized the "jurymen for ignoring the evidence and their instructions," and a new trial began immediately after summoning a second jury.[56] This time the court did not risk letting Niles defend himself. Millbrook lawyers T. T. Tillotson and H. J. Harwi served as Niles's counsel for defense. The county attorney was C. W. Smith with the assistance of W. H. Barnes for the state. E. P. McCabe was one of eight men subpoenaed to appear at this trial, but it is not clear whether McCabe appeared for the prosecution or the defense. This time the state fared even worse. Nine voted for acquittal and three for conviction. *Millbrook Times* editor Graves said he knew no "precedent for holding a man for a third trial for such a trifling offence." Niles was a free man.[57]

Exhilarated by the trial and his growing reputation as a gifted public speaker, Niles seized every opportunity to stay in the limelight. Graves covered all of Niles's orations and escapades and reported on an extravagant speech to Greenbackers in which Niles "painted the colored colony in this county in glowing colors." Niles then switched to "solid science and showed how great showers of refreshing rain could be brought down on this great American desert by filling the hills with powder and blowing them up thus creating a concussion." According to the *Times*, he was cheered and time and again by the "immense audience," with calls of "Encore!" and "the air . . . rent with shouts for NILES."[58]

In October 1881, the editor of the *Logan (Kans.) Enterprise* was quite taken with Niles when he called at the paper and expressed his views on the assassination of President Garfield. He printed all of Niles's comments on the front page. Although Garfield had been shot in July, he did not die until September, and historians now attribute his death to the intervention of sixteen doctors, all of whom thrust unwashed hands into Garfield's wound while probing for the bullet. The *Enterprise* referred to Niles as "Graham county's famed orator," and the *Graham Republican* reprinted the column.[59] Niles held the unorthodox view that Garfield's death was for the best, because it "united the Republican party and not only the party but the nation."[60] He also suggested that tar and feathers and a sharpened rail be used to punish the assassin, Charles Guiteau.

The following spring, Niles went from Graham County to Lee County, Arkansas. There he posed as a lawyer and "claimed to have authority from the United States Land Office to locate homestead entries." He secured an appointment as a special land agent of the Memphis and Little Rock Railway Company, persuaded African Americans to buy tracts of nonexistent railroad lands, then pocketed the money with the promise that the "land department" would send out a surveyor and attorney as soon as a certain number of tracts were sold.[61]

While in Arkansas, Niles founded the Indemnity Party, and promoted his dream of establishing an all-black town, to be called Progress. The Indemnity Party sought separation of the two races and demanded land to form a new state as restitution for time spent in slavery. In short, he exploited blacks' anger over years spent in slavery. He founded black lodges with secret signals, grips, and passwords, reminiscent of white fraternal organizations, and, in a bizarre reversal of racial dominance, he insisted that blacks should now rule and "that the two races must intermarry."[62] His propensity toward self-aggrandizement never flagged.

In 1882, alarmed by rumors of another Civil War, one instigated by blacks, Helena, Arkansas, formed a strong military company—the Lee Guards—composed of the best veterans the town could muster.

Because the rumors were gaining credibility nationwide a reporter from the *New York Herald* was sent to investigate. He concluded that the tension might be the beginning of a "revolution as extensive and bloody as that of John Brown [at] Harper's Ferry." The reporter interviewed Niles in a jail cell where the entrepreneur was being held for selling corn whiskey without a license (rather than for swindling). He had been fined $1,200, but, unable to pay, then ordered to labor on a convict farm near Helena. In custody three or four days before his African American friends collected money to pay his fines and get him out of jail, he was immediately rearrested, this time on federal charges of selling liquor without a license. Niles's friends rallied again and posted a placard throughout Lee County: "Notis hir given to all de white men of Lee County Arkansas, if Mr. Niles air not turn out Lee County Arkansas will be burnt up." Niles pleaded guilty to four charges in federal court, and was fined four hundred dollars and sentenced to four months in prison.[63]

Niles wrote to Benjamin Graves from Arkansas on December 20, 1882, giving an account of his arrest by federal authorizes. His letter, which Graves published under the headline "The Great Unterrified," claimed that the Indemnity Party was growing so fast that both Democrats and Republicans had taken it upon themselves to "kill us off." In this letter he gave a dramatic but implausible account of his house being surrounded "at the dead hour of midnight" by some "three hundred masked men, the half of whom were armed with needle guns, shooting from sixteen to eighteen times." Niles claimed he had fired back and held everyone off, surrendering only at the request of his mother. He enclosed a circular "embracing the policy of the Indemnity Party."[64]

The *Arkansas Gazette* gave a different account of Niles's arrest in a long article headlined "Niles Nailed" ("The Chief of the 'Indemnity party,' a colored Rogue and Swindler, Placed in the Penitentiary"). The *Gazette* described Niles as a "burly and muscular negro . . . light in color with features rather Caucasian than Senegambian and with a cunning and self-confident rather than an intelligent expression." The editor referred, with scathing disdain, to blacks' gullibility, then castigated prominent white male landowners in the community who had been similarly deceived by Niles's presentations and letters, which had convinced them that he would be a valuable colleague.⁶⁵

Upon his release from the Arkansas state prison, Niles resumed his political activities. Now convinced that separation of the races would result in a better life for African Americans, he urged the State of Arkansas and the U.S. government to satisfy his petition for slave reparations by giving his Indemnity Party a tract of land—one hundred fifty miles from east to west, extending forty miles from north to south—bounded by Indian Territory on the east, Texas on the south, New Mexico on the west, and Colorado and Kansas on the north.

Niles traveled to Washington, D.C., in late July 1883 to make his case. He went with letters of introduction from the chairman and secretary of the Indemnity Party of Arkansas to present to two prominent advocates of rights for blacks, Frederick Douglass and Richard T. Greener, the first African American to graduate from Harvard. In *Niles of Nicodemus*, Chambers writes that "metropolitan dailies contained notice of an eloquent colored orator who gave nightly talks on the streets of Washington, D.C. . . . in which he demanded a stupendous indemnity for ex-slaves because of the deprivation of their liberty and the wages of their enforced toil."⁶⁶

The *Millbrook Times* reprinted the following from the *Philadelphia Times*, under the headline "John W. Niles," datelined Washington, September 9 (1883):

> The Rev. Mr. Niles, a colored evangelist from Arkansas, who came here in the interests of a scheme to separate the blacks from the whites, has experienced up-hill work. He was refused the use of a public hall at the hands of the colored men here, who have antagonized his scheme from the start. Considerable ill-feeling has grown out of his efforts. Defeated in securing a hearing in a hall he made application to the police authorities for permission to speak in the streets today. This permission was granted and at half-past three several thousand people assembled at the intersection of Seventh street and Pennsylvania avenue, curious to hear the views of Mr. Niles on colonization, but he failed to put in an appearance. About an hour later he came,

but was then shut off by the police, because it was not the time designated in the permit and the assembly broke up in disgust. Mr. Niles says the separation scheme has many followers among his race in the South, but they are afraid of it here.[67]

Niles ran into difficulties explaining his plan to blacks at two mass meetings in Washington, D.C. The *Wheeling Register* in Wheeling, West Virginia, reported that he was choked by a "cry of crank" when he tried to expound on his beliefs.[68] The *Atlanta Constitution* condensed its view of Niles's venture into a fourteen-word headline— "The Colored Dupes: Efforts of Schemers to Get the Ignorant Blacks into More Trouble"—but other prominent newspapers also denounced Niles schemes.[69] The *Arkansas Mansion,* an African American paper, wrote that Niles had no following except in Lee and St. Francis Counties, "where the masses are exceedingly ignorant." The editor concurred with whites that "Niles was a fraud, humbug, and in every particular unworthy of confidence."[70] This opinion was shared by the prominent Arkansas African American lawyer, J. Pennoyer Jones. The *People's Advocate,* an African American newspaper published in Washington, D.C., also advised blacks to "take no stock in the Utopian scheme."[71] Then Niles claimed his travel plans were thwarted because the fifty dollars which was to be sent him weekly by his supporters was blocked by the post office in Arkansas because people there opposed his schemes. The post office investigated.

T. Thomas Fortune, at that time editor of the *New York Globe*, an African American weekly, published a succinct and spirited criticism of Niles's plans:

> Mr. J. W. Niles of Arkansas, thinks that the colored people of the South should take themselves up bag and baggage and flee into some community where there are no white men. . . . We would advise Mr. Niles to keep cool. The colored people are not going to run away from the South or from the United States to satisfy the whim of Mr. Niles or the earnest desire of many white men. We did not ask the white men to fetch us to this country and we do not ask them to take us away. We are part and parcel of the American people, and we propose to exercise an equal's

prerogative in deciding for ourselves whether we will go to that place or remain in this.[72]

While in Washington, Niles wrote an outrageous letter to President Chester Arthur listing a catalog of mistreatment by the State of Arkansas. Niles claimed that members of the Indemnity Party had filed on public land, that about $5,000 of fees had been confiscated, and that their village had been demolished, their land seized, and women forced into prostitution. He claimed party members were "manacled and whipped with red-hot hand saws dipped in boiling oil." His account of his arrest in Arkansas in this letter was even more hair-raising than the one printed in the *Millbrook Times*. He begged Arthur for "protection and such aid as be lawfully given" and asked him "to present our cause to Congress, and urge an act to allow us the use of the United States courts, as we cannot get justice in the State courts, if allowed to prosecute there, and to give us such other measures of relief as may be necessary to life, liberty, and the pursuit of happiness."[73]

President Arthur referred the letter to the U.S. attorney general, Benjamin Harris Brewster. Brewster replied immediately, saying that the public lands of which Niles spoke were under the control of the State of Arkansas and that the United States "cannot interpose for your relief." Brewster emphasized that Niles's appeals had to first go through the highest court in the state, and "from that to the Supreme Court of the United States. The Executive of the United States has no power whatever in the premises."[74] A number of major national newspapers printed Brewster's letter in full. The *New Haven Register* reported that after receiving the reply Niles had proclaimed that blacks' only salvation "is to leave the country they are in."[75] The *Logansport Journal*, after quoting Brewster, reported that Niles was preparing an address regarding this decision.[76]

Niles quickly published a pamphlet containing the two letters and a lengthy dissertation regarding race, titling this *A New Religion: J. W. Niles' Address to the Colored People of the United States*. In it he wrote,

> Hence the States can pass laws and apply them to the colored people alone, or apply them with unequal severity; then can by

craft and power, impose upon us disabilities, as they have done, and we have no redress!

After twenty years of almost fruitless endeavor many of our brethren, and especially the Indemnity Party, which I represent, have become satisfied that we must be forever at a disadvantage in our present relations; that we are attempting what never has been done, the union of two types of mankind in equal number in different states or degrees of development upon a basis of political, commercial and intellectual equality.

Niles ended with a call for money: "Send in your subscriptions to aid the cause. Direct to J. W. Niles, Agent of the Indemnity Party, No. 1212 R. Street, Washington, D.C."[77]

During Niles's stay in Washington, the Supreme Court, in a landmark decision announced October 15, 1883, declared the Civil Rights Act of 1875 to be unconstitutional. The act had guaranteed African Americans equal treatment in public accommodations and public transportation, and ensured blacks' rights to serve on a jury. Justice John Marshall Harlan was the lone dissenter. The Court held that the Fourteenth Amendment prohibited discrimination by the state regarding privileges and immunities, but did not apply to private individuals, and that racial discrimination in public accommodations was not contrary to the Constitution. Stripped of judicial support, the post–Civil War constitutional amendments became meaningless in the South, and the way was clear for the adoption of Jim Crow laws, which imposed racial segregation.[78] African Americans and white allies across the country considered this ruling retrogressive and hastened to express their opinions.

Frederick Douglass, in a speech to a group of African Americans holding a meeting at Lincoln Hall in the District of Columbia, expressed his grief over this decision: "We cannot . . . overlook the fact that though not so intended, this decision has inflicted a heavy calamity upon seven millions of the people of this country, and left them naked and defenseless against the action of a malignant, vulgar, and pitiless prejudice from which the Constitution plainly intended to shield them."[79] The register of the treasury, Blanche Kelso Bruce, formerly having served as U.S. senator, declared that it would "give the colored race a setback of at least a decade." Bruce, who became one of only five African Americans whose names would appear on treasury bills, enjoyed enormous status as an African American spokesman.

Niles, however, thought otherwise about the Supreme Court ruling. When a reporter asked Niles, calling him a "separationist," what he thought about the decision, Niles gave "evidence of great glee."[80] Niles said he welcomed the decision because it strengthened the cause of separation. He said the decision was further evidence that African Americans would never receive equal treatment, the point he had made in his *New Religion* pamphlet.

Niles made surprising headway in getting his agenda through Congress. The *Rooks County Record* reported that Niles had presented a petition to Senator John Sherman of Ohio on December 5, 1883.[81] Senator Sherman was the brother of the famous general William Tecumseh Sherman and author of the Sherman Anti-Trust Act. Senator Sherman also later served as secretary of the treasury and secretary of state. Niles's petition sought relief from "unlawful combinations of the whites of Arkansas" to prevent him and "his colored brethren from making entries of public lands."[82] The physical copy of the petition no longer exists in the National Archives.[83] Nevertheless, the *Senate Journal* of the first session of the Forty-Eighth Congress states that "Mr. Sherman presented a petition of J. W. Niles and certain colored citizens of Arkansas, praying the equal protection of the laws in securing homesteads; which was referred to the Committee on Public Lands when appointed."[84]

In his biography of Niles, Chambers scoffed at Niles's claim that Senator John J. Ingalls had once favored him with a visit and "cordially endorsed negro-indemnity." Chambers found Niles's claim to recognition from "so high a source" absurd.[85] But Ingalls *was* involved in Niles's petition—he helped defeat it. The *Senate Journal* for the second session of the Forty-Eighth Congress on January 26, 1885, recorded that the members consented to implement a motion by Senator Ingalls "that the Committee on the Judiciary be discharged from the further consideration of the memorial of J. W. Niles, representing the association of colored people, known as the 'Indemnity Party,' and other citizens

Senator John James Ingalls (R-KS). Courtesy of Library of Congress, Prints & Photographs Division.

of Kansas, praying the equal protection of the Laws in securing homesteads, and that it lie on the table."[86]

In late December 1883, several newspapers around the country announced the formation of an immigrant organization in Washington created by "colored residents of the city." J. W. Niles, it was reported, had been elected treasurer. The organization's constitution promised the head of every household 160 acres of land, and it was said that those paying ten dollars to the association will receive help in migrating and have assistance for one year afterward.[87]

There are no extant records about the remainder of John Niles's life. At that point he simply disappears from the pages of history. Regrettably, one of the founders of Nicodemus, who was instrumental in securing the colony's survival, acted fraudulently in many areas of his personal life. Niles began his political career on a local level and rose to prominence on the national scene. A gifted orator, he outwitted the best legal minds in Kansas during his trial for mortgaging nonexistent corn. He persuaded one of Kansas's most respected congressmen, James Legate, to introduce a resolution on his behalf. He founded the Indemnity Party, attracted a crowd of over three thousand in Washington, D.C., and convinced the venerable Senator John Sherman to present a petition seeking reparations for the time African Americans spent in slavery.

For all his dubious methods, Niles was a hero to many of the colonists of Nicodemus. On a national level, he was the first proponent for slave reparations to persuade the Senate to consider a formal petition. Niles's approach to achieving equality differed from Abram Hall's emphasis on racial uplift and E. P. McCabe's determination to forge equal rights through legislation, but his belief that African Americans should receive compensation for years spent in slavery has endured.

Chapter 11
I Will Not Touch the Unclean Thing

> *They offered resolutions that they would prevent the landing of colored paupers, as they call them, peaceable, if they could; forcibly if they must. It was suggested by law-abiding citizens that that was a good deal like a vigilance committee, and for the reputation of the town did not want that to go on record; and the resolutions at their second meeting, at which another chairman presided, were to the effect that the mayor use means to raise money and send them away.*
>
> Testimony of W. J. Buchan

THE TESTIMONY OF W. J. BUCHAN, a Kansas state senator from Wyandotte, illustrates how much Kansans wanted to protect their reputation as champions of liberty, morally superior to the South. But in reality the citizens of Wyandotte—as well as other overwhelmed areas where refugees were landing—did not want blacks in their own community. Buchan described the organization of committees to "provide for their temporary wants and with which to get them away."[1] Meanwhile, African Americans in sparsely populated western Kansas were developing an entirely different, partially integrated relationship with whites. The men and women shopped in white towns, were elected to offices traditionally held by white candidates, and gained political recognition.

E. P. McCabe, certainly a beneficiary of western Kansas's more sophisticated interracial relationships, became the best known of the three African American men who shaped Nicodemus. Four years after arriving in Graham County, he would be elected state auditor of Kansas.

McCabe was born in Troy, New York, on October 10, 1850. His parents moved to Fall River, Massachusetts, then to Newport, Rhode Island, and then to Bangor, Maine, where he attended public schools until the death of his father. McCabe then left school to support his sister and mother. Later, in New York City, he worked as a clerk for Shreve and Kendrick on Wall Street, then moved to Chicago. After working in Chicago as a clerk for Potter Palmer, the hotel king, he was appointed clerk in the Cook County office of the federal treasury. Inspired by articles in "race" newspapers in 1878, he joined his friend Abram Hall, Jr., to seek his fortune in Kansas.[2]

McCabe agreed with Hall's emphasis on education, racial uplift, and brokering intelligent compromises with whites but he did not believe these accomplishments were enough to secure civil rights. Neither did he share John Niles's rancor against whites. Instead McCabe believed that blacks could only achieve justice through aggressive pursuit of their agenda via legislative means. Eventually, however, he would endorse a policy of black separatism.

In contrast to the amiable Hall, McCabe easily took umbrage and was quick to suspect racial bias. He was highly principled and reluctant to compromise his agenda to secure the best results for African Americans. Argumentative and confrontational, he was adept at lampooning whites and blacks alike with his sarcastic, biting wit.

McCabe's foray into Kansas politics began with his appointment on August 14, 1878, through Rooks County, as the second notary public to serve the unorganized county of Graham. N. C. Terrell, a Millbrook attorney, preceded him as the first notary public by two days. By law, when McCabe took his oath he had to file a bond for one thousand dollars. Clearly he and Hall were prospering in their land location business to be able to offer surety for this bond. As a notary public, McCabe could acknowledge the legitimacy of deeds and other instruments of writing, validate official acts, and administer oaths. McCabe's commission was a tremendous benefit for the citizens of Graham County. They no longer had to make the long trip to Stockton to record business transactions. By extension, becoming a notary public was a boon for his and Hall's land location business as it cut down on trips to Stockton to validate their contracts.[3]

After Governor St. John issued a proclamation designating Millbrook as the county seat, he appointed McCabe to the office of temporary county clerk and John Inlow, O. J. Nevens, and A. E. Moses as county commissioners. In the view of Benjamin Graves, McCabe was "well and favorably known all over the county."[4] As county clerk, McCabe had to guarantee a bond for $2,000. In this position he was required to appoint a deputy and attend sessions of the county commissioners to record their business. He also had many responsibilities related to the establishment and maintenance of county roads. Dassler's *Compiled Laws* lists the salaries for county clerks, based on population. At the time of McCabe's appointment, the Graham County clerk would have been paid $700 a year. According to *Compiled Laws*, fees charged for clerks' service ranged from five cents to a dollar. McCabe was required to turn the money over to the commissioners at specified intervals along with a detailed report listing each transaction.[5]

McCabe appointed Niles as his deputy clerk, although they would seem an unlikely pair. However, the two men's signatures were on the 1879 announcement in the *Colored Citizen* that the colonists were discontinuing "this community now known as the Nicodemus Graham County Colony" and had "dissolved its officers and members to become citizens of Graham County in common with all others."[6] The colony was disbanded following Hall's accusation that Niles had sold solicited supplies and kept the money.[7] Although Hall's words no doubt spurred the colonists to action, Nicodemians had also become increasingly anxious to dissociate their image from that of the needy Exodusters pouring into the state.

St. John's appointments of Graham County officials were valid only until the first special election, scheduled for June 1, 1880. Since the county clerk's annual salary was lucrative, there were a number of candidates vying for the position. The other seven townships would also elect township clerks. (After Hall had filed his petition to create Nicodemus Township in July 1879, the white population began organizing additional townships.)

In anticipation of the upcoming election, Graham County Republicans met on April 16 to nominate a full slate of county officers.[8] Following a rather contentious meeting, the gathering agreed on a nominating committee and endorsed the state platform of the Republican Party and agreed to distribute the county offices equally throughout the county regardless of quarrels on township issues. The biracial committee on credentials reported that the following men from each township were entitled to seats at the convention: H. J. Harwi (Millbrook), Thomas Beaumont (Hill City), A. T. Hall, Jr. (Nicodemus), G. M. Dodge (Gettysburg), H. J. Scott (Indiana), I. N. Boyle (Bryant), L. W. Ingram (Graham), and F. Bullard (Moreland). These men nominated the following candidates for the general election: J. L. Walton (representative), J. R. McCoun (county attorney), H. J. Harwi (register of deeds), John DePrad (county clerk), J. E. Staples (sheriff), L. Thomas (treasurer), F. E. Bowers (superintendent of public instruction), James Gordon (probate judge), Lewis Pritchard (surveyor), and T. H. McGill (clerk of the district court).[9]

In addition to electing county officers, this all-important special election would also decide the location of the permanent county seat. Hall and McCabe were still touting the virtues of Roscoe, and they spoke on this topic at the Houston schoolhouse. The *Graham County Lever* printed a snide account of the meeting: "Dr. Butterfield, of Roscoe, did the slow and monotonous part of the programme and A. T. Hall, of Nicodemus, the brilliant and effective part. Charley Warren made the usual blunder and McCabe played the sarcastic part. All were most effectively answered by our candidate for Representative, J. L. Walton. . . . As far as the Roscoe 'boom' is concerned the meeting was a failure."[10] By that time, McCabe had clearly reversed his early rejection of involvement with county politics, when he had denied signing a county seat petition, telling the governor he refused to "touch or handle the unclean thing."[11]

Hill City's chances to become the county seat might have been better if W. R. Hill had not been so controversial. Hill would never overcome the antipathy of the colonists who felt deceived by his original propaganda calling blacks to Kansas. Then too, the colonists still bore him ill will from their having seen him pawn their goods in WaKeeney to pay the freight bill, which Hill had promised would be paid in advance. Even one of his staunchest supporters, W. H. Smith, who helped found Nicodemus, said that although Hill had selected ground for the colony, nothing was done legally, and that "everything is at odds and ends, without any means of command."[12]

Two charges of embezzling—plus arson to destroy the evidence—ruined Hill's credibility in promoting Hill City for county seat. On Saturday evening, September 20, 1879, the printing office in Hill City caught on fire. Although the flames were easily extinguished, the next night an armed mob went to Hill's residence and accused him of setting the fire to burn papers implicating him in embezzlement. Hill met the vigilantes with armed resistance. The men then sent a neutral party, Lew Bell, into the house with a note ordering Hill to "leave Hill city and the vicinity, and never return." Hill agreed immediately. Postmaster Crawford, accused of receiving money from Hill to set the fire, received a similar note. Crawford, however, told them to "go to hell, and if one of them enters my door he will go out as a corpse."[13]

In a surprisingly objective account, Benjamin Graves presented two other views of the incident. One was that the fire had been entirely accidental, the other that certain parties had wanted to raise a mob and drive Hill and Crawford out of Hill City long before the fire, and the fire was a pretext to do this.[14] Regardless, Hill and Crawford left, reportedly going as far as WaKeeney, but returned Tuesday night with two deputies. The *Stockton News* reported that even as Hill was showing "a bullet hole through the lapel of his coat" and swearing an oath "that his life was threatened," the deputies learned that the Trego County sheriff "was in search of Mr. Hill, having a warrant for his arrest on the charge of embezzlement."[15] Hill, who was in Stockton at the time, immediately pleaded guilty to another charge that had been filed with a justice of the peace there so he would "be safely jailed" in Rooks County when the Trego County sheriff arrived. However, the Trego County sheriff got "Hill's body out of jail on a writ of habeas corpus, had him discharged, then rearrested him. Hill [then] escaped on the road with just a light scratch from the sheriff's revolver."[16]

Graves in Millbrook later reported that "all but two of the male citizens of Hill City were taken to Stockton again last week, either as prisoners or witnesses, but they are getting things so mixed up in riots and rascality over there that people don't care anything about the particulars."[17] The *Graham County Lever* gleefully printed a letter from "Consistency" charging that if "the so-called Hill City rioters" succeeded in driving Hill out of town "they would rid this county of one of the meanest, most contemptible lying thieves that ever disgraced this state."[18] Nevertheless, Hill would be acquitted.[19]

The other county seat contenders had their share of rogues. The *Lever* in Gettysburg jeered at Millbrook's ambitions due to the town's difficulty in obtaining water. Gettysburg also launched a relentless negative publicity campaign against one of Millbrook's prominent citizens, N. C. Terrell, and his "noble mule." The editor reported that Terrell and his infamous mule had held a secret meeting with a "few colored men on the open prairie" to elude eavesdroppers and said that Terrell's hirelings were reporting that the two factions of Nicodemus had settled their differences and intended to vote solidly for Roscoe for the county seat. The *Lever* editor scoffed at this notion and believed it was another of Terrell's schemes to insure Millbrook's future.[20]

Graves in the *Millbrook Times* accused Gettysburg backers of promising potential voters of building a stone bridge across the river or "anything else you may wish," sarcastically adding, "They will readily promise to liquidate the national debt . . . or have a railroad built from that place direct to your farm and give you a free pass for life."[21] The *Roscoe Tribune* did not begin publication until after the June election or the town might have fared better. Also, at that time there was clearly division among the African American men in Nicodemus.

Despite the indecisive vote for county seat, county officers receiving a valid majority would replace those with temporary appointments, and McCabe was concerned about his wages under these circumstances. On June 10, 1880, he wrote Willard Davis, the Kansas attorney general, to inquire if he would receive wages during the interval between the election and the certification of the new Graham County clerk.[22] Elected officials had to establish their qualifications within twenty days of election. Davis replied that McCabe's salary would continue from election day until his replacement, John DePrad, was qualified, which could be as early as the day after the election. One of DePrad's requirements for certification was meeting the demand for a $2,000 bond.[23]

McCabe did not run for county clerk in the June election. In fact, he asked the *Millbrook Times* to publish a letter denouncing those accusing him of subverting DePrad's attempts to file his official bond. McCabe wrote that this accusation was a "malignant lie," saying, "I am no candidate for any office, nor have I used any influence to such an end."[24] At the July 30, 1880, meeting of the newly elected Graham County commissioners, the board allowed McCabe his requested payment of $221.47 for services as temporary county clerk from the time of St. John's appointment on April 5 to June 20. At this meeting, Niles was present in his capacity as McCabe's deputy clerk. Later DePrad also appointed Niles as his deputy clerk.[25]

The year 1880 was tumultuous for McCabe, as it was for Hall. In addition to the acrimonious atmosphere of the special election and Niles's inflammatory speeches on slave reparations, an African American correspondent signing as "Scipio" targeted Hall in the *Roscoe Tribune*. Scipio acknowledged that "the correspondent with Greek non-de-plume," Acribus (as Hall sometimes signed his letters), had other responsibilities, but said subscribers missed his "imaginative articles, true chronicles of occurrences in his own mind, just to see how close he can come to the truth without touching it."[26] The following week, inspired by Scipio's boldness, "On Dit" wrote from Nicodemus accusing Acribus (Hall) of sending false information to the *Tribune*.[27] Hall was too busy taking the federal census to reply publicly until July 30. Then Hall claimed to be amused by their "quaint humor" and the inference that they "were the sole personification of the truth." He wrote that "like Brutus in the quarrel scene with Cassius, I can say their charges 'pass by me as the idle wind which I heed not.'"[28] Hall then proceeded with his usual cheery general summary of Nicodemus news. Hall would leave Kansas for St. Louis before the national election held November 2.

In the 1880 election, L. P. Boyd won the coveted position of Graham County clerk. John Niles was also a candidate for this office but by that time had little credibility. The *Lever* pointed out that the defeat of Granville Lewis, the African American candidate for sheriff, was partly due to a "prejudice created by the incompetence of DePrad and the consequent irregularities in connection with the office of county clerk."[29]

L. P. Boyd appointed one C. Fountain, an attorney, as his deputy. Benjamin Graves, who had also been a county clerk candidate, would charge in an editorial a year later that Fountain "has done nearly all the business of the clerk's office without a cent's pay, while the dummy who was elected to the office has drawn the salary, schemed for county seat, practiced at the bar (?) and speculated in county script."[30] Animosity toward Boyd set the stage for McCabe's entry into the contest for county clerk the following year.

After Hall left Nicodemus in October 1880, McCabe continued with the land location business and law firm. Deprived of Hall's presence, the *Tribune* reported that McCabe looked "happy, but wan." That fall he married Sarah Bryant of Phillipsburg. According to Lulu Craig, the wedding took place on a rainy, windy night, and McCabe had asked the Reverend John Samuels to wait for him at his new two-story stone house while he went to Kirwin to fetch Sarah. Samuels made coffee and waited for the drenched couple to arrive. He stopped them at the threshold, "and in the dim night with the rain sweeping in, he read the Marriage Ceremony." According to Craig, Sarah could barely whisper the words, and McCabe then carried his dripping wet bride across the threshold. Samuels presented them with a chicken and a cake, courtesy of his wife. However, Sarah was chilled and nervous and declared she wasn't hungry. She drank a cup of coffee, went to bed, and tried to warm up while McCabe and Samuels visited until morning.[31]

In 1881, McCabe asked the state legislature for changes that would be advantageous for the residents of Graham County. He shared the sentiments of others in the area who wanted reduce the time it took to prove up homesteads from five to two years. Counties would benefit from the taxes and there would be less time for speculators to exploit settlers. McCabe wrote a letter to Congressman John A. Anderson lobbying for the amended legislation, and Anderson promised to press for a bill.[32]

The voters of Graham County were subjected to another election in 1881. This was the regularly scheduled state general election in November. By this time, Graham County was fed up with incompetent county clerks. DePrad had been accused of irregularities by the *Lever*, and editor Graves asserted that L. P. Boyd drew the salary but turned all the work over to his deputy. When McCabe ran for the office, voters remembered his superior performance after St. John appointed him temporary clerk. He won by a sound majority.

Everett Dick wrote that among the reasons for "the death of a thriving town" were that the county seat was established in a rival town.[33] After towns' failed bids to secure status as county seat, newspapers in the losing towns also went out of business. With the official placement of the county seat in Millbrook, the *Roscoe Tribune*, the *Graham County Lever*, the *Graham Republican*, and the *Hill City Times* would no longer exist when McCabe began his campaign for state office the next year. Benjamin Graves first proposed McCabe's candidacy for state auditor in the March 17, 1882, edition of the *Millbrook Times*.[34] He pointed out that the Republican Party "owed a lot of its existence to the northwest . . . and to colored voters," and nominating McCabe would do justice to both those interests.[35] J. H. Downing, editor of the *Star-Sentinel*, published in Hays, Kansas, immediately objected, declaring that he wanted a "more worthy colored man" than McCabe.[36] *WaKeeney Weekly World* was not in favor of a black man, let alone one "never struck by piety very hard."[37] But Graves insisted, "There's many a blacker white man than McCabe."[38] While McCabe wanted it "distinctly understood" that he was also a candidate for re-election to the office of county clerk, Graves was disappointed by this, as he interpreted this decision as "lack of faith" on McCabe's part.

By May, papers outside Kansas were aware of the bold move from this African American outlier. The *Chicago Conservator*, in an article undoubtedly written by Abram Hall, maintained that McCabe could bring as "many qualifications as the next man" and that Kansas would show sister states that "a colored republican if qualified for the place can aspire to and attain the position the same as [do] his white compatriots."[39] Not all Nicodemians supported McCabe's bid for auditor, however. A painfully written letter from "J.J. uv Wild Hoss" commented on McCabe's candidacy. It was a poignant testimony to both blacks' facility with spoken language and their struggle to communicate ideas through inadequate (and distracting) writing. J. J. stated that he "rite you in a spearit ov luv & not anymosytie" but said the *Millbrook Times* was "slitely off ure base, or barkin up the rong tree as it were, in tryng to boost McCabe onto a limb too 'high fur his equilybrim.'" J. J. recommended the "Hon. Samuil Gasline" and asserted that at the recent Kansas Convention of Colored Men, "Gasline" "swade them konventionirs to hiz oan swete wil with his bootyful wit, kute sarkazum, patryotick flourishes, staitsmumlike dyplomacie, impressive geschers, deep paythoz, and undying loity to the flag . . . becides there ain't no sort of cents in wun man gobblin' all the fat ophices."[40]

Nationwide, African Americans continued to criticize the Republican Party for its token recognition of blacks' contribution. Hall, who kept a close watch on Kansas politics, blasted the Convention of Colored Men in a stinging column in *Chicago Conservator.* Under the headline "The Colored Man's 'Whereas,'" Hall noted that after a long recitation of injuries inflicted by the Republican Party, "these political giants, these Samsonian colored representatives resolve to reaffirm their devotion to the party. Jawbone magnificent! Backbone sublime!"[41]

All across western Kansas, editors began weighing in on McCabe's candidacy. His ethnicity was a formidable obstacle. However, his light complexion enhanced his chances with most of the white community and some of the blacks. His run for office brought forth some vicious existing intraracial and interracial prejudices, and the *Weekly Kansas Chief* (Troy) commented, "The nomination of McCabe will not satisfy most of the colored voters. He was never a slave, but was born free, in Troy, New York."[42] Socially, "freemen" were on a different plane than "freedmen," former slaves. Many of the prewar black elite were wealthy, light-skinned slaveholders themselves and opposed the movement for racial uplift. So acrimonious was this intraracial prejudice that in some cases, historian Ira Berlin reports, "the old free Negro elite, rather than attend church with the freedmen, formed their own congregation, hired a white minister, and let it be known that 'no black nigger' was welcome."[43]

Even in interracial western Kansas there was acute sensitivity to the "intra-color" line. State census records differentiated between blacks, whites, and mulattos. When McCabe campaigned for the office of state auditor, the *Stockton Record* enthusiastically declared that McCabe was a man well qualified to fill the office of auditor and was "what you might call a smoked Irishman." The *Record* assured its subscribers that "Mr. McCabe has so little colored blood in his veins that it can only be detected with a microscope."[44]

In the *Afro-American Encyclopaedia*, compiled by James T. Haley with comments by Booker T. Washington, and published in 1895, colored people in the United States were traditionally graded according to the greater or less predominance of "Negro" blood as follows:

Mulatto, one-half black, white and Negro
Quarteron (Quadroon), one-fourth black, white and mulatto
Metis, or *Metif*, one-eighth black, white and quarteron
Meamelouc, one-sixteenth black, white and metis
Demi-meamelouc, one-thirty-second black, white and meamelouc
Sang-mele, one sixty-fourth black, white and demi-meamelouc
Griffe, three-fourth black, Negro and mulatto
Marabou, five-eights black, mulatto and griffe
Sacatra, seven-eights black, griffe, and Negro.[45]

Across the country some formerly enslaved African Americans did not appreciate having light-complexioned men who had been born free step forward to champion their interests, and that included residents of Nicodemus. Historian Nell Painter wrote, "Late nineteenth century newspapers, black and white, spoke of assimilated Negroes as 'representative colored men,' meaning that they represented the best the race had to offer." Blacks who advocated assimilation, however, infuriated others who preferred to emphasize their African heritage. Benjamin Singleton, who proclaimed himself father of the Exoduster movement and certainly was the instigator of the black colonization movement into Kansas, scathingly denounced "representative" Negroes: "I am now compelled to say something to the leading men of our race that sit in high places and get their living off of our poor laboring class. . . . Such men as this should not be leaders of our race any longer."[46] McCabe, Hall, and Niles were classified as mulattos on the federal census record. However, even with their distinctly racial agenda, like all the other settlers in Nicodemus—whether freeborn or formerly enslaved—they were never "representative Negroes" who courted the approval of whites.

At first McCabe's candidacy for state auditor was so implausible that he had not attracted wide attention. State auditor was a fiercely competitive position requiring enormous skills and staggering responsibility. Moreover, the state auditor received a handsome annual salary of $2,000. It was not simply that a black man was seeking state office but the fact that McCabe was seeking that *particular* office that would eventually galvanize the Republican Party. It would be difficult to imagine any one man capable of overseeing the office's volume of detailed work in the 1880s during McCabe's tenure. Kansas abolished the position in 1975 and no comparable position exists today. The state auditor was required to keep track of Kansas's transactions with any other state or territory. The auditor validated any claims against the state, recorded all warrants drawn, and accounted for all taxes received and other money entering the treasury. The auditor planned the management of public revenues and provided the treasury office with a two-year estimate of expenses. The auditor supervised the copious files maintained by the chief clerk, a land office clerk, and other clerks as needed. Twice a year the auditor examined the books and accounts of the treasurer. In short, the job required tireless energy and a first-class mind with a genius for details.[47]

Naturally, the *Colored Patriot* immediately got behind McCabe's candidacy. From the *Chicago Conservator* it reprinted these words that probably were Hall's: "Let the people of Kansas practice the doctrine of true Republicanism they have preached for so many years, and thus show to her sister states the cheerful spectacle of one northern state, where a colored Republican, if qualified for the place, can aspire to and attain the position the same as [do] his white compatriots."[48]

One of the biggest factors that enabled McCabe's nomination was the party's fury over St. John seeking a third term as governor. The *Atchison Champion* believed the "Constitution of the United States, and the Constitution of every state in the Union, ought to limit the Chief Executive office to two terms," saying that "any President or Governor wanting more than two terms is a 'political hog.'"[49]

The governor had already made enemies due to several unpopular positions: his advocacy of women's rights, his championing of the rights of African Americans, and his unyielding middle-of-the-road position on prohibition. Many prominent Republicans, such as Senator John J. Ingalls, made it quite clear that they did not care for the governor. Ingalls afforded St. John only minimal courtesy. At the beginning of St. John's first term, the newly elected governor received a telegram from Ingalls asking St. John to send the required credentials certifying his reelection to the U.S. Senate. In a subsequent sarcastic letter, Ingalls stated that while his credentials had arrived, "They look as if they had been painted with cat's tail dipped alternately in a thunder cloud and the burnished tints of the setting sun." He pointed out that also the dates of the credentials were wrong and enclosed a draft in proper form, which he urged St. John to emulate. He arrogantly provided instructions as to the placement of the "Great Seal of the State."[50]

Convinced that a black man did not stand a chance of winning the nomination and therefore it was not necessary to expend much energy in campaigning against him, a large number of Kansas Republicans ignored McCabe and focused on thwarting St. John's nomination. The Hays *Star-Sentinel* warned, "If the State Convention re-nominates John P. St. John, 20,000 Republicans stand ready to scratch his name from the ticket, and either vote for a democrat or no one at all."[51]

By logic, prohibition advocates should have been the most stalwart supporters of St. John's candidacy. However, St. John had originally supported "local option," gaining him acquired many enemies among prohibitionists who viewed this as a timid approach. The local option law allowed any voting entity, such as a city, township, or county, to vote in unique liquor regulations. Consequently the Republicans unintentionally created an alliance of anti–St. John radical prohibitionists who wanted statewide prohibition, with no local option, and anti-prohibitionists who didn't like anyone very much, let alone St. John. No Graham County paper—or other paper—seems to have printed McCabe's formal stance on prohibition, but an early circular promoting Nicodemus stated that "no saloons or other houses of ill-fame will be allowed on this town site within five years of the date or this organization." The five years were up when McCabe ran for office.[52]

There were rumors that a run for a third term was not St. John's idea. The *Star-Sentinel* reprinted a letter published in the *New York Witness*, which St. John had supposedly written to a friend, saying, "You can scarcely imagine how anxious I am to be once more free entirely from the cares incident to an official position. While friends are pressing me for a third term in this State, I say to you frankly that I do not want it."[53] However, there is no evidence that he made serious attempts to withdraw his name from consideration, and St. John continued to give speeches advocating temperance, which endeared him to a large number of Kansans. He paraphrased Lincoln's well-known comment that no government could endure "half slave and half free" by saying that Kansas could not exist "half drunk and half sober. It must eventually become all one or the other."[54]

St. John provided another distraction from McCabe's campaign in being a passionate champion of women's rights. In August 1881 he received a long letter from the famous suffragist Susan B. Anthony, lamenting that both Kansas senators were against allowing women the vote. Anthony cleverly linked women's right to vote as a key strategy for advancing prohibition, and she wrote, "Happy will it be for Kansas if all *free whiskey* foreigners will stay outside her borders; at least until her women are enfranchised." Anthony suggested that Kansans had the "cart before the horse" but if the state would vote in women's suffrage first, "Prohibition would be easily executed."[55] However, despite the state's enthusiasm for temperance, many communities considered the push for suffrage an assault on home and family. And while a good number of women regarded St. John as saintly, men thought otherwise. The *Weekly Kansas Chief*, linking suffrage with prohibition, acknowledged that "some good Christian women . . . descended on Topeka to support the prohibitionary amendment." However, the editor asserted that most suffragists were "divorced women, women who had deserted their husbands, women whose husbands had been divorced or deserted them, and women who almost publicly carried on prostitution." The *Wichita Eagle* quoted the *Atchison Champion* in describing an earlier convention of suffragists as an invasion of a "horde of long-haired men and short-haired women, who roamed about like a walking pestilence, filling the air with their howls."[56]

An anecdote recalled by temperance leader Francis Willard hints at the link between the powder keg issues of women's suffrage and temperance. As Willard recalled, an amendment to the Kansas Constitution banning liquor was one vote short, when a woman was seen going "down that aisle where woman never trod before." "She goes straight to her husband, takes his big hands into her little ones, lifts her dark eyes to his face, and speaks these thrilling words: 'My darling, for my sake, for the sake of our sweet home, for Kansas' sake and God's. I beseech you change your vote.' When lo! Upon the silence broke a man's deep voice: 'Mr. Speaker . . . I wish to change my vote from no to aye!'"[57] Thus Kansas became the first state in the Union amending its constitution to ban liquor. However, even many teetotalers resented this amendment limiting their freedom to decide for themselves what to drink. Politicians were uneasy. German Democrats were livid and referred to prohibition advocates as "water fools."

Meanwhile, many saw suffragists as disrupting the "natural order" of male dominance, and suffragists did at least implicitly reject the concept that a woman's place was at home. Male scientists argued that because there was only so much blood in the human body, if this blood were drawn to the head through hard thinking about politics, their ovaries would shrink.[58] In short, the fate of the nation's children depended on denying women the vote—and Governor St. John was an advocate for women's suffrage. With a number of prominent Republicans determined to block his nomination, it is not surprising that an obscure black man from western Kansas running for state auditor bypassed the scrutiny he would have received under different circumstances. McCabe was now receiving endorsements from prominent publications such as the Mankato-based *Kansas Jewellite*, and in August, the *Topeka Capital* warned that "McCabe had more delegates instructed for him than any other candidate in the field except St. John."[59] St. John was the odds-on favorite to win the nomination by a large margin, despite rumblings in the general populace. There were still a majority of electors who believed his passionate advocacy of temperance was more important than either the third-term issue or his support of the weakening local option provision. Republican leaders, however, foolishly minimized signs of trouble. They ought to have taken it seriously in March when the *Commonwealth* printed a letter noting that "the people have set their seal of disapproval so emphatically on even the idea of third term that it would be the next thing to madness in anybody to boost himself up."[60] They should have noted the disapproval between the lines when the Hays *Star-Sentinel* scoffed that "nothing of the kind had ever been heard of in Kansas before."[61]

In May 1882, Kansas Republicans decided that "the interests of the party" called for two conventions. The first would be held in July to agree on rules and a platform, while the second, in August, would nominate state officers. Having accomplished the purpose of the July convention, the official delegates of the Grand Old Party met in Topeka on August 9 to select candidates. The next day, despite the embarrassment of many of the delegates at having wasted the previous night in "too much singing," the 384 attendees were determined to finish their work by noon.[62] Wild cheers greeted all the agreed-upon resolutions, including the controversial prohibition plank. The governor easily achieved renomination and then delivered an eloquent address.[63] Earlier the *Anthony Journal* had gleefully predicted, "Thousands of Democrats all over the state will cast their ballots for him."[64]

Other nominations went smoothly until it was time to select the candidate for auditor. In addition to McCabe, nominees were L. P. Stover (Allen County), W. T. Nicholas (Rice County), Edward Spaulding (Osage County), Samuel McFadden (Shawnee County), W. H. Taylor (Sedgwick County), Martin Mohler (Osborne County), and state senator Albert Greene (Douglas County).[65]

On the first ballot, McCabe received far more support than anyone probably expected. The candidates stood as follows: Stover 25, McFadden 34, Mohler 77, Taylor 49, Nicholas 43, Spaulding 34, Greene 1, and McCabe an astonishing 106.[66] The establishment discounted this support as a one-time wonder. A majority of votes cast was required in order to win. However, after the second ballot, the delegates received an even larger jolt. The votes this time: Stover 22, McFadden 30, Mohler 83, Taylor 16, Nicholas 19, Spaulding 24, Greene 0, and McCabe a jaw-dropping 169. The outlier lacked only thirteen votes of being the nominee. A Mr. Pickering called for the unanimous nomination of McCabe, but delegates loudly rejected this move with cries of "no, no, no."[67]

The state auditor was responsible for staffing prestigious and lucrative positions and could make or break careers. When Republicans realized the party was in danger of nominating an African American, they panicked, as they thought McCabe was unlikely to win the general election.

Judge Joel Holt, a friend of Governor St. John, asked for an adjournment until two o'clock. The maneuver was later reported to have been an attempt to "kill off McCabe," the hope being that a recess would chill the unexpected enthusiasm for a black man.[68] Friends of McCabe fought against the adjournment but were outvoted. Then "St. John's friends, including the state house staff, commenced tearing around devising ways to beat McCabe."[69] Antics at the convention were so convoluted and Machiavellian that it is impossible to determine if St. John himself moved to block McCabe's nomination or whether his loyal cohorts took action without his knowledge. St. John did not have the same camaraderie with McCabe as he had experienced with Hall. This was evident in McCabe's letter to the governor over denial of aid to blacks in WaKeeney in 1880 and the governor's scolding of McCabe's underscoring with double lines the word "black." Regardless, when the convention reassembled at two thirty, the third ballot proved even more disastrous for McCabe's foes. And on the fifth ballot—for the first time in the North, the Republicans nominated an African American for a state office. At a celebratory bonfire afterward, McCabe was "vehemently called for" and then came forward and made a few remarks: "Fellow-citizens of Shawnee county: Never in the history of my life can I recall an incident in which I take more pride than that of to-day, and I am very grateful for it. My race, too, are grateful. I think that you will excuse me from making any further remarks, as I am unwell, and there are other speakers to follow."[70]

Kansas newspaper editors jumped in with an immediate analysis of what had happened and reported on subsequent attempts to get McCabe off the ticket. Several papers reported that McCabe had been offered five thousand dollars to withdraw, saying that he had declined. There was also an immediate cascade of derogatory letters to editors. Some prominent Republicans believed that anti–St. John men had achieved McCabe's nomination. They alleged that electing an African American was a trick to the put the pro–St. John delegates in a bind with the black community. They reportedly "compelled the St. John fellows either to take him" or go back on their promises to "their colored brethren" to acknowledge the importance of their vote through awarding a member of the race a place on the ballot.[71]

The *Smith County Pioneer* reported that it had received fifty letters from all parts of the state in regard to the McCabe nomination. "All regret it—some will oppose him, and most of them advise the Central Committee to investigate him and remove him for cause if any exist."[72] The *Iola Register* warned that the "party needs to prepare itself for attacks against McCabe" but said that "McCabe was not the loose-jointed gangling African that some have tried to make him out [to be]."[73]

Some editors printed racial jokes and slurs. The editor of *Fort Scott Daily Tribune* reported that there was now a "conflict of races" between men of Irish descent and men of African descent claiming McCabe, as the Irish said his name implied he was "descended from the old stock of Donnegal, Limerick or Down."[74] And another editor wrote, "The Germans being whiskeyites, they got no representation on the state ticket. McCabe, the candidate for Auditor, appears to be an Irish darkey."[75]

The pressure for McCabe to withdraw never let up. The *Wichita Eagle* insisted, "Evidence accumulates, day by day, that the St. John gang considers the colored man, McCabe, a disgrace to the ticket, and that they mean to get rid of him, or defeat him. . . . Mohler, of Osborn, was the man they intended to nominate." The *Eagle* pointed out: "North-Western Kansas appears to be eternally yawping for something. It is now howling over the defeat of Mohler, of Osborne, for Auditor of State. They say that North-Western Kansas was solid for Mohler, yet the Convention nominated McCabe. Who gave North-Western Kansas a right to dictate who should be nominated for Auditor. . . . The delegates of the whole state had a say in this matter and if a majority preferred McCabe to Mohler, the North-West has no right to bellow and paw the ground."[76]

Some editors moved on from racial slurs to raising doubts about McCabe's abilities and integrity. The editor of the *Weekly Kansas Chief* denounced the editor of the *Kirwin Chief* and reprinted an article viciously assailing McCabe's character and qualifications:

> The question of color has nothing to do with the dissatisfaction. The fact that he is a saddle-colored "man and brother," cuts no figure in the case. The potent causes of the trouble are: First— The Northwest was entitled to the nomination, and expressed their preference almost solidly for Mr. Mohler. . . . But the Chief [Kirwin] learns from people who know him thoroughly, that he is totally unfitted for the arduous and responsible duties of the office. We have conversed with citizens of Graham County and their evidence is: "He is a shrewd, unscrupulous, impudent fellow, without character or moral standing. He is not a prohibitionist in principle or practice, and his opinion of people who believe in churches, is that they are all lunatics. That such a man should be foisted on the Republican party of Kansas for one of the most responsible State offices, is a disgrace to all who assisted in the nomination.[77]

The *Millbrook Times* immediately rushed to McCabe's defense. Its editor, Graves, urged all Graham County voters to set aside party loyalty and "vote for E. P. McCabe, not necessarily because he is a republican, or greenbacker or democrat, but simply because he is a Graham county pioneer homesteader and possesses every necessary qualification for the place."[78] The *Times* printed letters of support from all over the state:

> The nominee for Auditor, E. P. McCabe, county clerk of Graham county, is a young colored man of more than ordinary talents and ability, a college graduate—in fact the most brilliant colored man of his age in Kansas. An extended acquaintance with him enables us to say that he is thoroughly qualified for the position. A thorough-going and experienced business man, a neat and

correct book keeper, an elegant penman, honest and conscientious, eminently trustworthy and a courteous gentleman, we have no hesitancy in saying that he will perform the duties of the Auditor of State in as satisfactory a manner as any of his predecessors. That he will be elected by a handsome majority, there can be no doubt. We rejoice in his success.—*Jamestown Kansas.*

We are personally acquainted with McCabe, the colored candidate for Auditor and know him only as a perfect gentleman—sharp, well educated and competent.—*Crocker Journal.*

In spite of the malicious falsehoods circulated at Topeka last week in regard to McCabe's incompetency to fill the office of Auditor, his friends were able to pull him through safely. There is not a better qualified man in state than this same E. P. McCabe and his traducers know it, which can be abundantly proven by examining his reports on file in the archives at Topeka.
—*Millbrook Herald.*

McCabe was just as fairly nominated as any other candidate on the ticket, and is just as fairly entitled to the party support. It is not alleged that he is incompetent, and nothing has been established discreditable to him. It is about time, therefore, that this talk about removing him from the ticket or opposing him should stop. The *Smith County Pioneer* is owned by one of Gov. St. John's secretaries, and edited by one of his most ardent supporters, and these gentlemen should therefore, set a better example for Republicans than this.—*Atchison Champion.*[79]

A number of newspapers in the East had been intensely interested in all things coming out of Kansas since the border wars. The *Boston Herald* commented on the unexpected results of the Kansas State Republican Convention, saying, "They proclaim their intemperate devotion to temperate principles. . . . They stand up perpendicular for women's suffrage. They are against monopolies and name railroads as requiring strict supervision. They heartily endorse the president's veto of the river and harbor bill, and they ended up by nominating a colored man for state auditor."[80]

Other papers ignored the implications of McCabe's nomination and focused on the party's surprise endorsement of the right of women to vote. "The Republicans of Kansas have taken an advance and bold step. Not contented with the nomination of the great living Temperance apostle, they have endorsed woman suffrage, and put a colored man on the ticket for State Auditor. This is the farthest step yet taken in political acrobatics. . . . Yet, it is believed so thoroughly St. Johnish was the convention, that had an available Chinaman appeared on the scene he would have been taken up and put before the people as a champion bearer."[81]

But the Republican Party was deeply split over prohibition, women's suffrage, and its black candidate for auditor, and a governor seeking a third term would soon face Democrats more united in ideology. The Democratic convention, which met in Emporia on August 30, 1882, first chose John Martin of Topeka as the candidate for governor, and delegates were disappointed when he declined the nomination. By the second day, Democrats had carefully constructed a platform that included an enthusiastic endorsement of temperance in theory but with a strenuous objection to the "oppressive and tyrannical" provisions of the prohibition amendment. The party insisted that the amendment be resubmitted to the people.

Throughout the state, Democrats were still indelibly associated with Missouri border ruffians—largely southern Democrats—flooding Kansas before the Civil War. Still fighting their image as "whisky-party drinking, degraded, foul-mouthed marauders," the Democrats were nevertheless in general agreement that people had the right to choose whether or not to drink alcohol.[82] After Martin declined to run, on the basis that "offering myself as a sacrifice for the purpose of harmonizing the differences of the party in the state of Kansas would be suicide," the party recessed, then reassembled to nominate George Washington Glick, a lawyer from Atchison.[83]

Further complicating the general election would be the entry of the controversial Greenback candidate for governor, Charles Robinson, who had been Kansas's last territorial governor and its first state governor. Robinson and Glick had the same stance on alcohol: pro-temperance but against the prohibition amendment. Ironically, St. John, a stalwart champion of prohibition, became the most vilified by ardent prohibitionists because of his support for local option.

Republicans gave McCabe a brief reprieve from campaign scrutiny while they quarreled over prohibition. Editor Downing of the *Star-Sentinel* scoffed that "the firm of St. John and God have taken on a new partner—James F. Legate of Leavenworth."[84] Legate, one of the most esteemed legislators, had already endangered his popularity by supporting Niles's campaign for slave repatriations. Legate explained his views on temperance at a talk in Leavenworth, August 23, 1882.[85] He said that he had opposed the prohibition amendment because of the difficulty of enforcement and favored strict licensing of saloonkeepers. Nevertheless, he firmly believed that since the amendment had passed in 1880, then "the only course for the people of Kansas to pursue is to follow the law."

As the election grew nearer, Republican leaders became increasingly nervous, and the slurs against McCabe intensified. The editor of the *Weekly Kansas Chief* reminded voters "of the treatment of McCabe by St. John and his strikers. They tried to defeat him for nomination; and when he was nominated, they tried to force him to withdraw. Failing in that, they threatened to defeat him, and offered to trade him off for votes for St. John. . . . St. John does not deserve the vote of a single colored man."[86] There was even a movement afoot to vote only for McCabe and no other Republican candidate.[87]

Despite the accelerated attacks, those who knew McCabe well were the most likely to support his candidacy. Abram Hall, on a visit back to Kansas, assured a *Commonwealth* reporter that he knew McCabe "all the time he was in Chicago and was with him eighteen months in Graham county, and a more straightforward square man don't live."[88]

On Tuesday, November 7, the people of Kansas marched to the polls and cast a historic vote, electing E. P. McCabe as state auditor with a large plurality over his Democratic opponent. But stunned Republicans reeled from the defeat of St. John by Glick, a Democrat, and bitter recriminations followed. According to the *Commonwealth*, St. John was on record as saying "that a large slush fund, treachery and fraud have accomplished what the opposition set out to accomplish."[89] The *Atchison Champion* scolded the Republican Party, citing all the errors it had made. The *Wichita Eagle* tried to sum up the reasons St. John had failed to gain a third term and offered this advice for the next election: "When the party turns a deaf ear to the whisperings of the Bosses and opens a willing ear to the whisperings of the masses, it will be on the road to success." "As Republicans have been made sadder," the paper added, "it is hoped they have also become wiser."[90]

In a speech George Glick gave after the election, he "rejoiced to think that it was a triumph of Kansas in favor of individual liberty of the citizen as opposed to sham prohibition and sham government by which manhood was degraded and trampled down."[91] The citizens of Graham County meanwhile were ecstatic over McCabe's election. Benjamin Graves denounced all the Republicans who had attempted to solicit his support in removing McCabe from the ticket simply because Graves was a Greenbacker. Graves also revealed that the *Times* had been offered $5,000 if he would launch a "vigorous fight and open a bitter feeling against [McCabe] in his home county." The *Times* offered a tribute to Sarah McCabe, describing her as "a faithful and devoted wife and mother" who attended strictly to the affairs of her household.[92] Lulu Craig later wrote of the pride the colonists felt that "the first colored man elected to a state office was E. P. McCabe of Nicodemus."[93]

By June 1883, the correspondent of the *Kansas City Times* reported that "inquires" had been made at the statehouse, and "E. P. McCabe makes as good an Auditor as Kansas has ever had."[94] If there were any doubts about McCabe's abilities, they were laid to rest with the publication of the "Fourth Biennial Report of the Auditor of the State and Register of State Land Office," an accounting of the fiscal years ending June 30, 1883, and June 30, 1884. After the work was "Respectfully submitted to Governor Glick," McCabe concluded:

> The relations with my fellow-officers have been pleasant and cordial, and I take this occasion to express my appreciation for courtesies received.
>
> To the people and press of the State I hereby convey my grateful acknowledgment for the generous support and considerate treatment extended during my initial term, and will

add that I have made every effort to deserve their confidence by a conscientious discharge of the duties of this office.

My assistants have creditably acquitted themselves in the places assigned them respectively.[95]

By 1884, as McCabe's term was nearing a close, his race was not a serious hindrance. However, Republicans were still smarting from losing the governorship to a Democrat, and some charged that McCabe "did not labor for Gov. St. John's re-election as he should have done." There was a also movement among some African Americans to replace McCabe with the well-known John Milton Brown of Eskridge, who had worked tirelessly to provide relief for the Exodusters. Nevertheless, as the *Topeka Capital* pointed out, "It has been the custom of the Republican party to renominate a man for a second term when he was made a good record during the first term." The *Capital* vouched for McCabe as being "capable, courteous, industrious, and a credit to his race."[96] Further, McCabe still had solid support in Graham County. In fact, he had kept his house there, and from time to time his family still went from Topeka back to western Kansas to visit friends. The McCabes had two daughters, Lenore and Edwina. A son, Eddie, had died when he was twelve days old.

McCabe easily won the Republican nomination and the subsequent general election in 1884. St. John was the Prohibition Party's candidate for the U.S. president, as New York Democrat Grover Cleveland narrowly defeated Republican James Blaine of Maine.

Then, in 1886, McCabe made the same mistake that St. John had made in 1882. He attempted to run for a third term. He was immediately and bitterly opposed by many in the Republican Party. However, the *Saline County Journal* was in favor of nominating an African American candidate, saying, "if not McCabe it should be Col. Brown, or some other colored man," as though all black men had an equal ability to perform the exhausting duties required of the state auditor. That year had already been a tumultuous one for Kansas blacks, and racial issues, minimized in the 1884 campaign, emerged again. The furor began after President Cleveland nominated William C. Matthews for recorder of the District of Columbia and the Republican-dominated

U.S. Senate refused to confirm him, one of Leavenworth's most revered African Americans. Kansas's own Senator Ingalls cast a negative vote, allegedly because Matthews was a former Republican who had switched to the Democratic Party. D. L. Strothers, the Democratic editor of the *Abilene Reflector*, a white man, accused Ingalls of racial bias and urged African Americans to switch parties.[97] The editor of the *Fort Scott Tribune* charged, "Whatever right is conferred upon the negro by the amended constitution, the right to be a Democrat was not one of them."[98]

Kansas Democrats exploited the outrage over Matthews to move race to the forefront. The *Reflector* wrote, "'Thank God we are rid of the nigger,' is the exulting cry . . . coming up among Republicans throughout Kansas."[99] However, refuting this allegation, in addition to John Milton Brown, other African American candidates suggested by various factions of the Republican Party were William Twine and C. H. Langston.[100] Even some of the most loyal Republican editors, who had high praise for McCabe, objected to his seeking a third term. They also denounced the white secretary of the treasury, Samuel T. Howe, who was running for a third term. Curiously, both McCabe and Howe ended their required reports to the governor (now John Martin) with farewell messages, as though they did not intend to run again. However, since both men had rendered exceptional service, supporters had urged both men to seek a third term.

The Republican state convention met at Topeka, on July 7, 1886. In a caucus meeting called by J. R. Burton, 123 delegates signed a resolution in opposition to endorsing any third-term candidate. Burton praised both Howe and McCabe for their performance while in office and assured them that the resolution was "devoid of malice."[101] McCabe was not presented for renomination, and the convention nominated Timothy McCarthy for state auditor. Delegates proudly sported his adopted badge, picturing three heads of timothy grass bound with green ribbon in honor of his Irish background. The exuberant Republicans unanimously nominated Governor Martin for a second term, A. P. Riddle as lieutenant governor, and E. B. Allen for secretary of state, but the nomination for secretary of the treasury did not proceed as smoothly. Preceding the adoption of the resolution barring third-term candidates, Samuel Howe stayed in the running through the fifth ballot but was defeated by J. H. Hamilton of Sumner County.

In a surprise move that July, the Prohibition Party convention in Lawrence nominated C. H. Langston for state auditor. At the August 4 Democratic convention in Emporia, Democrats nominated by acclamation another African American candidate, William D. Kelley, of Leavenworth County, for the same position. The *Abilene Reflector* heartily endorsed Kelley, noting his "modest and eloquent manner." In his acceptance speech he declared that "from the time he had cast his vote for Horace Greeley [a presidential candidate in 1872] he had voted with the Democratic Party." Kelley's nomination prompted vitriolic letters from some hard-line Democratic Party members, such as one written by G. H. Bliss, entitled "A White Democrat" and published in the *Iola Register*, that would be considered too viciously racist for publication today.[102] McCarthy easily defeated Kelley that November, with 161,052 votes to Kelley's 92,824 and Langston's 8,366.

McCabe's work as auditor continued throughout the remainder of 1886. His term ended January 10, 1887. Shortly thereafter the *Wichita Globe* reported that McCabe and his family had made a trip to the Pacific coast.[103] After returning to Kansas, the family remained in Topeka and never returned to Nicodemus to live. Nicodemus was rapidly declining. Despite the presence of two newspapers "booming" the town (*Nicodemus Cyclone* and *Nicodemus Enterprise*) and a brief period of wild land speculation in 1886, Nicodemus was bypassed by three railroads. Then the Union Pacific dealt a fatal blow: the company created its own town, Bogue, just six miles south of Nicodemus, and a number of businesses moved from Nicodemus to the new railroad town.

In Topeka, McCabe resumed his lobbying for black equality. In October, he became a member of a convention to form an Afro-American State League and was appointed to its credentials committee. The committee reported that that African Americans were being denied the right to suffrage in a large section of the United States and reduced to a condition scarcely more endurable than they suffered under slavery. The league denied the rumor that it intended to use "force of arms" but said it instead wanted to explore options for securing blacks' natural rights.[104]

At the party's state convention in 1888, McCabe was nominated as a delegate at large to the Republican National Convention. He was defeated, receiving only four votes.[105] In 1889 he went to Washington with a delegation of prominent African Americans to ask new president Benjamin Harrison for patronage for qualified blacks. It was reported that he was among the office seekers and hoped to gain the position of register of the U.S. Treasury. McCabe denied that he had been seeking the job, but the Topeka *American Citizen* reprinted a letter of endorsement from the *Gate City Press*, located in Kansas City, Missouri, as though his candidacy was a fact.[106] He was accompanied on this trip by his wife, Sarah, and their daughter, Lenore. While there, Sarah was quite ill, reportedly with "phthisic pulmonalis."[107] This archaic medical term signified pulmonary tuberculosis.

During the time McCabe served as Kansas auditor, according to the *Kansas City Evening News*, "influences were at work in every state and every territory in the union inducing immigration to Oklahoma."[108] Organizations emerged, and after McCabe's second term as state auditor expired, he became increasingly caught up in a new role as head of the movement to make Oklahoma an all-black state.[109] There were rumors that McCabe hoped to be appointed governor. After being denied the federal treasury appointment, McCabe moved to Oklahoma and established a law office in Guthrie. He specialized in land claims and founded Langston City, named after John M. Langston, Virginia's first black congressman (and brother of C. H. Langston). Blacks were thwarted, however, in their goal of obtaining an all-black state, and land promotion there was not a prosperous venture for McCabe.

Whether McCabe's motive in exploiting the colonization of Oklahoma Territory was purely for profit or an extension of his belief that justice for African Americans could be achieved only through the courts and racial separation, he eagerly pursued this avenue. He had certainly profited by aggressive land promotion techniques in Kansas. His efforts to colonize Oklahoma were supported by William Eagleson, the former editor of the *Colored Citizen*, and McCabe and Eagleson began publishing the *Langston City Herald* in 1891.[110] As a result of McCabe's efforts, the territorial legislature established the Colored Agricultural and Normal University of the Oklahoma Territory at Langston.

In 1895, McCabe was appointed assistant auditor (assistant chief clerk) of the territorial assembly. When Oklahoma became a state in 1907, however, he lost his position. The Democratic-controlled legislature severely curtailed positions blacks had held during the territorial period. McCabe railed against this, as his status and financial stability began to decline.

McCabe made one more stand for African American civil rights. The first state legislature of Oklahoma passed a bill requiring segregation in railroad stations and cars. The Oklahoma Separate Coach Law inferred constitutionality from the 1896 *Plessy v. Ferguson* decision establishing the doctrine of separate but equal facilities. McCabe filed a court case in 1914 against the Atchison, Topeka and Santa Fe Railway Company. He argued that the railroad line was denying him his constitutional right by not providing "separate but equal accommodations." He was among five black men who filed suits against railroad companies, and their joint appeal went all the way to the U.S. Supreme Court. They lost the case because none of the five could prove that they personally had been denied accommodations. The right to protection under the law was that of the right of an individual. In short, they had jumped the gun. The Separate Coach Act had not yet taken effect when they filed the lawsuit, and they could not assume there would be no remedy at hand when they were passengers.

McCabe died a pauper in Chicago on February 23, 1920, at the age of seventy-one. His remains were brought to Topeka for burial in the Topeka Cemetery. The *Topeka Plaindealer* lamented that Sarah McCabe could not bear to have it known that McCabe had died in an almshouse, so only she and a white undertaker were in attendance.[111] Ironically, despite her lifelong history of illness, her husband preceded her in death. Sarah would live until 1938. The McCabes' three children, Eddie, Jr., Edwina, and Lenore, are also now buried in the family plot. In 1985, the Kansas Historical Society received a request from Oklahomans to disinter McCabe's body and move it to the campus at Langston. Some Kansans objected, however, and launched a fund drive to provide a suitable marker for the gravesite.

Despite his inglorious end, McCabe was a trailblazer for other African Americans. His election in 1882 as Kansas state auditor inspired other blacks to seek public office and fight to overcome racial barriers. He thrived in the political climate created by Kansas governor John St. John, and he vigorously promoted his belief that political equality for blacks would be best achieved through legislation.

Kansas was the perfect venue for a man with McCabe's abilities. After his sense of adventure led him to the state, his legal training enabled him to develop a county in need of qualified attorneys. His successful financial partnership with Abram Hall as land locater allowed McCabe to make frequent trips to Topeka, where he became acquainted with influential members of its African American community. His thriving legal practice and temporary appointment as Graham County clerk—followed by formal election—solidified the county's trust in his honesty and attention to detail. His election to state auditor challenged Kansans to look beyond race and consider politicians based on their real qualifications. Ever since then, countless African Americans have validated McCabe's belief that blacks can best achieve justice through political activism.

Epilogue

ON JUNE 1, 1880, the U.S. Senate Select Committee to Investigate the Causes of the Removal of the Negroes from the Southern States to the Northern States—the Voorhees Committee—issued seventeen hundred pages of testimony. There were two separate reports assessing the causes for the migration. The Majority Report was submitted by Democratic senators Daniel W. Voorhees, Zebulon Baird Vance, and George Hunt Pendleton. The Minority Report was submitted by Republican senators William Windom and Henry W. Blair. Both reports are ample evidence of the partisan nature of the investigation.

The Majority Report concluded that the migration had been induced "to a great degree by Northern politicians, and by negro leaders in their employ, and in the employ of railroad lines." These three men believed that the black exodus was basically a political movement resulting from a vigorous campaign to lure black voters to northern states. Their report concluded, "The causes of discontent among those people could not have arisen from any deprivation of their political rights or any hardship in their condition." The committee found no denial of justice "in theory or in practice." True, educational facilities in the South were found to be inferior to those in the North, but they said, "We found in every case that the blacks had precisely the same advantages that the whites enjoyed." As to the relationships between landlords and tenants, the report pointed out that "your committee is not aware of spot on earth where the cunning and the unscrupulous do not take advantage of the ignorant." Testimony about politically based outrages was dismissed as hearsay: "That there have been clashings of the races in the South, socially and politically, is never to be denied nor to be wondered at: but when we come to consider the method in which these people were freed, as the result of a bitter and desolating civil war; and that for purposes of party politics these incompetent, ignorant, landless, homeless people, without any qualifications of citizenship, without any of the ties of property or the obligations of education were suddenly thrown into political power."

The Majority Report ended with words of admiration for the number of black witnesses "who were intelligent, sober, industrious, and respectable men, who testified to their own condition, the amount of property they had accumulated since their emancipation, the comfort in which they lived, the respect with which they were regarded by their white neighbors." The three men wrote that "if one black man could attain to this degree of prosperity and respectable citizenship, others could, having the same capacity for business and practicing the same sobriety and industry."[1] The report concluded:

> Your committee is further of the opinion that Congress having enacted all the legislation for the benefit of the colored people of the South which under the Constitution it can enact, and having seen that all the States of the South have done the same: that by the Constitution of the United States and the constitutions of the various States these people are placed upon a footing of perfect equality before the law, and given the chance to work out their own civilization and improvement: any further attempts at legislation or agitation of the subject will but excite in them hopes of exterior aid that will be disappointing to them, and will prevent them from working out diligently and with care their own salvation; that the sooner they are taught to depend upon themselves, the sooner they will learn to take care of themselves: the sooner they are taught to know that their true interest is promoted by the friendship of their white neighbors instead of their enmity, the sooner they will gain that friendship; and that friendship and harmony once fully attained, there is nothing to bar the way to their speedy civilization and advancement in wealth and prosperity, except such as hinder all people in that great work.

The two senators who submitted the Minority Report, Windom and Blair, maintained that three volumes of testimony proved the absurdity of the charge that the exodus was a political movement induced by northern partisan leaders. Blair and Windom derided the idea that

Kansas would lure black voters into a heavily Republican state where the outcome of elections was already assured. They pointed out the wastefulness of devoting six months, 159 witnesses, and over $30,000 just to disprove a political basis. This report was considerably longer than the Majority Report, as the two men reviewed various categories of atrocities and went back over some of the testimony regarding voting rights, schools, land ownership, protection against random violence, and wrongful incarceration.[2] The report offered entirely different reasons for the black exodus than the Democratic senators had put forth. "Thousands of colored people," they wrote,

> unable any longer to endure in intolerable hardship, injustice, and suffering inflicted upon them by a class of Democrats in the South, had, in utter despair, fled panic stricken from their homes and sought protection among strangers in a strange land. Homeless, penniless, and in rags, these poor people were thronging the wharves of Saint Louis, crowding the steamers on the Mississippi River, and in pitiable destitution throwing themselves upon the charity of Kansas. . . . The newspapers were filled with accounts of their destitution, and the very air was burdened with the cries of distress. Their piteous tales of outrage, suffering and wrong touched the hearts of the more fortunate members of the race in the North and West, and aid societies designed to afford temporary relief and composed largely, almost wholly, of colored people, were organized in Washington, Saint Louis, Topeka, and in various other places. That they were organized to induce migration for political purposes, or to aid or encourage these people to leave their homes for any purpose, or that they ever contributed one dollar to the end, is utterly untrue, and there is absolutely nothing in the testimony to sustain such a charge.

The remainder of the Minority Report was a scathing denouncement of the conclusions reached by Voorhees, Vance, and Pendleton. The report listed and summarized vast crimes committed against blacks and then stated that "the only remedy for the exodus is in the hands of Southern Democrats themselves, and if they do not change their treatment of the negro and recognize his rights as a man and a citizen, the movement will go on, greatly to the injury of the labor interests of the South, if not the whole county."

Since the purpose of the committee was to explore the reasons why blacks were leaving the South, there was no discussion of the positive contributions that would be made by black immigrants. There was also no discussion of the positive factors that attracted to Kansas black northerners such as Abram Hall and E. P. McCabe and white immigrants from the upper Midwest and New England. The appeal of free land was universal and knew no racial barriers. Land and the emphasis on acquiring property came up time and again throughout the testimony. Land denoted security and self-worth.

No legislation would be proposed as a result of this painful investigation, nor would the reports result in any changes in the personal lives of blacks. The committee was in session during the time Hall, McCabe, and John Niles were in Nicodemus. Despite the deceitful if not altogether fraudulent publicity campaigns that drew African Americans to Nicodemus, the community prospered for a time. The colony would not have been the same without the talents and wisdom of Hall and McCabe, but neither would it have thrived without the native intelligence and wit of its ex-slaves, such as the parents of Lulu Craig, who had risked all to come to a strange land. Hall and McCabe had arrived with Niles in early 1878, at which time the colonists had survived the savage first winter. The immigrants had figured out much of what they needed to do to make a life on the prairie. The two northerners then provided knowledge of the law and the ability to negotiate with the surrounding whites.

The *Voorhees Committee Report* noted the importance of Nicodemus.[3] If the colony succeeded, it would prove that blacks had the wherewithal to thrive on their own in a region that was considered to be uninhabitable. There has been a great deal of speculation by historians as to whether this town attracted unusually determined and resourceful blacks to begin with, or whether the frontier brought forth those qualities in blacks as well as whites.

In 1881 there was a meeting of the early settlers of Nicodemus. A committee on resolutions decided to declare September 17 as a

Lulu Sadler Craig, age 102. Courtesy of Alice Craig McDonald private collection.

holiday to be observed in memory of their arrival in Nicodemus, and "nearly all hands proclaimed their faith in Kansas."[4] Thomas Johnson claimed that "by coming to the state he had decidedly bettered his condition in life." Grant Harris, who "came here penniless," had accumulated sixty head of stock and had forty acres under cultivation.[5]

Anderson Boles said "he don't want a better country . . . and never will return to old Kentucky." Samuel Garland "held that negro immigration was no longer a problem, that the Nicodemus colony had solved it." Niles and McCabe summed up with a few words of encouragement.[6] In a nutshell, three distinct philosophies emerged during the shaping of Nicodemus, and they were embodied in three men who profoundly influenced the future of the colony. Hall's letters from Nicodemus alerted Kansans elsewhere to the abilities of the blacks populating this community and galvanized Graham County when he forced its organization. Hall and McCabe, referred to as "the grand Moguls of Western Kansas" by the editor of the *Colored Citizen*, went from being pelted with derogatory remarks upon their arrival to being addressed by whites as "sir" two years later, with race infrequently mentioned regarding local politics.[7] Whites courted the black vote by putting together multiracial political parties that were forced to consider issues important to African Americans.

McCabe was the first black state official elected in Kansas and opened the political field to African Americans statewide. And despite ethical concerns about Niles's behavior, he was the first to persuade Congress to take formal action on a petition for slave reparations. Although many of the colonists would move from Nicodemus to Bogue after the railroad was built to the south, a good many of the original settlers who had acquired homesteads stayed and prospered. Though sparsely populated, Nicodemus lives on today and is under the protection of the National Park Service. Each year, the last weekend of July, proud descendants of the original settlers "come home to Nicodemus" and celebrate the founding of the town. Nicodemus was declared a national historic site in 1976, and the exhibition in the town hall receives visitors from across the United States.

The three men who were most instrumental in shaping the future of Nicodemus—Hall, Niles, and McCabe—may have left the community, but their actions and ideas had lasting impact. The men were archetypes for three differing approaches to relations with whites in the post-Reconstruction era. Even today, in the twenty-first century, we can see that Niles's pleas for reparations, McCabe's search for social justice through legislation and the courts, and Hall's well-reasoned incremental pursuit of equal rights on an individual level represent persistent patterns. The success of African Americans in every political and financial field bolsters Hall's idea that equality could only be gained through individual achievement. The stark necessity of McCabe's emphasis on legislative measures was demonstrated by the progress made by African Americans during and after the 1960s civil rights movement. And, sadly, the continuation of racially motivated violence against African Americans seems to validate Niles's belief that blacks cannot obtain justice in the United States. These differing philosophies not only live today, they continue to have an affect—on blacks and on all Americans.

Notes

Introduction

1. Nell Irvin Painter, *Exodusters: Black Migration to Kansas after Reconstruction* (New York: W. W. Norton, 1976), xvi.

2. Damani Davis, "Exodus to Kansas: The 1880 Senate Investigation of the Beginnings of the African American Migration from the South," *Prologue* 40, no. 2 (Summer 2008), www.archives.gov/publications/prologue/2008/summer/exodus.html; U.S. Congress, Senate, *Report and Testimony of the Select Committee of the United States Senate to Investigate the Causes of the Removal of the Negroes from the Southern States to the Northern States,* 46th Cong., 2nd sess. (Washington, D.C.: Government Printing Office, 1880); hereafter cited as *Voorhees Committee Report.*

3. Painter, *Exodusters*; Nell Irwin Painter, *Sojourner Truth: A Life, a Symbol* (New York: W. W. Norton, 1996); Robert G. Athearn, *In Search of Canaan: Black Migration to Kansas, 1879–80* (Lawrence: Regents Press of Kansas, 1978).

4. *Promised Land on the Solomon: Black Settlement at Nicodemus, Kansas,* Washington, D.C.: U.S. Department of the Interior, 1984; Clayton Fraser, "Nicodemus: The Architectural Development and Decline of an American Town," in ibid., 35–61; La Barbara W. Fly, "Into the Twentieth Century," in ibid., 65–83.

5. Steven Hahn, *A Nation under Our Feet: Black Political Struggles in the Rural South from Slavery to the Great Migration* (Cambridge, Mass.: Harvard University Press, 2003).

6. Nell Waldron, "Colonization in Kansas" (PhD diss., Northwestern University, 1932).

7. William J. Belleau, "The Nicodemus Colony of Graham County, Kansas" (master's thesis, Fort Hays State College, 1943).

8. Orval L. McDaniel, "A History of Nicodemus, Graham County, Kansas" (master's thesis, Fort Hays State College, 1950).

9. Van Burton Shaw, "Nicodemus, Kansas: A Study in Isolation" (PhD diss., University of Missouri, 1951), 125, 138. According to another Nicodemus resident, the fact that Shaw's daughter "showed no reluctance about being the only white child in a group of Negro playmates was greeted with respect and admiration by the Negro people." Ibid., 138.

10. Glen Schwendemann, "Negro Exodus to Kansas: First Phase, March–July, 1879" (master's thesis, University of Oklahoma, 1957); Glen Schwendemann,

"Nicodemus, Negro Haven on the Solomon," *Kansas Historical Quarterly* 34 (Spring 1968): 10–31.

11. Claire O'Brien, "'With One Mighty Pull': Interracial Town Boosting in Nicodemus, Kansas," *Great Plains Quarterly* 16 (Spring 1996): 117–29.

12. Antoinette Broussard Farmer, "Craig, Lulu Sadler," Antoinettebroussard.com, http://antoinettebroussard.com/pdfs/LuluSadlerCraig.pdf.

13. There is no way to assess the undeniable role played by those who worked behind the scenes.

14. Charlotte Hinger, "Pioneer Editors: The Alchemists of the Prairie," *Kansas Territorial* 3 (March 1983): n.p.

15. Don W. Wilson, "Barbed Words on the Frontier: Early Kansas Newspapers," *Kansas History* 3 (Autumn 1978): 147–54.

16. Nyle H. Miller, Edgar Langsdorf, and Robert W. Richmond, eds., *Kansas in Newspapers* (Topeka: Kansas State Historical Society, 1963), iii.

17. David Dary, *Red Blood and Black Ink: Journalism in the Old West* (New York: Alfred A. Knopf, 1998), 37.

Chapter 1. Passing into a New Civilization

Epigraph: Testimony of Isaiah Wears, *Voorhees Committee Report*, part 3, 151–52.

1. Belleau, "The Nicodemus Colony of Graham County," 55–56; Lulu Sadler Craig, "Early Settlement," Craig Manuscript Collection, Graham County Historical Society Archives, Hill City, Kansas (hereafter: Craig manuscript); Nicodemus Historical Society, Nicodemus, Kansas; Graham County Historical Society Archives, Hill City, Kansas. Craig's manuscript of topically arranged material about Nicodemus contains a detailed narrative from Hall. In her foreword, Craig thanked A. T. Hall, W. L. Sayers, Annie Hickman Comer, and Betty Kirtley Lewis for "suggestions and data." As was the custom then, Hall was identified as "Sr." rather than "Jr." after his father's death.

2. *Colored Citizen*, July 26, 1878; Craig Miner, *West of Wichita: Settling the High Plains of Kansas, 1865–1890* (Lawrence: University Press of Kansas, 1986), 84–85; McDaniel, "History of Nicodemus," 35.

3. For an overview of African American post-Reconstruction political activity in Kansas, see Nell Irvin Painter, *Exodusters: Black Migration to Kansas after Reconstruction* (New York: W. W. Norton, 1976); Miner, *West of Wichita*; Norman Crockett, *The Black Towns* (Lawrence: Regents Press of Kansas, 1979); Robert G. Athearn, *In Search of Canaan: Black Migration to Kansas, 1879–80* (Lawrence: Regents Press of Kansas, 1978); Quintard Taylor, *In Search of the Racial Frontier: African Americans in the American West* (New York: W. W. Norton, 1998); Steven Hahn, *A Nation under Our Feet: Black Political Struggles in the Rural South from Slavery to the Great Migration* (Cambridge, Mass.: Harvard

University Press, 2003); Ira Berlin, *Slaves without Masters: The Free Negro in the Antebellum South* (New York: Free Press, 1974); Claire O'Brien, "'With One Mighty Pull': Interracial Town Boosting in Nicodemus, Kansas," *Great Plains Quarterly* 16 (Spring 1996): 117–29.

4. *Voorhees Committee Report*, part 3, 151–52.

5. Craig manuscript, "Settlement," 8–10. Some of Craig's pages are numbered. Most are not. Numbers are noted whenever they appear.

6. Daniel Chu and Bill Shaw, *Going Home to Nicodemus: The Story of an African American Frontier Town and the Pioneers Who Settled it* (Morristown, N.J.: Silver Burdett Press, 1994): 7.

7. Kenneth Marvin Hamilton, "The Origins and Early Promotion of Nicodemus: A Pre-Exodus All-Black Town," *Kansas History* 4 (Winter 1982): 220–42. Breaking sod was an arduous task and could only be accomplished with any degree of efficiency with a special sod-breaking plow.

8. Craig manuscript, "Settlement," n.p., quoting from Hall's narrative.

9. *Leavenworth Daily Times*, March 28, 1878.

10. Craig manuscript, "Settlement," n.p., quoting from Hall's narrative. For more on William D. Matthews and William B. Townsend, both longtime residents of Leavenworth and influential leaders of the African American community, see Roger D. Cunningham, "Douglas's Battery at Fort Leavenworth: The Issue of Black Officers during the Civil War," *Kansas History* 23 (Winter 2000–2001): 204–16; Brent M. S. Campney, "W. B. Townsend and the Struggle against Racist Violence in Leavenworth," *Kansas History* 4 (Winter 2008–2009); "Capt. Matthews, Pioneer Colored Kansan, Is Dead," *Leavenworth Times*, March 3, 1906; "Brief Biographical Sketches, of State Officers, Members of Congress, and Officers and Members of the Legislature of Kansas, for the Year 1879," *Topeka Commercial*, March 5, 1879; "W. B. Townsend Is Prosperous," *Topeka Plaindealer*, March 14, 1902.

11. Cunningham, "Douglas's Battery," 202–203; *Republican Daily Journal*, October 15, 1878.

12. Campney, "W. B. Townsend," 261–63.

13. Craig manuscript, "Settlement," 9–10; *Leavenworth Times*, April 11, 1878.

14. Craig manuscript, "Settlement," 12.

15. Craig manuscript, "Settlement," 13. Hall's account of the church meeting and the controversy over Niles's credentials is verified in the *Leavenworth Times*. The versions of this meeting contained in the Craig manuscript have been typed on various typewriters produced by typists of varying ability. None are dated. Therefore, I cleaned up obvious typos.

16. Testimony of Dr. F. M. Stringfield, *Voorhees Committee Report*, part 3, 373–76, introducing one of Reynolds's columns "The Hegira of the Negro"; Craig manuscript, "Nicodemus," 8.

17. "Secretary of State—Second Biennial Report," in *Public Documents: Kansas, 1879–1880* (Topeka: Geo. W. Martin, Kansas Publishing House, 1881), 125. McCabe was the second person commissioned as notary in Rooks County. He was preceded two days earlier by N. C. Terrell, a Millbrook man, who would later play a crucial part in Graham County politics.

18. Painter, *Exodusters*, 6.

19. "American Freedmen's Inquiry Commission, Preliminary Report," June 30, 1863, Shotgun's Home of the American Civil War, www.civilwarhome.com/prelimcommissionreport.htm.

20. Testimony of Benjamin Singleton, *Voorhees Committee Report*, part 3, 382.

21. Ibid., 383; Athearn, *In Search of Canaan*, 6.

22. Hahn, *Nation under Our Feet*, 132–48.

23. Ibid., 136.

24. Waldron, "Colonization in Kansas," 125.

25. *Voorhees Committee Report*, "Minority Report," xii; George F. Marlowe's written report introduced by the testimony of John Henri Burch, part 3, page 136–37.

26. Ibid.

27. Shaw, "Nicodemus, Kansas," 24.

28. Waldron, "Colonization in Kansas from 1861 to 1890," 124.

29. Athearn, *In Search of Canaan*, unpaged illustration, approximately page 101.

30. Quoted in Ibid., 134. In this speech, Windom denied that the movement was politically inspired.

31. Ibid., 79.

32. Craig Miner, *Kansas: The History of the Sunflower State, 1854–2000* (Lawrence: University Press of Kansas, 2002), 1.

33. Theodore Davis, "A Stage Ride to Colorado," *Harpers New Monthly Magazine* 35, no. 206 (July 1867): 137–51.

34. *Wyandotte Constitution*, article V, section 1.

35. Testimony of Isaiah Wears, *Voorhees Committee Report*, part 3, 151–52.

Chapter 2. Ho for Kansas!

Epigraph: Testimony of Henry Adams, *Voorhees Committee Report*, xi.

1. *Voorhees Committee Report*, "Minority Report," x.

2. Darlene Clark Hine, William C. Hine, and Stanley Harrold, *The African-American Odyssey* (Upper Saddle River, NJ: Prentice Hall, 2002), 301. Adams's testimony encapsulated the devastating consequences of pulling federal

troops out of the South following the Compromise of 1877. The North concentrated on industrialization and abandoned all attempts to reconstruct the South.

 3. Brent M. S. Campney, "'This is Not Dixie': The Imagined South, the Kansas Free State Narrative, and the Rhetoric of Racist Violence," *Southern Spaces*, September 6, 2007, www.southernspaces.org/.

 4. James N. Leiker, "Race Relations in the Sunflower State," *Kansas History* 25 (Autumn 2002): 216.

 5. *Voorhees Committee Report*, "Majority Report," iv.

 6. *Voorhees Committee Report*, "Minority Report," xxv.

 7. Testimony of Jacob Stevens, *Voorhees Committee Report*, part 3, 57.

 8. Testimony of Emile Auspitz, *Voorhees Committee Report*, part 3, 52.

 9. Testimony of Henry Adams, *Voorhees Committee Report*, part 2, 104.

 10. Testimony of William Twine, *Voorhees Committee Report*, part 3, 319.

 11. Angela Bates, "People of Nicodemus" (lecture, Fort Hays State University, February 2004).

 12. W. E. B. Du Bois, *Black Reconstruction in America* (New York: Atheneum, 1992), 43.

 13. Painter, *Exodusters*, 8; Craig manuscript, "Leaving the Old Plantation," 17.

 14. Craig manuscript, "Leaving the Plantation," 19. Craig refers to the narrator as "Beverly"—probably Beverly Carr or Beverly Herring. The man who was referred to as "Ben" on the Town Company Certificate may have been Beverly Carr. Chambers manuscript, "Niles," n.p.

 15. Craig manuscript, "Leaving the Plantation," 19.

 16. Ibid.

 17. Craig manuscript, "The Spring of 1878," n.p.

 18. *Kentucky Gazette*, January, 10, 1877.

 19. Ibid.

 20. Athearn, *In Search of Canaan*, back cover.

 21. *Commonwealth* (Topeka), April 29, 1879.

 22. Testimony of Charlton H. Tandy, affidavit from John Cummings, *Voorhees Committee Report*, part 3, 59.

 23. Testimony of Charlton H. Tandy, affidavit from Edward Parlor, *Voorhees Committee Report*, part 3, 43.

 24. Hamilton, "The Settlement of Nicodemus," 7

 25. Ibid.; Angela Bates, interview, August 16, 2015; Waldron, "Colonization in Kansas," 125. Citations of exact numbers and the origin of colonists varies among sources. This study relies on the Waldron dissertation for colonization statistics due to her methodology. However, some scholars believe there were fifty persons—and only one woman—in the original group. Waldron

documents five separate colonies migrating, three from Kentucky and two from Mississippi.

26. *Ellis County Star*, March 21, 1878.

27. "Harvesting the River," Illinois State Museum, www.museum.state.il.us/RiverWeb/harvesting/transportation/boats/steamboats.html. See also William L. Crothers, *American-Built Packets and Freighters of the 1850s: An Illustrated Study of Their Characteristics and Construction* (Jefferson, N.C.: McFarland, 2013).

28. Kittie Dale, "Ballad of Nicodemus': Kansas Town's Theme," *Wichita Eagle Magazine*, August 21, 1960, 14. Dale's information is based on an interview with Lena Penney, age ninety-two, who recalled making the trip from Georgetown, Scott County, Kentucky, with her grandparents.

29. Everett Dick, *Sod House Frontier: A Social History of the Northern Plains from the Creation of Kansas and Nebraska to the Admission of the Dakotas* (Lincoln, Neb.: Johnsen, 1954), 54.

30. Hamilton, "The Settlement of Nicodemus," 1.

31. Quoted in Athearn, *In Search of Canaan*, 76.

32. Hamilton, "The Settlement of Nicodemus," 8.

33. McDaniel, "A History of Nicodemus," 33. McDaniel's information was derived from an article in *Hill City Times*, August 22, 1940.

34. McDaniel, "A History of Nicodemus," 46.

35. *Hays City Sentinel*, September 7, 1877. The editor mixes his opinions with those of the *Stockton News*.

36. *Stockton News*, July 19, 1877.

37. Throughout his stay in Nicodemus, Hall wrote numerous letters to the *Stockton News, Stockton Record, Atchison Daily Champion, Millbrook Times, Colored Citizen, Topeka Commonwealth*, and *Roscoe Tribune*.

38. W. L. Chambers, *Niles of Nicodemus: Exploiter of Kansas Exoduster, Negro Indemnity and Equality of Black with Whites His Obsession, Beats Bankers, Bench and Barristers; Counter League to Post-War K.K.K. Riots and Finally Prison* (Los Angeles: Washington High School, 1930), n.p.; Craig manuscript, "Settlement," 9; George A. Root, "Biographical Sketch of Daniel Hickman," 6, in George A. Root Collection, Kansas Historical Society.

39. John W. Niles, letter, February 25, 1880, Correspondence Received, Governor John Pierce St. John, box 1, folder 14, Kansas Historical Society, Topeka; John Pierce St. John, letter, March 2, 1880, Letter Press Books, box 7, no. 24, Kansas Historical Society.

40. Quoted in Chambers, "Niles of Nicodemus," n.p.

41. Ibid.

Chapter 3. Kansas—Sure but Slow Poison

Epigraph: Testimony of Philip Brookings, *Voorhees Committee Report*, part 3, 107–11.

1. *Hays City Sentinel*, March 30, 1878.
2. Dary, *Red Blood and Black Ink*, 37.
3. *Hays City Sentinel*, March 30, 1878.
4. Testimony of A. J. Allen, *Voorhees Committee Report*, part 3, 128–29; *Kentucky Gazette*, June 11, 1879.
5. Miner, *West of Wichita*, 84.
6. Chu and Shaw, *Home to Nicodemus*, 34.
7. Craig manuscript, "The First Winter," n.p.
8. Fraser, "Nicodemus," 37.
9. Testimony of A. S. Johnson, *Voorhees Committee Report*, part 3, 121.
10. Quoted in Shaw, "Nicodemus, Kansas," 99.
11. *Hays City Sentinel*, September 21, 1877. Many of the persons writing letters and columns in the early papers used pen names or nicknames. Several Sheridan County African Americans favored either Greek pen names or those of historical figures who played an important role in forming their black heritage. Writers are identified by their real names in the notes whenever possible. Speculation is labeled as such.
12. Craig manuscript, "The First Christmas 1877," n.p.
13. *Hays City Sentinel*, October 12, 1877.
14. *Stockton Record*, June 5, 1880.
15. *Stockton News*, July 7, 1880.
16. *Roscoe Tribune*, June 30, 1880.
17. *Norton County Advance*, December 29, 1880.
18. Ibid., February 6, 1879; David M. Bartholomew, *Pioneer Naturalist on the Plains: The Diary of Elam Bartholomew 1871 to 1934* (Manhattan, Kans.: Sunflower University Press); "Elam Bartholomew," *Kansapedia*, Kansas Historical Society, www.kshs.org/kansapedia/elam-bartholomew/18648. Elam Bartholomew's fungi and plant collections are now housed in such far-flung institutions as the Egyptian Ministry of Agriculture in Cairo, the Cawthron Institute in New Zealand, Harvard University, and the New York Botanical Garden. More than forty thousand of his original specimens, mycological and otherwise, were acquired by Harvard University after his death.
19. *Atchison Daily Champion*, October 24, 1878.
20. Testimony of J. W. Wheeler, *Voorhees Committee Report*, part 3, 7.
21. Craig manuscript, "Light," n.p.
22. Fraser, "Nicodemus," 37.
23. Barbara Oringderff, *True Sod* (North Newton, Kans.: Mennonite Press, 1976), 25.

24. Craig manuscript, "The First Winter 1877–78," n.p.
25. Waldron, "Colonization in Kansas,"126.
26. Craig manuscript, "The First Winter," n.p.
27. Root, "Biographical Sketch of Daniel Hickman," 4–6.
28. Myrtle D. Fesler, *Pioneers of Western Kansas* (New York: Carlton Press, 1962), 191.
29. The second group, which came from Kentucky, is often referred to as the first group because it was quite large—about 350 persons. The first group came from Topeka. It was small, with from thirty to fifty men and only one female.
30. Fesler, *Pioneers of Western Kansas*, 193.
31. As reported in *Hays Daily Sentinel*, May 18, 1878.
32. *Hays Daily Sentinel*, April 6, 1878. One such "sharper" to whom they referred was W. R. Hill.
33. Hamilton, "The Origins and Early Promotion of Nicodemus," 8.
34. John Joseph Mathews, *The Osages: Children of the Middle Waters* (Norman: University of Oklahoma Press, 1961), 624.
35. "Tribal History," Prairie Band Potawotami Nation, n.d., www.pbpindiantribe.com/tribal-history.aspx.
36. McDaniel, "A History of Nicodemus," 43.
37. Testimony of John D. Knox, *Voorhees Committee Report*, part 3, 411.
38. *Topeka Capital*, October 22, 1879.
39. Testimony of J. W. Wheeler, *Voorhees Committee Report*, part 3, 12.
40. *Stockton Record*, March 20, 1880, quoting the *Atchison Champion*.
41. Kenneth M. Stampp, *The Peculiar Institution: Slavery in the Anti-Bellum South* (New York: Vintage Books, 1989), 169–70.
42. Craig, "The First Christmas 1877," n.p.
43. Root, "Biographical Sketch of Daniel Hickman," 6. Root incorrectly identified victim John Landis as "John Landers."
44. *Norton County Advance*, August 1, 1978; ibid., September 5, 1878.
45. *Hays City Sentinel*, September 21, 1878.
46. *Millbrook Times*, August 1, 1879.
47. Du Bois, *Black Reconstruction in America*, 143.
48. James R. Shortridge, *Peopling the Plains: Who Settled Where in Frontier Kansas* (Lawrence: University Press of Kansas, 1995).
49. Root, "A Biographical Sketch of Daniel Hickman," 5.
50. Dale, "Ballad of Nicodemus," 14.
51. Miner, *Kansas*, 12.
52. John Ise, *Sod and Stubble: The Story of a Kansas Homestead* (Lincoln: University of Nebraska Press, 1936).
53. Ruth Kelley Hayden, *The Time That Was: The Courageous Acts and Accounts of Rawlins County, Kansas 1875–1915* (Colby, Kans: Colby Community College, 1973), 49–50.

54. Frederick Jackson Turner, "The Significance of the Frontier in American History," in *Does the Frontier Experience Make America Exceptional?*, ed. Richard W. Etulain (Boston: Bedford/St. Martin's, 1999), 40.

55. Howard Ruede, *Sod-House Days: Letters from a Kansas Homesteader, 1877–78* (Lawrence: University Press of Kansas), xix.

56. Craig manuscript, "Settlement," n.p.

Chapter 4. Unconsidered Trifles

Epigraph: Testimony of T. C. Sears, *Voorhees Committee Report*, part 3, 161–62.

1. Richard R. Wright, *Centennial Encyclopaedia of the African Methodist Episcopal Church* (Philadelphia: Book Concern of the African Methodist Episcopal Church, 1916), 103. An electronic edition is available through the Documenting the American South project of the University of North Carolina at Chapel Hill: http://docsouth.unc.edu/church/wright. References to the senior Hall's first name vary between "Abraham," "Abram," and "A. T. Hall, Sr." The junior Hall's brother Charles, who was ten years old when Abram came to Nicodemus, became a statistician and wrote an 845-page book, *Negroes in the United States*, for the Bureau of the Census.

2. Quoted in Craig manuscript, "Settlement," n.p.

3. Burton D. Meyers, *The History of Medical Education in Indiana* (Bloomington: Indiana University Press, 1956), 52–53. Information about the College of Physicians and Surgeons and the Medical College of Indiana was supplied by Nancy L. Eckerman, special collections librarian at the Ruth Lilly Medical Library, Indiana University, Indianapolis.

4. Ruth A. Siegrist, "Nicodemus," paper presented at regional Daughters of the American Revolution meeting, Russell, Kansas, May 15, 1982, located at Graham County Historical Society.

5. Jere W. Roberson, "Edward P. McCabe and the Langston Experiment," *Chronicles of Oklahoma* 51 (Fall 1973): 343–55; Craig manuscript, "Settlement," n.p.; Martin Dann, "From Sodom to the Promised Land: E. P. McCabe and the Movement for Oklahoma Colonization," *Kansas Historical Quarterly* 40 (Autumn 1974): 370.

6. Craig manuscript, "On the Prairie," n.p.

7. Ibid., "First Stores," n.p.; Siegrist, "Nicodemus," n.p.

8. Siegrist, "Nicodemus," n.p.

9. Craig manuscript, "McCabe," n.p.; Theodosia E. Fenner, "Black Leadership in 1889," in *Oklahoma's Historical Edition*, vol. 3, ed. Dessie M. Ritter (Oklahoma City, C. E. Ritter, 1982), n.p.; C. F. W. Dassler, *Compiled Laws of Kansas* (St. Louis: W. J. Gilbert, 1879), 113; Robert W. Richmond, *Requisite Learning and Good Moral Character: A History of the Kansas Bench and Bar* (Topeka: Kansas Bar Association, 1982), 37–70; Michael H. Hoeflich, "Why

the History of Kansas Law Has Not Been Written," *Kansas History* 26 (Winter 2003–2004): 264–71; Robert C. Haywood, *Cowtown Lawyers: Dodge City and Its Attorneys, 1876–1888* (Norman: University of Oklahoma Press, 1988), 49–50; D. M. Valentine, "Roll of Attorneys," in *Reports of Cases Argued and Determined in the Supreme Court of the State of Kansas*, vol. 29 (Topeka: Kansas Publishing House, 1883), xiv–xv. Valentine recorded seven hundred persons admitted to practice before the Kansas Supreme Court by 1883. Out of the plethora of attorneys in Graham and Rooks Counties—identified as such through business cards and letterheads—only the names of Thomas Beaumont and T. T. Tillotson appear on Valentine's roll. My communication from the Kansas Law Library verified that there are no historical lists of attorneys practicing in the various counties in Kansas. The Kansas Bar Association was not established until 1883. However, Hall and McCabe are named as attorneys in numerous documents, and the Kansas Historical Society has a record of Hall and McCabe as attorneys in Abram T. Hall, Jr., and E. P. McCabe, "Brief of the attorneys for the Roscoe Petition," filed March 30, 1880, 27-04-01-7, folder 23, Gov. John P. St. John, Correspondence Received, Kansas Historical Society, Topeka, Kansas (hereafter cited as "folder 23, St. John Correspondence").

10. Craig manuscript, "Settlement," n.p.; Craig manuscript, "E. P. McCabe," n.p.

11. Craig manuscript, "Settlement," n.p.

12. Craig manuscript, "First Things," n.p.

13. *Kirwin Chief*, July 23, 1879; Craig manuscript, "Settlement," n.p.

14. *Hays City Sentinel*, April 6, 1878; Craig manuscript, "Others Came Also," n.p.

15. *Stockton News*, January 26, 1881; *Graham County Republican*, January 7, 1882; Craig manuscript, "Others Came Also," n.p.

16. Craig manuscript, "The Colony," n.p.

17. *Colored Citizen*, August 23, 1878.

18. *Norton County Advance*, September 12, 1878.

19. *Hays City Sentinel*, April 6, 1878.

20. Shaw, "Nicodemus, Kansas," 99–100.

21. *Roscoe Tribune*, July 30, 1880.

22. *Colored Citizen*, July 5, 1878; *Stockton News*, February 6, 1879.

23. *Colored Citizen*, May 10, 1878. Hall's first letter, written about two weeks after his arrival in Nicodemus, contains a wealth of information, with dates and details. Due to his training as a journalist, his reports are likely the most accurate among conflicting accounts regarding the founding of the colony.

24. *Stockton News*, June 13, 1878. This first regional letter written by Hall, composed June 10, 1878, published June 13, is printed in its entirety because it

illustrates A. T. Hall's sensitivity to white's perceptions and contains important political implications. "Inst." is an archaism meaning "in the present or current month" (literally an abbreviation for "instant").

25. Craig, "Settlement," n.p.
26. *Colored Citizen*, July 5, 1878.
27. *Colored Citizen*, December 5, 1878.
28. Taylor Gordon, *Born to Be* (Lincoln: University of Nebraska Press, 1995), 234.
29. Walter Prescott Webb, *The Great Frontier* (Boston: Houghton Mifflin, 1952), 49, 50.

Chapter 5. Black Republicans

Epigraph: Testimony of F. M. Stringfield, *Voorhees Committee Report*, part 3, 373–76. Dr. Stringfield inserted into his testimony a newspaper article, "The Hegira of the Negro," by M. W. Reynolds (Kicking Bird) of Parsons, Kansas.

1. *Colored Citizen*, August 8, 1878, quoting from a letter written by W. B. Townsend.
2. Painter, *Exodusters*, 161.
3. William H. Chafe, "The Negro and Populism: A Kansas Case Study," *Journal of Southern History* 3 (August 1968): 411.
4. Testimony of John Milton Brown, *Voorhees Committee Report*, part 2, 358.
5. Thomas C. Cox, *Blacks in Topeka, Kansas, 1865–1915* (Baton Rouge: Louisiana State University Press, 1982) 33–36.
6. Ibid. In Hall's letter to the *Colored Citizen* of September 20, 1878, following the state Republican Convention, he scolded black delegates who put race above the "good of the commonwealth." Until his death at the age of ninety-nine he wrote for a number of white as well as black publications.
7. Campney, "W. B. Townsend," 260–73.
8. *Colored Citizen*, May 17, 1878.
9. Richard B. Sheridan, "Charles Henry Langston and the African American Struggle in Kansas," *Kansas History* 4 (Winter 1999): 281.
10. *Colored Citizen*, August 16, 1878. This observation comes from A. H. Walton who wrote a column for the *Citizen* following his visit to Nicodemus during its Fourth of July celebration.
11. Cox, *Blacks in Topeka*, 30.
12. "Eagleson, William Lewis (1835–1899)," *Online Encyclopedia*, http://encyclopedia.jrank.org/articles/pages/4225/Eagleson-William-Lewis-1835-1899.
13. *Colored Citizen*, June 7, 1878.

14. *Colored Citizen*, April 26, 1878.
15. *Colored Citizen*, April, 19, 1878.
16. *Colored Citizen*, July 5, 1878.
17. *Colored Citizen*, July 23, 1878.
18. *Colored Citizen*, August 2, 1878.
19. Waller quote from Randall B. Woods, "After the Exodus: John Lewis Waller and the Black Elite, 1878–1900," *Kansas History* 2 (Summer 1977): 173; *Colored Citizen*, May 10, 1878.
20. *Colored Citizen*, July 26, 1878. The paper quoted the *New Orleans Observer*, which wished Henderson well in the upcoming election.
21. *Colored Citizen*, August 2, 1878.
22. Ibid.
23. Campney, "W. B. Townsend," 261; *Colored Citizen*, April 26, 1878.
24. *Colored Citizen*, August 23, 1878.
25. *Colored Citizen*, September 6, 1878.
26. *Wichita City Eagle*, August 29, 1878.
27. *Emporia News*, August 30, 1878.
28. *Wichita City Eagle*, August 29, 1878.
29. *Colored Citizen*, August 30, 1878.
30. Ibid.
31. *Colored Citizen*, September 20, 1878, quoting the *Valley Falls (Kans.) New Era*.
32. *Colored Citizen*, September 20, 1878.
33. Ibid.
34. *Colored Citizen*, October 11, 1878.
35. *Colored Citizen*, October 26. 1878
36. Ibid. In this lengthy column rebuking James, he initially mistakenly refers to James as Jones.
37. *Colored Citizen*, October 4, 1878.
38. Testimony of A. J. Allen, *Voorhees Committee Report*, part 3, 132, 133.
39. *Colored Citizen*, November 2, 1878.
40. *Colored Citizen*, October 26, 1878.
41. *Colored Citizen*, October 10, 1878.
42. "Bruce, Blanche Kelso," History, Art and Archives, U.S. House of Representatives, http://history.house.gov/People/Detail?id=10029.
43. *Colored Citizen*, December 12, 1878.
44. *Atchison Champion*, November 27, 1878.
45. Testimony of Benjamin Singleton, *Voorhees Committee Report*, part 3, 384.
46. Testimony of Benjamin Singleton, *Voorhees Committee Report*, part 3, 379.

47. Painter, *Exodusters,* 15

48. Ibid., 16; Randall B. Woods, "Integration, Exclusion or Segregation? The Color Line in Kansas, 1878–1900," in *African Americans on the Western Frontier,* edited by Monroe Lee Billington and Roger D. Hardaway (Boulder: University Press of Colorado, 1998), 128–46.

49. *Colored Citizen,* December 7, 1878. Embry's account of his trip included transportation details. He started on the Missouri Pacific Railroad and switched to Ohio & Mississippi at St Louis after tending to business and visiting friends. In Cincinnati, he went by "bus" to the Marietta Depot where he spent some time "looking around," before he boarded the train bound for Washington. When he arrived he hired a hack to take him to the house of "brother and sister Simms."

50. *Colored Citizen,* December 12, 1878.

51. *House Journal, State of Kansas,* 1879, 37, 52; *Colored Citizen,* January 25, 1878; *Leavenworth Weekly Public Press,* publication date for "Henderson's prayers" comment not given in the *Colored Citizen.*

52. *Colored Citizen,* February 15, 1879.

53. Ibid.

Chapter 6. The Needs of the Race

Epigraph: Testimony of H. Ruby, *Voorhees Committee Report,* part 3, 414. Ruby, who emigrated from Texas to Kansas, specifically cited educational discrimination as one of the reasons for leaving.

1. Quoted in Du Bois, *Black Reconstruction in America,* 641–42. The fact that Du Bois quoted Washington, with whom he had many differences, illustrates African American unity regarding the importance of education.

2. Testimony of R. C. Badger, *Voorhees Committee Report,* part 1, 397.

3. Quoted from labor convention reports inserted into testimony of John Henri Burch, *Voorhees Committee Report,* part 3, 142.

4. Testimony of Gilbert Myers, *Voorhees Committee Report,* part 2, 582.

5. Testimony of John G. Lewis, *Voorhees Committee Report,* part 2, 437.

6. *Colored Citizen,* February 1, 1879. In this talk, delivered on January 21, there are a number of literary allusions and French phrases, demonstrating the breadth of Hall's education.

7. Ibid.

8. Testimony of John G. Lewis, *Voorhees Committee Report,* part 2, 426.

9. *Colored Citizen,* February 1, 1879.

10. Testimony of J. H. Shepherd, *Voorhees Committee Report,* Part 3, 193. Shepherd was a lawyer and a school inspector.

11. Scott N. Morse, editor, "'Knowledge Is Power': The Reverend Grosvenor Clarke Morse's Thoughts on Free Schools and the Republic during the Civil War," *Kansas History* 31 (Spring 2008): 9, 10.

12. Quoted from labor convention report inserted into testimony of John Henri Burch, *Voorhees Committee Report*, part 3, 142.

13. Henry Adams clipping of *Franklin (La.) Enterprise*, August 6, 1874, in Testimony of Henry Adams, *Voorhees Committee Report*, part 2, 170. The statement from Christian members of the White League protested blacks being granted any civil rights.

14. Ruby, *Voorhees Committee*, part 2, 53.

15. Testimony of J. H. Shepherd, *Voorhees Committee Report*, part 3, 192.

16. Testimony of George E. Gillespie, *Voorhees Committee Report*, part 3, 353.

17. Testimony of James T. Rapier, *Voorhees Committee Report*, part 2, 475.

18. Testimony of Andrew Currie, *Voorhees Committee Report*, part 3, 76.

19. Shepherd, *Voorhees Committee*, part 3, 190. The Freedman's Savings and Trust Company was headquartered in Washington, D.C., but a number of states, including Alabama, had a branch bank.

20. Ibid.

21. Burch, *Voorhees Committee*, part 3, 145. Burch included Rapier's comments when he seconded the resolutions of the Committee on Education. Burch testified in both parts 1 and 2, and Rapier testified separately in part 3.

22. John Milton Brown, *Voorhees Committee Report*, part 2, 353.

23. Lewis, *Voorhees Committee Report*, part 2, 248.

24. Quoted from labor convention reports inserted into testimony of John Henri Burch, *Voorhees Committee Report*, part 3, 142.

25. V. Dell, *Voorhees Committee Report*, part 3, 256.

26. Burch, *Voorhees Committee Report*, part 2, 217–18.

27. Brown, *Voorhees Committee Report*, part 2, 386.

28. *Colored Citizen*, September 20, 1878.

29. *Colored Citizen*, February 1, 1879.

30. Dassler, *Compiled Laws of Kansas*, 839, 846.

31. James Carper, "The Popular Ideology of Segregated Schooling: Attitudes toward the Education of Blacks in Kansas, 1854–1900," *Kansas History* 1 (Winter 1978–79): 272.

32. *Session Laws of Kansas*, 1877, 225.

33. *Stockton News*, March 14, 1878. There is no information on the location and composition of these schools. A number of the settlers had some form of home schooling. However, because they were acknowledged in the paper, these seem to indicate more substantial organization.

34. Craig manuscript, "The Hemp Factory," n.p.

35. Ibid.

36. Ibid.; Craig manuscript, "Nicodemus School Organized July 1879," n.p.

37. Craig manuscript, "Keber [sic] Schools," n.p. This spelling should be "Kebar."
38. Craig manuscript, "The Kebar Country," n.p.
39. *Colored Citizen*, July 5, 1878.
40. *Stockton News*, December 8, 1878. Hall's letter was dated December 1.
41. Craig, "The Kebar Country," n.p.
42. *Stockton News*, February 13, 1879.
43. Craig manuscript, "Nicodemus School Organized July 1879," n.p.
44. Craig manuscript, "Vanduvall and School," n.p.; Craig manuscript, "Nettie Craig Teacher," n.p.
45. Dassler, *Compiled Laws of Kansas*, 824.
46. Dick, *Sod House Frontier*, 118, 119.
47. "Report of the Superintendent of Public Instruction," in *Public Documents-Kansas, 1879–1880*, 72.

Chapter 7. Leave This Godforsaken Country

Epigraph: Testimony of John Henri Burch, *Voorhees Committee Report*, part 2, 237.

1. Testimony of John Davis, *Voorhees Committee Report*, part 3, 226.
2. Gayle K. Berardi and Thomas W. Segady, "The Development of African American Newspapers in the American West, 1880–1914," in *African Americans on the Western Frontier*, ed. Monroe Lee Billington and Roger D. Hardaway (Boulder: University Press of Colorado), 217–30.
3. Testimony of John C. New, *Voorhees Committee Report*, part 2, 21–23.
4. Testimony of O. S. B. Wall, *Voorhees Committee Report*, part 1, 27.
5. Testimony of Samuel L. Perry, *Voorhees Committee Report*, part 1, 287.
6. Testimony of O. S. B. Wall, *Voorhees Committee Report*, part 1, 26. The Freedmen's Bureau was established by the War Department in 1865 to provide relief to former slaves. Its massive task was to create a new social order for thousands of impoverished blacks. See the African American records of the National Archives for complete information.
7. Testimony of Henry Adams, *Voorhees Committee Report*, part 2, 156. See Painter, *Exodusters*, chapters 6–8 for an overview of Henry Adams's extensive efforts to remove blacks from the South to Liberia.
8. Testimony of Henry Adams, *Voorhees Committee Report*, part 2, 192–214. These accounts are numbered and simply stated. For instance, "582d. Barrett Telley, colored, killed by white men, on Mr. Rogers's plantation, 1874."
9. Ibid., 192.
10. Testimony of Samuel L. Perry, *Voorhees Committee Report*, part 1, 287.
11. Painter, *Exodusters*, 93.

12. See Nudie E. Williams, "Black Newspapers and the Exodusters of 1879," *Kansas History* 4 (Winter 1985), 217–25, for an overview of the intensity of the emigration debate and the role of the *Colored Citizen* in shaping opinion.

13. *Colored Citizen*, May 24, 1879.

14. Testimony of Isaiah Wears, *Voorhees Committee Report*, part 3, 157.

15. *Colored Citizen*, May 17, 1879.

16. *Republican Daily Journal*, October 15, 1878. Matthews gave an address in Lawrence later that year that traced the history of African American Masonry and bitterly refuted the legitimacy of a rogue movement of states rights' Masonry. The Prince Hall Masons are the oldest and largest group of Masons of African origin in the world. Today there are forty Grand Lodges of Prince Hall Freemasonry in the United States, Canada, the Bahamas, and Liberia. These Grand Lodges preside over more than five thousand lodges. All of them claim descent from the Prince Hall Grand Lodge of Massachusetts, which is traced back to the African Lodge No. 459. See more at: http://www.blackpast.org/aaw/prince-hall-masons-1784#sthash.wmZ1424E.dpuf

17. *Colored Citizen*, January 18, 1879.

18. Ibid.

19. Ibid.

20. *Colored Citizen*, February 1, 1879

21. *Colored Citizen*, February 25, 1879.

22. *Colored Citizen*, February 8, 1879.

23. *Colored Citizen*, February 8, 15, 22, 1879.

24. *Colored Citizen*, February 22, 1879.

25. Ibid.

26. *Colored Citizen*, March 1, 1879.

27. *Colored Citizen*, March 8, 1879.

28. *Colored Citizen*, March 15, 1879.

29. *Colored Citizen*, January 25, 1879.

30. *Colored Citizen*, February 1, 1879

31. *Colored Citizen*, February 8, 1879.

32. *Colored Citizen*, March 1, 1879.

33. *Colored Citizen*, March 29, 1879.

34. *Colored Citizen*, April 19, 1879. Eagleson claimed that "propriety forbids its publication" and that "time would bring all to light."

35. *Colored Citizen*, March 1, 1879.

36. *Colored Citizen*, July 26, 1879.

37. Testimony of James T. Rapier, *Voorhees Committee Report*, part 2, 482.

38. *Colored Citizen*, April 5, 1879.

39. *Colored Citizen*, April 19, 1789.

40. *Colored Citizen*, May 17, 1789.

41. Ibid.

42. *Colored Citizen*, May 17, 1879.

43. Proceedings of the National Conference of Colored Men of the United States, Held in the State Capitol at Nashville, Tennessee, May 6, 7, 8 and 9, 1879 (Washington, D.C.: Rufus H. Darby, 1879), available at www.hathitrust.org/.

Chapter 8. Give No Aid to the Sharks

Epigraph: Testimony of M. Bosworth, *Voorhees Committee Report*, part 3, 292.

1. Painter, *Exodusters*, 225; "Tandy, Charleton (1836–1919)," Bryan M. Jack, *The Online Reference Guide to African American History*, BlackPast.org, www.blackpast.org/aah/tandy-charleton-1836-1919.

2. Bryan M. Jack, *The St. Louis African American Community and the Exodusters* (Columbia: University of Missouri Press, 2007), 29.

3. Leiker, "Race Relations in the Sunflower State," 204–36.

4. *Colored Citizen*, March 29, 1879.

5. Quoted in ibid.

6. *Colored Citizen*, May 3, 1879.

7. *Proceedings of the National Conference of Colored Men of the United States*, appendix N.

8. *Colored Citizen*, May 31, 1879.

9. Henry Worrall, "Exoduster Illustrations," *Harper's Weekly*, July 5, 1879.

10. *Daily Democrat* (New Orleans), April 24, 1879.

11. Ibid.

12. *Commonwealth* (Topeka), April 18, 1879.

13. Ibid.

14. Bosworth, *Voorhees Committee Report*, part 3, 292.

15. *St. Louis Globe Democrat*, reprinted in *Leavenworth Times*, March 19, 1879.

16. *Vicksburg Herald*, March 25, 1879.

17. Ibid.

18. *Commonwealth* (Topeka), March 21, 1879.

19. *North Topeka Times*, March 28, 1879.

20. *Commonwealth* (Topeka), May 1, 1879.

21. Ibid.

22. *Articles of Corporation and Bylaws of the Kansas Freedmen's Relief Association* (Topeka: F. F. Baker & Sons, 1879); Athearn, *In Search of Canaan*, 57.

23. *Commonwealth* (Topeka) May 1, 1879; *Kansas Freedmen's Relief Association*, 2.

24. *Commonwealth* (Topeka), April 29, 1879.

25. *Daily Capital*, June 28, 1879.

26. *Commonwealth* (Topeka), June 14, 1879. When W. J. Buchan testified at the Voorhees hearings, Senator Windom asked him if the immigrants understood that were not going to get forty acres of land free. Buchan responded that "they did not seem to rely upon the promises made by the people at all. . . . It was sort of a myth through the air; but none of them had any such expectations." Testimony of W. J. Buchan, *Voorhees Committee*, Part 3, 481. The "forty acres and a mule" myth stemmed from a field order given by Union general William Tecumseh Sherman's Special Field Order No. 15 in 1865 that promised to distribute forty acres of confiscated land and an army mule to blacks living along the coasts of South Carolina, Georgia, and Florida. President Andrew Johnson rescinded the order, but the myth persisted. Henry Louis Gates, Jr., "The Truth behind '40 Acres and a Mule,'" *The Root*, January 13, 1013, www.theroot.com/.

27. Cox, *Blacks in Topeka*, 68.
28. Ibid.
29. *Evening Gazette* (Worcester, Mass.), July 2, 1879.
30. Dassler, *Compiled Laws of Kansas*, 140.
31. *Commonwealth* (Topeka), July 30, 1879.
32. *Salina Herald*, August 2, 1879.
33. Athearn, *In Search of Canaan*, 65. Quoted from the *Weekly Clarion*, Jackson, Mississippi, July 30, 1879. There was no mention of the source of the *Clarion*'s quote.
34. Kansas Freedmen's Relief Association, *Articles of Corporation and By-Laws* (Topeka: F. P. Baker & Sons, 1879); David H. Finke, "Introducing Chicago Area Quakers," Street Corner Society, www.strecorsoc.org/docs/chicago.html; *Commonwealth* (Topeka), June 6, 1880; *Topeka Capital*, July 16, 1879.
35. Haviland, *A Woman's Life Work*, 66.
36. *Commonwealth* (Topeka), April 14, 1880.
37. *Stockton News*, March 26, 1879.
38. *Colored Citizen*, April 12, 1879.
39. James Himes to St. John, November 6, 1880, in St. John, Correspondence Received, 1879–82, box 1, Kansas Historical Society, Topeka; A. J. R. Smith to St. John, May 8, 1880, box 1, in St. John, Correspondence Received, 1879–82.
40. *Herald of Kansas*, March 19, 1880. Eagleson was forced to change the name of his new paper because a *Kansas Herald* already existed in Hiawatha, Kansas.
41. *Millbrook Times*, January 2, 1880.
42. *Western Star*, February 5, 1880.
43. Ibid.
44. John Inlow, letter, January 17, 1880, box 1, folder 9, in St. John, Correspondence Received, 1879–82.

45. J. A. Keeney, letter, January 10, 1880, box 1, folder 11, in St. John, Correspondence Received, 1879–82.

46. Jay Gould, telegraph, January 11, 1880, and letter, January 12, 1880, box 1, folder 7, in St. John, Correspondence Received, 1879–82.

47. E. P. McCabe, letter, January 26, 1880, box 1, folder 13, in St. John, Correspondence Received, 1879–82.

48. John Pierce St. John, letter, January 29, 1880, box 7, no. 24, in St. John, Letter Press Books, Kansas Historical Society.

49. A. R. George, letter, February 2, 1880, box 1, folder 7, in St. John, Correspondence Received, 1879–82; *Western Star*, February 12, 1880.

50. E. P. McCabe, Letter, February 14, 1880, box 1, folder 13, in St. John, Correspondence Received, 1879–82.

51. John Pierce St. John, Letter, February 21, 1880, box 7, no. 19, in St. John, Letter Press Books.

52. *Western Star*, February 12, 1880.

53. *Millbrook Times*, February 20, 1880.

54. *Graham County Lever* (Gettysburg, Kans.), February 27, 1880.

55. *Millbrook Times*, December 10, 1880 quoting the *Leavenworth Times*.

56. Miner, *Kansas*, 3–4.

57. *Topeka Weekly Times*, May 13, 1881, quoting the *Huntington (W.Va.) Advertiser*.

58. Ibid.

Chapter 9. The Colored People Hold the Key

Epigraph: Testimony of John Henri Burch, *Voorhees Committee Report*, part 3, 132. Burch inserted an extract from a black labor convention held in Montgomery, Alabama, January 2, 1872, part of a statewide movement of "Negro conventions" in Alabama. See Judy Bissell Leforge, "Alabama's Colored Conventions and the Exodus Movement, 1871–1879," *Alabama Review* 61, no. 1 (January 2010): 3–29.

1. Dassler, *Compiled Laws of Kansas*, 265.

2. Dick, *Sod House Frontier*, 459.

3. *Stockton News*, December 5, 1878; *Atchison Daily Champion*, December 19, 1878.

4. *Stockton News*, December 5, 1878.

5. *Atchison Daily Champion*, January 2, 1879. Hall's letter was written December 30, 1878.

6. *Stockton News*, February 13, 1879.

7. "Graham County Commissioners Journal, Docket 1 (incomplete), March 7, 1881–February 3, 1887," in *Historical Records Survey* (Topeka: Federal

Works Agency, n.d.), 69; Homer E. Socolofsky and Huber Self, *Historical Atlas of Kansas* (Norman: University of Oklahoma Press, 1975), 40.

8. The Kansas Historical Society has appointment books for Governor George T. Anthony, who preceded St. John, and for Governor George W. Glick, who followed him, but there is no extant appointment book for Governor St. John. Both Hall and St. John alluded to this January meeting in correspondence. Abram T. Hall and E. P. McCabe to Governor John P. St. John, April 11, 1879, folder 1, St. John Correspondence; St. John to Abram T. Hall and E. P. McCabe, April 17, 1879, box 5, no. 15, Letter Press Books, Kansas Historical Society (hereafter cited as box 5, no. 15, Letter Press Books).

9. St. John to Abram T. Hall and E. P. McCabe, April 17, 1879, box 5, no. 15, Letter Press Books.

10. Public Documents of Kansas, 1879–80, 112.

11. *Stockton News*, May 7, 1879; *Session Laws of Kansas*, chap. 73, sect. 3; *Stockton News*, May 21, 1879. Attorney General Willard Davis wrote to Benjamin B. F. Graves on July 30, 1879, that in his opinion "some clerk made a mistake." Davis's letter was sent to W. R. Hill but was "in answer to the letter of yourself, Hall, McCabe and others." "Report of the Attorney General," in *Public Documents, Kansas, 1879–1880*, 111, 112. In fact, changing county boundaries required a majority of votes by the legal voters of both counties. See Dassler, *Compiled Laws of Kansas* (1879), chap. 24, sects. 1369–73, 124–28.

12. *Millbrook Times*, August 22, 1879.

13. "Townships and Township Officers," in Dassler, *Compiled Laws of Kansas*, chap. 110, sect. 3.

14. Dassler, *Compiled Laws of Kansas*, chap. 24, sect. 137.

15. *Rooks County Commissioners Minutes*, July 7, 1879, and July 29, 1879, J. N. Mitchell, Rooks County Clerk, Office of the County Clerk, Rooks County Courthouse, Stockton, Kansas; Dassler, *Compiled Laws of Kansas*, chap. 24, sect. 137

16. *Millbrook Times*, July 11, 1879.

17. Shortridge, *Peopling the Plains*, 82–92. The Greenback Labor Party favored monetary inflation and so supported increasing the number of paper dollars in circulation. *Millbrook Times*, July 11, 1879.

18. *Millbrook Times*, July 18, 1879.

19. Ibid.

20. *Millbrook Times*, July 25, 1879.

21. Benjamin B. F. Graves to St. John, July 29, 1879, folder 1, St. John Correspondence; Governor John P. St. John to Benjamin B. F. Graves, July 31, 1879, box 5, no. 17, Letter Press Books.

22. F. E. Bowers to St. John, July 10, 1879, folder 1, St. John Correspondence.

23. "Petition for the Organization of Graham County," received in the office of John P. St. John, October 11, 1879, folder 4, St. John Correspondence; Dassler, *Compiled Laws of Kansas*, chap. 24, sect. 114. In 1881 Ida Tillotson would become the fourth female admitted to practice law in Kansas. See *Graham County Lever*, April 22, 1881. In the June 16, 1881, *Hill City Lively Times*, editor Thomas McGill mentioned borrowing a law book from Ida that was inscribed "To Ida Tillotson, att'y at law, Millbrook, Kans., from her friend and Sabbath School teacher, John P. St. John."

24. Abram T. Hall to St. John, November 3, 1879, folder 1, St. John Correspondence. Affidavits were enclosed with this letter.

25. St. John to Hall, November 6, 1879, box 6, no. 20, Letter Press Books.

26. "Petition from Gettysburg for County Officers," received in the office of John P. St. John, November 5, 1879, folder 5, St. John Papers; Thomas Beaumont to St. John, May 23, 1879, and T. H. McGill to St. John, May 29, 1879, folder 1, St. John Papers.

27. Rev. John S. Henry to St. John, November 7, 1879, folder 1, St. John Correspondence; *Western Star*, quoted in *Millbrook Times*, August 1, 1879; Root, "Biographical Sketch of Daniel Hickman." Root incorrectly refers to Landis to as "Landers." The *Norton Advance* stated there had been two previous attempts on Landis's life. A correspondent from Nicodemus, when commenting on the "Roscoe riot," implied that there were racial factors in the murder of John Landis. See *Roscoe Tribune*, January 28, 1881.

28. I. O. Pickering, "The Administration of John P. St. John," *Kansas Historical Collections* 9 (1906): 670.

29. Testimony of G.W. Carey, *Voorhees Committee Report*, part 1, 391.

30. Shortridge, *Peopling the Plains*, 82–92. Shortridge stated that Missourians settled as clustered groups in Phillips, Rooks, and Graham Counties. The *Hays City Sentinel* quoted from the *Troy (Kans.) Chief* and referred to these Missourians as "rebel bushwhackers" when discussing the murder of John Landis (*Hays City Sentinel*, September 21, 1878).

31. Governor John P. St. John to Abram T. Hall, Jr., November 21, 1879, box 6, no. 20, Letter Press Books.

32. *Millbrook Times*, December 5, 1879.

33. "Townships and Township Officers," in Dassler, *Compiled Laws of Kansas*, chap. 110; *Millbrook Times*, January 2, 1880; *Stockton Record*, January 10, 1880, quoting from the *Ness County Pioneer*; *Western Star*, January 8, 1880. Graham County would hold the mandatory second Nicodemus Township election on February 3.

34. *Millbrook Times*, January 23, 1880.

35. Thomas Allison to St. John, March 22, 1880, and J. J. Bell to St. John, March 22, 1880, folder 2, St. John Correspondence.

36. Abram T. Hall, Jr., "Census Report of Graham County," March 6, 1880, State Archives, Kansas Historical Society. Hall reported that Graham County had a population of 3,570, with 1,084 householders, 1,026 voters, 1,101 schoolchildren, and 17,709 acres under cultivation.

37. "Petition for the Designation of Hill City as the Temporary County Seat of Graham Co.," received in the office of John P. St. John, March 4, 1880, folder 9, St. John, Correspondence; "Petition from Millbrook," received in the office of John P. St. John, March 5, 1880, folder 10, St. John Correspondence; E. P. McCabe to St. John, March 3, 1880, folder 2, St. John Correspondence.

38. "Petition for the Designation of Roscoe as the Temporary County Seat of Graham Co.," March 20, 1880, folder 13, St. John Correspondence. Roscoe was the last town of the four county-seat contenders to acquire a paper: the *Roscoe Tribune*, edited by F. P. Kellogg and first published on June 13, 1880.

39. L. P. Boyd to St. John, March 12, 1880, folder 2, St. John Correspondence.

40. R. H. Lyman, H. Williams, and J. B. Gregory to St. John, March 5, 1880, folder 2, St. John Correspondence; *Stockton News*, April 6, 1881.

41. Thomas Beaumont to St. John, March, 17, 1880, folder 2, St. John Correspondence; St. John to Thomas Beaumont, March 18, 1880, box 7, no. 25, Letter Press Books.

42. The law in question is cited in Dassler, *Compiled Laws of Kansas*, chap. 24, sect. 1338; Hall and McCabe, "Brief of the attorneys for the Roscoe Petition," folder 23, St. John Correspondence.

43. Ibid.

44. Willard Davis to Governor John P. St. John, "Report of the Attorney General," March 18, 1880, in *Public Documents, Kansas 1879–80*, 131.

45. "Proclamation of Governor John Pierce St. John Organizing the County of Graham, April 1, 1880," in *Proclamations and Messages*, vol. A, Governor's Office, John P. St. John, Kansas Historical Society; "Historical Sketch," in *Inventory of the County Archives of Kansas* (Topeka: Historical Records Survey, Works Progress Administration, 1938), 5.

46. "Historical Sketch," in *Inventory of the County Archives of Kansas* (Topeka: Historical Records Survey, Works Progress Administration, 1938), 5. Hill City was never a serious contender during the first vote for the seat of Graham County. The town even failed to poll a majority in its own township on June 1.

47. *Millbrook Times*, June 4, 1880; Graham *County Lever*, June 11, 1880; *Roscoe Tribune*, June 23, 1880. This was the *Roscoe Tribune*'s first issue.

48. *Graham County Lever*, November 5, 1880.

49. *Graham County Commissioners' Journal*, Docket I, 1881, 58.

50. Ibid., 67.

51. Dassler, *Compiled Laws of Kansas*, chap. 26, sect. 7.

52. *Graham County Commissioners' Journal*, Docket I, 1881 (Topeka, Kansas: Historical Records Survey, Works Progress Administration), 59, 69; Kansas History Records Survey, *Inventory of the County Archives of Kansas*, no. 33, *Graham County (Hill City)* (Topeka: Works Progress Administration, Division of Women's and Professional Projects, 1938), 6; *Western Star* editor McGill qtd. in *Hill City Lively Times*, July 28, 1881.

53. *Atchison Daily Times* quoted in the *Roscoe Tribune*, November 12, 1880.

54. For Hall's letter to Henri, see Belleau, "The Nicodemus Colony of Graham County, Kansas." Quotation from the *Atchison Daily Champion* in the *Roscoe Tribune*, November 12, 1880.

55. There are only four extant issues of the *Chicago Conservator*. The publication dates of the existing copies are November 18, 1882; December 16, 1882; September 8, 1883; and December 18, 1886. The Halls are mentioned all these issues. A. T. Hall, Jr., is listed as the city editor on the masthead of the first two issues, his wedding is described in the third issue, and his father is mentioned in the fourth. Anti-lynching crusader and pioneer black feminist Ida B. Wells would purchase the paper in 1895.

56. *Chicago Conservator*, September 8, 1883.

57. Ibid.

58. Ibid.

59. *Pittsburgh Post-Gazette*, August 10, 2010.

60. Ibid.

61. *Pittsburgh Press*, January 10, 1951. Hall's book of poetry, *En Emeritus*, is located in the Jeanne Boger Jones Collection at the Vivian G. Harsh Research Collection of Afro-American History and Literature, Chicago Public Library.

62. For analysis of the causes of county seat fights, see Dick, *The Sod-House Frontier*, 459; Steven L. Scott, "Great Plains Hamlet County Seat," *Heritage of the Great Plains* 19 (Spring 1986): 1–14; Homer Socolofsky, "County Seat Wars in Kansas," *Trail Guide* 9 (1964): 1–25; James A. Schellenberg, *Conflict between Communities: American County Seat Wars* (New York: Paragon House, 1987), 27; Robert K. DeArment, *Ballots and Bullets: The Bloody County Seat Wars of Kansas* (Norman: University of Oklahoma Press, 2006), 5.

Chapter 10. One Tree Bore Bread, Another Bore Lard

Epigraph: Testimony of Louis Stubblefield, *Voorhees Committee Report*, part 3, 520.

1. Craig manuscript, "Colonization," n.p.

2. Quoted in Root, "Biographical Sketch of Daniel Hickman," 4.

3. *New York Herald*, "The Indemnity Party a New Secret Political Organization in Arkansas," May 27, 1882.

4. *Stockton News*, March 26, 1879.
5. Chambers, "Nile of Nicodemus," n.p.
6. Chambers, "Niles of Nicodemus," n.p.
7. Craig manuscript, "Settlement," 14.
8. Hamilton, "Settlement of Nicodemus," 9.
9. *Roscoe Tribune,* June 23, 1880.
10. Hamilton, "Settlement of Nicodemus," 9.
11. *Herald of Kansas*, April 9, 1880.
12. *Herald of Kansas*, April 23, 1880.
13. Ibid.
14. Ibid.
15. *Herald of Kansas,* April 16, 23, 30, 1880.
16. *Herald of Kansas*, April 16, 1880. Hall undoubtedly penned this letter. Hall and McCabe had barely arrived home from the state Republican convention when the Convention for Colored Men took place.
17. *Herald of Kansas*, June 11, 1880.
18. *Millbrook Times*, September 3, 1880.
19. *Millbrook Times*, April 25, 1880.
20. *Millbrook Times*, November 12, 1880.
21. *Graham County Lever,* September 24, 1880.
22. *Millbrook Times*, June 11, 1880.
23. *Millbrook Times*, July 2, 1880.
24. *Millbrook Times*, June 25, 1880.
25. *Millbrook Times*, July 9, 1880.
26. *Millbrook Times*, July 23, 1880.
27. *Millbrook Times*, November 12, 26, 1880.
28. *Stockton News*, July 21, 1880.
29. Chambers, *Niles of Nicodemus*, n.p.
30. *Millbrook Times*, December 24, 1880.
31. *Millbrook Times*, August 27, 1880.
32. *Millbrook Times*, October 28, 1881.
33. *Millbrook Times*, October 28, 1881.
34. *Millbrook Times*, August 20, 1880.
35. Lowell Beecher, *The Spring Creek Valley* (Hill City, Kans.: L. Beecher, 2009), available at Graham County Historical Society, Hill City, Kansas. *The Spring Creek Valley* contains original scholarship about regional social and economic issues.
36. Ibid., 69.
37. *Roscoe Tribune*, December 31, 1880.
38. *Roscoe Tribune*, January 4, 1881.
39. *Topeka Commonwealth*, January 13, 1881.

40. *Stockton News*, January 5, 1881
41. *Roscoe Tribune*, January 28, 1881.
42. Craig manuscript, "First Officers," n.p.; Painter, *Exodusters*, 152. Regrettably, this letter has disappeared from the Kansas Historical Society. Fortunately Painter's book preserved a portion of Roundtree's letter. Roundtree also wrote under the pseudonym Rough and Ready, or R&R.
43. *Roscoe Tribune*, January 28, 1881.
44. *Millbrook Times*, December 31, 1880.
45. *Millbrook Times*, January 14, 1881.
46. *Graham County Lever*, December 24, 1880.
47. *House Journal, State of Kansas*, 1881, 704.
48. Ibid., 1183.
49. Chambers, *Niles of Nicodemus*, n.p.
50. Quoted in ibid.
51. Ibid.
52. Ibid.
53. Ibid.
54. Hamilton, "Settlement of Nicodemus," 10; Chambers, *Niles of Nicodemus*, n.p. See Hamilton's quotes from Niles's defense recitation in his notes, p. 29.
55. *Millbrook Times*, May 20, 1881. The column was signed "Correspondent" but we can assume it was Graves because he was the one subpoenaed.
56. *Millbrook Times*, June 3, 1881.
57. *Graham County Lever*, May 27, 1881; *Millbrook Times*, June 3, 1881.
58. *Millbrook Times*, August 26, 1881.
59. *Graham Republican*, October 15, 1881.
60. Ibid.
61. *New York Herald*, May 27, 1882.
62. Chambers, *Niles of Nicodemus*, n.p.
63. *New York Herald*, May 27, 1882; *Arkansas Gazette*, June 3, 1882.
64. *Millbrook Times*, December 29, 1882.
65. *Arkansas Gazette*, June 3, 1882.
66. Chambers, *Niles of Nicodemus*, n.p.
67. *Millbrook Times*, September 21, 1883. Reprinted from the *Philadelphia Times*, September 9, 1883.
68. *Wheeling (W.V.) Register*, September 5, 1883.
69. *Atlanta Constitution*, August 31, 1883.
70. *Arkansas Mansion*, September 8, 1883.
71. *People's Advocate* (Washington, D.C.), August 25, 1883.
72. *New York Globe*, October 27, 1883. This *Globe* should not be confused with the *New York Globe* founded in 1904. Fortune subsequently renamed the

same paper the *Freeman*, then the *New York Age*, which became the country's leading black newspaper. Highly influential, Fortune was an outstanding editor, publisher, and civil rights leader.

73. John W. Niles, *A New Religion: J. W. Niles' Address to the Colored People of the United States* (New York: Indemnity Party, 1883). This rare publication is reprinted in T. DeWitt Talmage, *American Commerce and the New Orleans Exposition* (New York, 1884), held by the Rutherford B. Hayes Presidential Center, Fremont, Ohio.

74. Ibid., 3.

75. *New Haven Register*, October 13, 1883. Other papers that printed the letter include *Augusta Chronicle*, October 18, 1883; *Bridgeton (N.J.) Evening News*, October 19, 1883; *Summit County (Ohio) Beacon*, October 24, 1883; *San Francisco Bulletin*, November 9, 1883.

76. *Logansport (Ind.) Journal*, October 18, 1883.

77. Niles, *A New Religion*, 3.

78. "Frederick Douglass: A Powerful Voice for Abolition and Equal Rights," Louisville Free Public Library, http://www.lfpl.org/western/htms/douglass.htm.

79. *Boston Herald*, October 17, 1883.

80. Ibid.

81. *Rooks County Record*, December 14, 1883. The reporter interviewed a number of "leaders of the local colored people" to collect their opinion in regard to the civil rights bill.

82. Ibid.

83. Rodney A. Ross, Center for Legislative Archives, to Charlotte Hinger, Reference Request Number RR1–66158601, January 19, 2011.

84. *Journal of the Senate of the United States of America*, first sess., December 5, 1883, 34. A surprising number of newspapers across the country were aware of Niles's petition. Just to name a few: *Daily Illinois State Register* (Springfield), December 6, 1883; *Canton (Ohio) Repository*, December 7, 1883; *Sun* (San Diego), December 12, 1883.

85. Chambers, "Niles of Nicodemus," n.p.

86. *Journal of the Senate of the United States of America*, Forty-Eighth Cong., second sess., January 26, 1885. Senator Ingalls's resolution referred to J. W. Niles and other citizens of Kansas, rather than citizens of Arkansas, when he asked that the judiciary committee be discharged of this obligation.

87. The following papers reported on the formation of the immigration committee: *Daily Illinois State Register* (Springfield), December 27, 1883; *Times-Picayune* (New Orleans), December 27, 1883; *Cleveland Leader*, December 27, 1883; *San Francisco Bulletin*, December 27, 1883; *Canton (Ohio) Repository*, December 28, 1883.

Chapter 11. I Will Not Touch the Unclean Thing

Epigraph: Testimony of W. J. Buchan, *Voorhees Committee Report*, part 3, 473.

1. Buchan, *Voorhees Report*, 473.
2. A. T. Andreas, *History of the State of Kansas* (Chicago: A. T. Andreas, 1883), 570; Martin Dann, "From Sodom to the Promised Land: E. P. McCabe and the Movement for Oklahoma Colonization," *Kansas Historical Quarterly 40* (Autumn 1974): 370–78; Craig manuscript, "Settlement" n.p.
3. "Secretary of State, Biennial Report," in *Public Documents, Kansas, 1879–1880* (Topeka: George W. Martin, Kansas Publishing House, 1881), 125; Dassler, *Compiled Laws of Kansas*, 598.
4. *Millbrook Times*, April 9, 1880.
5. Dassler, *Compiled Laws of Kansas*, 281.
6. *Colored Citizen*, April 12, 1879.
7. *Stockton News*, March 26, 1879.
8. *Graham County Lever*, April 14, 1880.
9. *Graham County Lever*, May 7, 1880.
10. *Graham County Lever*, May 21, 1880.
11. E. P. McCabe to St. John, March 3, 1880, folder 2, St. John Correspondence.
12. *Commonwealth* (Topeka), July 8, 1879.
13. *Millbrook Times*, September 26, 1879.
14. Ibid.
15. *Stockton News*, November 12, 1879.
16. Ibid.
17. *Millbrook Times*, November 14, 1879.
18. *Graham County Lever*, October 10, 1879.
19. *Stockton News*, December 20, 1879.
20. *Graham County Lever*, April 28, 1880.
21. *Millbrook Times*, January 30, 1880.
22. "Report of the Attorney General," in *Public Documents, Kansas, 1879–1880*, 136.
23. Dassler, *Compiled Laws*, 280.
24. *Millbrook Times*, June 11, 1880
25. *Roscoe Tribune*, July 30, 1880.
26. *Roscoe Tribune*, June 23, 1880.
27. *Roscoe Tribune*, June 30, 1880.
28. *Roscoe Tribune*, July 30, 1880.
29. *Graham County Lever*, November 5, 1880.
30. *Millbrook Times*, July 28, 1881.
31. Craig manuscript, "E. P. McCabe," n.p. There were references in various newspaper about Sarah Bryant McCabe's ill health throughout her life.

32. *Graham Republican*, August 27, 1881.
33. Dick, *Sod House Frontier*, 54.
34. *Millbrook Times*, March 17, 1882.
35. Ibid.
36. *Star-Sentinel*, March 23, 1882. It would appear that by this time McCabe had switched his loyalty from Roscoe to Millbrook for the county seat.
37. *Millbrook Times*, May 12, 1882.
38. *Millbrook Times*, March 24, 1882.
39. Ibid., reprinted from the *Chicago Conservator*, May 19, 1882. By that time, Hall had moved from St. Louis to Chicago.
40. *Millbrook Times*, May 26, 1882.
41. *Millbrook Times*, June 23, 1882, reprinted from *Chicago Conservator*. Hall worked for the *Chicago Conservator* both before and after living in Nicodemus.
42. *Weekly Kansas Chief* (Troy), August 10, 1882.
43. Ira Berlin, *Slaves without Masters; The Free Negro in the Antebellum South* (New York: Free Press, 1974), 387, 388.
44. *Millbrook Herald*, June 20, 1882, quoting the *Stockton Record*.
45. James T. Haley and Booker T. Washington, *Afro-American Encyclopaedia; or, The Thoughts, Doings, and Sayings of the Race* (Nashville: Haley and Florida, 1895), 341.
46. Painter, *Exodusters*, 14, 114.
47. Dassler, *Complied Laws*, 896–98.
48. *Colored Patriot*, May 25, 1882. The *Colored Patriot* published for just two months: April 20, 1882 to June 22, 1882. Many black newspapers, including the *Patriot*, lacked a sufficient number of paying subscribers. The *Topeka Tribune* followed and quickly met the same fate.
49. *Star-Sentinel*, May 11, 1882. As with modern-day presses quoting the AP or other national wire services, newspapers freely reprinted from each other.
50. John J. Ingalls, to St. John, February 10 and 15, 1879, St. John Papers, Correspondence Received, box 1, folder 9.
51. *Star-Sentinel*, July 27, 1882.
52. "The Largest Colored Colony in Kansas," April 16, 1877, circular, Kansas Historical Society, Topeka.
53. *Star-Sentinel*, June 1, 1882.
54. *Star-Sentinel*, June 8, 1882.
55. Susan B. Anthony to John P. St. John, August 21, 1881, St. John Papers, Correspondence Received, box 1, folder 1.
56. *Wichita City Eagle*, August 24, 1882.
57. Quoted in Robert Smith Bader, *Prohibition in Kansas* (Lawrence: University Press of Kansas, 1986), 44. Kansas still has not ratified the 21st amendment.

58. Peter Conrad, *The Sociology of Health and Illness: Critical Perspectives* (NY: Worth Publishers, 2008), 108.
59. *Millbrook Times*, August 4, 1882.
60. *Topeka Commonwealth*, March 30, 1882.
61. *Star-Sentinel*, July 6, 1882.
62. *Leavenworth Times*, August 17, 1882.
63. Ibid.
64. *Anthony Journal* reprinted in *Leavenworth Times*, August 10, 1882.
65. William G. Cutler, *History of the State of Kansas* (Chicago: A. T. Andreas, 1883). The first names of the candidates for auditor were not given in the newspapers. Full name can be found under each county sketch.
66. *Leavenworth Times*, August 17, 1882.
67. *Topeka Commonwealth*, August 17, 1882.
68. *Leavenworth Times*, August 17, 1882.
69. *Topeka Commonwealth*, August 11, 1882.
70. Ibid.
71. *Weekly Kansas Chief*, August 10, 1882.
72. Ibid. The paper printed an excerpt from the *Smith County Pioneer*.
73. *Iola Register*, August 25, 1882.
74. *Fort Scott Daily Tribune*, August 12, 1882.
75. *Weekly Kansas Chief*, August 10, 1882.
76. *Weekly Kansas Chief*, August 24, 1882.
77. *Osborne County Farmer* reprinted in the *Weekly Kansas Chief*, August 24, 1882. The *Osborne County Farmer* was owned and edited by Martin Mohler, McCabe's rival for state auditor.
78. *Millbrook Times*, August 18, 1882.
79. *Wichita City Eagle*, September 7, 1882.
80. *Boston Herald* reprinted in *Millbrook Times*, September 8, 1882.
81. *Millbrook Times*, September 8, 1882.
82. *Leavenworth Times*, September 7, 1882; Robert Smith Bader, *Prohibition in Kansas: A History* (Lawrence: University Press of Kansas, 1986), 19.
83. *Leavenworth Times*, September 7, 1882.
84. *Star-Sentinel*, August 3, 1882.
85. *Leavenworth Times*, August 24, 1882.
86. *Weekly Kansas Chief*, November 2, 1882.
87. *Saline County Journal*, October 26, 1882.
88. *Topeka Commonwealth*, August 30, 1882.
89. *Topeka Commonwealth*, November 16, 1882.
90. *Wichita City Eagle*, November 16, 1882.
91. Ibid.
92. *Millbrook Times*, December 15, 1882.
93. Craig manuscript, "Edward P. McCabe," n.p.

NOTES TO PAGES 192–204

94. *Millbrook Times*, June 22, 1883.
95. "Fourth Biennial Report of the Auditor of State and Register of State Land Office, for the Fiscal Years Ending June 30, 1883, and June 30, 1884," in *Public Documents, Kansas, 1883–1884* (Topeka: George W. Martin, Kansas Publishing House, 1885), iv. The report was an accounting of every cent that passed through the state coffers. The majority of this document appears in 3-point type and focuses on "For what purpose" and "To whom paid."
96. *Millbrook Times*, April 25, 1884, quoting the *Topeka Capital*.
97. *Abilene Reflector*, July 29, 1886. This is the same William Mathews who became embroiled in the controversy with Niles over aid to Nicodemus.
98. Ibid., quoting from the *Tribune*.
99. Ibid.
100. Ibid. The *Kansas Democrat* promoted Parson Twine, an Atchison man. C. H. Langston was the grandfather of poet Langston Hughes.
101. *Wichita Daily Eagle*, July 9, 1886.
102. *Abilene Reflector*, August 12, 1886; *Iola Register*, October 22, 1886.
103. *Wichita Globe*, March 28, 1887.
104. *Benevolent Banner* (Topeka) October 8, 1887.
105. *Thomas County Cat*, May 17, 1888.
106. *American Citizen*, April 19, 1889.
107. *Leavenworth Advocate*, September 30, 1889. This diagnosis probably was not accurate, as Sarah McCabe outlived her husband.
108. *Kansas City Evening News*, March 4, 1890.
109. "Oklahoma Territory," The Encyclopedia of Oklahoma History and Culture, Oklahoma Historical Society, www.okhistory.org/publications/enc/entry.php?entry=OK085.
110. "Eagleson, William Lewis (1835–1899)," *African American History in the American West: Online Encyclopedia of Significant People and Places*, BlackPast.org, www.blackpast.org/aaw/eagleson-william-lewis-1835-1899.
111. *Topeka Plaindealer*, March 19, 1920.

Epilogue

1. *Voorhees Committee Report*, "Majority Report," iii–viii.
2. *Voorhees Committee Report*, "Minority Report," ix–xxv.
3. *Voorhees Committee Report*, part 3, 151–52.
4. *Graham Republican*, October 1, 1881.
5. Ibid.
6. Ibid.
7. *Colored Citizen*, October 23, 1879.

Bibliography

Primary Sources

"American Freedmen's Inquiry Commission, Preliminary Report," June 30, 1863. Shotgun's Home of the American Civil War, www.civilwarhome.com/prelimcommissionreport.htm.

Chambers, W. L. *Niles of Nicodemus: Nicodemus: Exploiter of Kansas Exoduster, Negro Indemnity and Equality of Black with Whites His Obsession, Beats Bankers, Bench and Barristers; Counter League to Post-War K.K.K. Riots and Finally Prison.* Los Angeles: Washington High School, 1930. Located at Graham County Historical Society, Hill City, Kansas.

Comstock, Elizabeth L. *A Statement by Mrs. E. L. Comstock, Correspondent of the Kansas Freedmen's Relief Association.* Topeka: Commonwealth Steam Printing Office, 1880. Located at Kansas Historical Society, Topeka.

Craig, Lulu Sadler. Craig Manuscript Collection. Graham County Historical Society Archives, Hill City, Kansas.

Dassler, C. F. W. *Compiled Laws of Kansas.* St. Louis: W. J. Gilbert, 1879.

"Fourth Biennial Report of the Auditor of State and Register of State Land Office, for the Fiscal Years Ending June 30, 1883, and June 30, 1884." In *Public Documents, Kansas, 1883–1884*, 1–402. Topeka: George W. Martin, Kansas Publishing House, 1885.

Graham County Commissioners' Journal. Topeka: Historical Records Survey, Work Projects Administration, n.d.

Grant, Ulysses S. *The Papers of Ulysses S. Grant*, vol. 1. Carbondale: Southern Illinois University Press, 1967.

Hall, Abram Thompson. *Census Report of Graham County.* March 6, 1880.

Historical Records Survey. Topeka: Federal Works Agency, n.d.

House Journal, State of Kansas, 1879. Topeka: Kansas Publishing House, 1881.

Inventory of the County Archives of Kansas. Topeka: Historical Records Survey, Works Progress Administration, 1938.

Journal of the Senate of the United States of America (Senate Journal).

Kansas Freedmen's Relief Association. *Articles of Corporation and By-Laws.* Topeka: F. P. Baker & Sons, 1879.

Kansas History Records Survey. *Inventory of the County Archives of Kansas*, no. 33, *Graham County (Hill City).* Topeka: Works Progress Administration, Division of Women's and Professional Projects, 1938.

Niles, J. W. *A New Religion: J. W. Niles' Address to the Colored People of the United State.* Marianna, Ark.: Indemnity Party, 1883.
Proceedings of the National Conference of Colored Men of the United States, Held in the State Capitol at Nashville, Tennessee, May 6, 7, 8 and 9, 1879 (Washington, D.C.: Rufus H. Darby, 1879), available at www.hathitrust.org/.
Public Documents, Kansas, 1881–1882. Topeka: George W. Martin, Kansas Publishing House, 1883.
Public Documents, Kansas, 1879–1880. Topeka: George W. Martin, Kansas Publishing House, 1881.
Rooks County Commissioner Notes, book 1. Transcript in the hand of J. N. Mitchell, County Clerk. Located at Rooks County (Kansas) Courthouse.
Root, George A. "Biographical Sketch of Daniel Hickman." Located in George A. Root Collection, Kansas Historical Society.
Rust, Horatio N. Scrapbook. Located at Kansas Historical Society, Topeka.
Session Laws of Kansas. Topeka: George W. Martin, State Printing Works, 1879.
Singleton, Benjamin. Scrapbook. Located at Kansas Historical Society.
St. John, John Pierce. Correspondence Received, 1879–82. Kansas Historical Society, Topeka.
———. Letter Press Books, boxes 4–14. Kansas Historical Society, Topeka.
U.S. Congress, Senate. *Report and Testimony of the Select Committee of the United States Senate to Investigate the Causes of the Removal of the Negroes from the Southern States to the Northern States.* 2 vols. in 3 parts. 46th Cong., 2d sess. Washington, D.C.: Government Printing Office, 1880. Cited throughout as *Voorhees Committee Report.*
Valentine, D. M. "Roll of Attorneys." In *Reports of Cases Argued and Determined in the Supreme Court of the State of Kansas*, vol. 29. Topeka: Kansas Publishing House, 1883.
Voorhees, Daniel W. *Forty Years of Oratory.* Indianapolis: Bowen Merrill, 1898.
Williams, Charles Richard, ed. *Diary and Letters of Rutherford Brichard Hayes.* 5 vols. Cincinnati: Ohio State Historical Society, 1922.
Wyandotte Constitution. Located at Kansas Historical Society, Topeka.

Secondary Sources
Books

Anoke, Akua Duku, and Jacqueline Brice-Finch. *Get It Together: Readings about African American Life.* New York: Longman, 2003.
Andreas, A. T. *History of the State of Kansas.* Chicago: A. T. Andreas, 1883.
Andrews, William L., and Henry Louis Gates, Jr., eds. *Slave Narratives.* New York: Penguin Putman, 2000.
Athearn, Robert G. *In Search of Canaan: Black Migration to Kansas, 1879–80.* Lawrence: Regents Press of Kansas, 1978.

Bader, Robert Smith. *Prohibition in Kansas: A History.* Lawrence: University Press of Kansas, 1986.

Bartholomew, David M. *Pioneer Naturalist on the Plains: The Diary of Elam Bartholomew, 1871 to 1934.* Manhattan, Kans.: Sunflower University Press, 1998.

Baugh, John. *Out of the Mouths of Slaves: African American Language and Educational Malpractice.* Austin: University of Texas Press, 1999.

Beecher, Lowell. *The Spring Creek Valley.* Hill City, Kans.: L. Beecher, 2009.

Berlin, Ira. *Slaves without Masters: The Free Negro in the Antebellum South.* New York: Free Press, 1974.

Billington, Monroe Lee, and Roger D. Hardaway, eds. *African Americans on the Western Frontier.* Boulder: University Press of Colorado, 1998.

Blackmar, Frank W. *Kansas: A Cyclopedia of State History.* Chicago: Standard Publishing, 1912.

Blassingame, John W. *Slave Testimony: Two Centuries of Letters, Speeches, Interviews, and Autobiographies.* Baton Rouge: Louisiana State University Press, 1977.

Blight, David W. *Race and Reunion: The Civil War in American Memory.* Cambridge, Mass.: Harvard University Press, 2001.

Bright, John D. *Kansas: The First Century.* New York: Lewis Historical Publishing, 1956.

Brooks, Roy L. *Integration or Separation? A Strategy for Racial Equality.* Norman: University of Oklahoma Press, 2011.

Burden, Don, Heather Lee Miller, Paul Sadin, and Dawn Vogel. *Historical Resources Study: Nicodemus National Historic Site.* National Park Service, Department of the Interior, 2011.

Campney, Brent M.S. *This Is Not Dixie: Racist Violence in Kansas, 1861–1927.* Champaign: University of Illinois Press, 2015.

Chalmers, David M. *Hooded Americanism: The History of the Ku Klux Klan.* Durham: Duke University Press, 1987.

Chu, Daniel, and Bill Shaw. *Going Home to Nicodemus: The Story of an African American Frontier Town and the Pioneers Who Settled It.* Morristown, N.J.: Silver Burdett, 1994.

Cohen, William. *At Freedom's Edge: Black Mobility and the Southern White Quest for Racial Control.* Baton Rouge: Louisiana State University Press, 1991.

Conrad, Peter. *The Sociology of Health and Illness: Critical Perspectives.* New York: Worth, 2008.

Cox, Thomas C. *Blacks in Topeka, Kansas, 1865–1915.* Baton Rouge: Louisiana State University Press, 1982.

Crockett, Norman. *The Black Towns.* Lawrence: Regents Press of Kansas, 1979.

Crothers, William L. *American-Built Packets and Freighters of the 1850s: An Illustrated Study of Their Characteristics and Construction.* Jefferson, N.C.: McFarland, 2013.

Cutler, William G. *History of the State of Kansas*. Chicago: A. T. Andreas, 1883.
Dary, David. *Red Blood and Black Ink: Journalism in the Old West*. New York: Alfred A. Knopf, 1998.
Davis, Kenneth S. *Kansas: A Bicentennial History*. New York: W. W. Norton, 1976.
DeArment, Robert K. *Ballots and Bullets: The Bloody County Seat Wars of Kansas*. Norman: University of Oklahoma Press, 2006.
Dew, Charles B. *Bond of Iron: Master and Slave at Iron Forge*. New York: W. W. Norton, 1994.
Dick, Everett. *The Sod House Frontier, 1854–1890: A Social History of the Northern Plains from the Creation of Kansas and Nebraska to the Admission of the Dakotas*. Lincoln, Nebr.: Johnsen, 1954.
Du Bois, W. E. B. *Black Reconstruction in America, 1860–1880*. New York: Atheneum, 1992.
———. *The Souls of Black Folks*. New York: Penguin, 1969.
———. *The Suppression of the African Stave-Trade to the United States of America, 1638–1870*. Mineola, N.Y.: Dover.
Etulain, Richard W. *Does the Frontier Experience Make America Exceptional?* Boston: Bedford/St. Martins, 1999.
Fesler, Myrtle D. *Pioneers of Western Kansas*. New York: Carlton Press, 1962.
Foner, Eric. *A Short History of Reconstruction, 1863–1877*. New York: Harper & Row, 1990.
Franklin, Jimmie Lewis. *The Blacks in Oklahoma*. Norman: University of Oklahoma Press, 1980.
Frazier, Thomas R. *Readings in African-American History*. Belmont, Calif.: Wadsworth/Thompson, 2001.
Gaspar, David Barry, and Darlene Clark Hine, eds. *More Than Chattel: Black Women and Slavery in the Americas*. Bloomington: Indiana University Press, 1996.
Gates, Henry Louis. *Africana: The Encyclopedia of the African and African-American Experience*. New York: Oxford University Press, 2005.
Genovese, Eugene D. *Roll, Jordan Roll: The World the Slaves Made*. New York: Vintage Books, 1976.
Glasrud, Bruce A., and Cary D. Wintz. *The Harlem Renaissance in the American West: The New Negro's Western Experience*. New York: Routledge, 2012.
Glasrud, Bruce A., and Charles A. Braithwaite, eds. *African Americans on the Great Plains: An Anthology*. Lincoln: University of Nebraska Press, 2009.
Glasrud, Bruce A., and Laurie Champion. *The African American West: A Century of Short Stories*. Boulder: University of Colorado Press, 2000.
Gordon, Taylor. *Born to Be*. Lincoln: University of Nebraska Press, 1995.
Hahn, Steven. *A Nation under Our Feet: Black Political Struggles in the Rural South from Slavery to the Great Migration*. Cambridge, Mass.: Harvard University Press, 2003.

Hall, Charles E. *The American Negro, His History and Literature: Negroes in the United States, 1920–1932.* New York: Arno Press, 1969.

Haviland, Laura Smith. *A Woman's Life Work: Including Thirty Years' Service on the Underground Railroad and in the War,* 5th ed. Grand Rapids, Mich.: L. B. Shaw, 1881.

Hayden, Ruth Kelley. *The Time That Was: The Courageous Acts and Accounts of Rawlins County, Kansas 1875–1915.* Colby, Kans.: Colby Community College, 1973.

Haywood, C. Robert. *Cowtown Lawyers: Dodge City and Its Attorneys, 1876–1886.* Norman: University of Oklahoma Press, 1988.

Hine, Darlene Clark, William C. Hine, and Stanley Harrold. *The African-American Odyssey.* Upper Saddle River, N.J.: Prentice Hall, 2002.

Hoogenboom, Ari A. *The Presidency of Rutherford B. Hayes.* Lawrence: University Press of Kansas, 1988.

Ise, John. *Sod and Stubble*: *The Story of a Kansas Homestead.* Lincoln: University of Nebraska Press, 1936.

Jack, Bryan M. *The St. Louis African American Community and the Exodusters.* Columbia: University of Missouri Press, 2007.

Katz, William Loren. *Black West: A Documentary and Pictorial History of the African American Role in the Westward Expansion of the United States.* New York: Harlem Moon, 2005.

Lemann, Nicholas. *The Promised Land: The Great Black Migration and How It Changed America.* New York: Alfred A. Knopf, 1991.

Lhamon, W. T., Jr. *Raising Cain: Blackface Performance from Jim Crow to Hip Hop.* Cambridge, Mass.: Harvard University Press, 1998.

Locke, Alain, ed. *The New Negro*: *An Interpretation.* New York: Atheneum, 1968.

Loewen, James W. *Sundown Towns: The Hidden Dimension of American Racism.* New York: New Press, 2005.

Logan, Onnie Lee. *Motherwit: An Alabama Midwife's Story.* New York: Dutton, 1991.

Mack, Dwayne A. *Black Spokane: The Civil Rights Struggle in the Inland Northwest.* Norman: University of Oklahoma Press, 2014.

Mathews, John Joseph. *The Osages: Children of the Middle Waters.* Norman: University of Oklahoma Press, 1961.

McPherson, James M. *Battle Cry of Freedom*: The Civil War Era: New York: Ballantine Books, 1988.

———. *What They Fought For: 1861–1865.* New York: Anchor Books, 1995.

Meyers, Burton D. *The History of Medical Education in Indiana.* Bloomington: Indiana University Press, 1956.

Miller, Nyle H., Edgar Langsdorf, and Robert W. Richmond. *Kansas in Newspapers.* Topeka: Kansas State Historical Society, 1963.

Miner, Craig. *Kansas: The History of the Sunflower State, 1854–2000*. Lawrence: University Press of Kansas, 2002.

———. *West of Wichita: Settling the High Plains of Kansas, 1865–1890*. Lawrence: University Press of Kansas, 1986.

Morrison-Reed, Mark D., and Jacqui James, ed. *Been in the Storm So Long*. Boston: Skinner House Books, 1991.

Moulton, Candy. *The Writer's Guide to Everyday Life in the Wild West: 1840–1900*. Cincinnati: Writer's Digest Books, 1999.

Nicodemus National Historical Site, Graham County, Kansas: Cultural Landscape Report. Prepared for National Park Service, Midwest Regional Office, Omaha, Nebraska. Charlottesville, Va.: OCULUS, 2003.

Northrup, David. *The Atlantic Slave Trade*. Boston: Houghton Mifflin, 2002.

Oringderff, Barbara. *True Sod*. North Newton, Kans.: Mennonite Press, 1976.

Painter, Nell Irvin. *Exodusters: Black Migration to Kansas after Reconstruction*. New York: Alfred A. Knopf, 1977.

———. *Sojourner Truth: A Life, a Symbol*. New York: W. W. Norton, 1996.

Porter, Kenneth W. *The Negro on the American Frontier*. New York: Arno Press, 1971.

Promised Land on the Solomon: Black Settlement at Nicodemus, Kansas. Washington, D.C.: Government Printing Office, 1984.

Ravage, John. *Black Pioneers: Images of the Black Experience on the North American Frontier*. Salt Lake City: University of Utah Press, 1997.

Reed, Christopher Robert. *Black Chicago's First Century*, vol. 1, *1833–1900*. Columbia: University of Missouri Press, 2005.

Richmond, Robert W. *Kansas: A Land of Contrasts*. Arlington Heights, Ill.: Forum Press, 1989.

———. *Requisite Learning and Good Moral Character: A History of the Kansas Bench and Bar*. Topeka: Kansas Bar Association, 1982.

Riley, Glenda. *The Female Frontier*. Lawrence: University Press of Kansas, 1988.

Ruede, Howard. *Sod-House Days: Letters from a Kansas Homesteader, 1877–78*. Lawrence: University Press of Kansas, 1983.

Rummel, Jack, and G. S. Prentzas. *African-American Social Leaders and Activists*. New York: Facts on File, 2011.

Schellenberg, James A. *Conflict between Communities: American County Seat Wars*. New York: Paragon House, 1987.

Shortridge, James R. *Peopling the Plains: Who Settled Where in Frontier Kansas*. Lawrence: University Press of Kansas, 1995.

Socolofsky, Homer E. *Kansas Governors*. Lawrence: University Press of Kansas, 1990.

Socolofsky, Homer E., and Huber Self. *Historical Atlas of Kansas*. Norman: University Press of Oklahoma, 1972.

Stampp, Kenneth M. *The Peculiar Institution: Slavery in the Ante-Bellum South*. New York: Vintage Books, 1989.

Sterling, Dorothy, ed. *We Are Your Sisters: Black Women in the Nineteenth Century.* New York: W. W. Norton, 1984.
Stuewe, Paul K., ed. *Kansas Revisited: Historical Images and Perspectives.* Lawrence: University of Kansas Press, 2004.
Talmage, T. DeWitt. *American Commerce and the New Orleans Exposition.* New York, 1884.
Taylor, Quintard. *In Search of the Racial Frontier: African Americans in the American West.* New York: W. W. Norton, 1998.
Taylor, Quintard, and Shirley Ann Wilson Moore, eds. *African American Women Confront the West, 1600–2000.* Norman: University of Oklahoma Press, 2003.
Terborg-Penn, Rosalyn. *African American Women in the Struggle for the Vote, 1850–1920.* Bloomington: Indiana University Press, 1998.
Trotter, Joe William, Jr. *The African American Experience.* Boston: Houghton Mifflin, 2001.
Vanepps-Taylot, Betti. *Forgotten Lives: African Americans in South Dakota.* Pierre: South Dakota Historical Society, 2008.
Webb, Walter Prescott. *The Great Frontier.* Boston: Houghton Mifflin, 1952.
Weiner, Marli F. *Mistresses and Slaves: Plantation Women in South Carolina, 1830–80.* Urbana: University of Illinois Press, 1998.
Woods, Randall Bennett. *A Black Odyssey: John Lewis Waller and the Promise of American Life, 1878–1900.* Lawrence: Regents Press of Kansas, 1981.
Wright, J. Earnest, and Laurence A. Glasco. *The WPA History of the Negro in Pittsburgh.* Pittsburgh: University of Pittsburgh Press, 2004.
Wright, Richard R. *Centennial Encyclopaedia of the African Methodist Episcopal Church.* Philadelphia: Book Concern of the African Methodist Episcopal Church, 1916.
Zornow, William Frank. *Kansas: A History of the Jayhawk State.* Norman: University of Oklahoma Press, 1957.

Articles

Berardi, Gayle K., and Thomas W. Segady, "The Development of African American Newspapers in the American West, 1880–1914." In *African Americans on the Western Frontier.* Edited by Monroe Lee Billington and Roger D. Hardaway, 217–30. Boulder: University Press of Colorado.
"Bruce, Blanche Kelso." History, Art and Archives, U.S. House of Representatives. http://history.house.gov/People/Detail?id=10029.
Campney, Brent M. S. "W. B. Townsend and the Struggle against Racist Violence in Leavenworth." *Kansas History* 4 (Winter 2008–2009): 261–73.
———. "'This Is Not Dixie': The Imagined South, the Kansas Free State Narrative, and the Rhetoric of Racist Violence." *Southern Spaces*, September 6, 2007. www.southernspaces.org/.

Carper, James C. "The Popular Ideology of Segregated Schooling: Attitudes toward the Education of Black in Kansas, 1854–1900." *Kansas History* 1 (Winter 1978–79): 254–65.

Chafe, William H. "The Negro and Populism: A Kansas Case Study." *Journal of Southern History* 3 (August 1968): 402–19.

Cheatam, Gary L. "'Slavery All the Time, or Not at All': The Wyandotte Constitution Debate, 1859–1861." *Kansas History* 3 (Autumn 1998): 168–87.

Cunningham, Roger D. "Douglas's Battery at Fort Leavenworth: The Issue of Black Officers during the Civil War." *Kansas History* 4 (Winter 2000): 200–17.

Dale, Kittie. "'Ballad of Nicodemus': Kansas Town's Theme." *Wichita Eagle Magazine*, August 21, 1960: 14, 22.

Dann, Martin. "From Sodom to the Promised Land: E. P. McCabe and the Movement for Oklahoma Colonization." *Kansas Historical Quarterly* 40 (Autumn 1974): 370–78.

Davis, Damani. "Exodus to Kansas: The 1880 Senate Investigation of the Beginnings of the African American Migration from the South." *Prologue* 40, no. 2 (Summer 2008). www.archives.gov/publications/prologue/2008/summer/exodus.html.

Davis, Theodore. "A Stage Ride to Colorado." *Harpers New Monthly Magazine*, July 1867: 137–50.

"Eagleson, William Lewis (1835–1899)." *African American History in the American West: Online Encyclopedia of Significant People and Places*, BlackPast.org, www.blackpast.org/aaw/eagleson-william-lewis-1835-1899.

"Eagleson, William Lewis (1835–1899)." *Online Encyclopedia*. http://encyclopedia.jrank.org/articles/pages/4225/Eagleson-William-Lewis-1835–1899.

"Elam Bartholomew." *Kansapedia*, Kansas Historical Society, www.kshs.org/kansapedia/elam-bartholomew/18648.

Farmer, Antoinette Broussard. "Craig, Lulu Sadler." Antoinettebroussard.com, http://antoinettebroussard.com/pdfs/LuluSadlerCraig.pdf.

Fenner, Theodosia E. "Black Leadership in 1889." In *Oklahoma's Historical Edition*, vol. 3. Edited by Cecil E. Ritter and Dessie M. Ritter. Oklahoma City, C. E. Ritter, 1982.

Finke, David H. "Introducing Chicago Area Quakers." Street Corner Society. www.strecorsoc.org/docs/chicago.html.

Fly, La Barbara W. "Into the Twentieth Century." In *Promised Land on the Solomon: Black Settlement at Nicodemus, Kansas*, 65–83. Washington, D.C.: Government Printing Office, 1974.

Fraser, Clayton. "Nicodemus: The Architectural Development and Decline of an American Town." In *Promised Land on the Solomon: Black Settlement at Nicodemus, Kansas*, 35–65. Washington, D.C.: Government Printing Office, 1984.

"Frederick Douglass: A Powerful Voice for Abolition and Equal Rights." Louisville Free Public Library. http://www.lfpl.org/western/htms/douglass.htm.

Garvin, Roy. "Benjamin or 'Pap' Singleton and His Followers." *Journal of Negro History* 33 (January 1948): 7–23.
Gates Henry Louis Gates, Jr. "The Truth behind '40 Acres and a Mule.'" *Root*, January 13, 1013. www.theroot.com/.
Hamilton, Kenneth Marvin. "The Origins and Early Promotion of Nicodemus: A Pre-Exodus All-Black Town." *Kansas History* 4 (Winter 1982): 220–42.
———. "The Settlement of Nicodemus: Its Origins and Early Promotion." In *Promised Land on the Solomon* (Washington, D.C.: Department of the Interior, 1984), 1–32.
Hardwick, M. Jeff. "Homesteads and Bungalows: African-American Architecture in Langston, Oklahoma." *Perspectives in Vernacular Architecture* 6 (1997): 21–32.
"Harvesting the River." Illinois State Museum, www.museum.state.il.us/RiverWeb/harvesting/transportation/boats/steamboats.html.
Hinger, Charlotte. "Black Renaissance in Helena and Laramie: Hatched on Top of the Rocky Mountains." In *The Harlem Renaissance in the American West.* Edited by Bruce A. Glasrud and Cary D. Wintz, 201–212. New York: Routledge, 2013.
———. "'The Colored People Hold the Key': Abram Thompson Hall Jr.'s Campaign to Organize Graham County." *Kansas History* 31 (Spring 2008): 32–47.
———. "Nicodemus: The Promised Land." *Witness* (Episcopal Church Publishing, Detroit) 75 (September 1992): 18–19.
———. "Pioneer Editors: The Alchemists of the Prairie." *Kansas Territorial* 3 (March 1983): n.p.
Hoeflich, Michael H. "Why the History of Kansas Law Has Not Been Written." *Kansas History* 26 (Winter 2003–2004): 264–71.
Leforge, Judy Bissell. "Alabama's Colored Conventions and the Exodus Movement, 1871–1879." *Alabama Review* 61, no. 1 (January 2010): 3–29.
Leiker, James N. "Race Relations in the Sunflower State." *Kansas History* 25 (Autumn 2002): 204–36.
Morse, Scott N. "'Knowledge is Power': The Reverend Grosvenor Clarke Morse's Thoughts on Free Schools and the Republic During the Civil War." *Kansas History* 1 (Spring 2008): 2–13.
O'Brien, Claire. "'With One Mighty Pull': Interracial Town Boosting in Nicodemus, Kansas." *Great Plains Quarterly* 16 (Spring 1996): 117–29.
Pickering, I. Q. "The Administration of John P. St. John." *Kansas Historical Collections* 9 (1906): 385–86.
Rice, Marc. "Frompin' in the Great Plains: Listening and Dancing to the Jazz Orchestras of Alphonso Trent, 1925–1944." In *African Americans on the Great Plains.* Edited by Bruce A. Glasrud and Charles A. Braithwaite, 256–72. Lincoln: University of Nebraska Press, 2009.
Roberson, Jere W. "Edward P. McCabe and the Langston Experiment." *Chronicles of Oklahoma* 51 (Fall 1973): 343–55.

Schwendemann, Glen. "Nicodemus: Negro Haven on the Solomon." *Kansas Historical Quarterly* 34 (Spring 1968): 10–31.
Scott, Steven L. "Great Plains Hamlet County Seat." *Heritage of the Great Plains* 19 (Spring 1986): 1–14.
Sheridan, Richard B. "Charles Henry Langston and the African American Struggle in Kansas." *Kansas History* 4 (Winter 1999): 268–83.
Socolofsky, Homer. "County Seat Wars in Kansas." *Trail Guide* 9 (1964): 1–25.
Taylor, Alrutheus A. "Negro Congressmen a Generation After." *Journal of Negro History* 7 (April 1922): 127–71.
"Tribal History." Prairie Band Potawotami Nation, n.d. www.pbpindiantribe.com/tribal-history.aspx.
Turner, Frederick Jackson. "The Significance of the Frontier in American History." In *Does the Frontier Experience Make America Exceptional?* Edited by Richard Etulain, 17–43. Boston: Bedford/St. Martin's, 1999.
Van Deusen, John G. "The Exodus of 1879." *Journal of Negro History* 21 (April 1936): 111–29.
Watts, Dale E. "How Bloody Was Bleeding Kansas? Political Killings in Kansas Territory, 1854–1861." *Kansas History* 3 (Summer 1995): 116–29.
Williams, Nudie E. "Black Newspapers and the Exodusters of 1879." *Kansas History* 4 (Winter 1985): 217–25.
Wilson, Don W. "Barbed Words on the Frontier: Early Kansas Newspapers." *Kansas History* 3 (Autumn 1978): 147–54.
Windom, William, and Henry W. Blair. "The Proceedings of a Migration Convention and Congressional Action Respecting the Exodus of 1879." *Journal of Negro History* 4 (January 1919): 51–92.
Wood, Forrest G. "On Revising Reconstruction History: Negro Suffrage, White Disfranchisement, and Common Sense." *Journal of Negro History* 51 (April 1966): 98–113.
Woods, Randall B. "After the Exodus: John Lewis Waller and the Black Elite, 1878–1900." *Kansas History* 2 (Summer 1977): 172–92.
———. "C. H. J. Taylor and the Movement for Black Political Independence, 1882–1896." *Journal of Negro History* 67, no. 2 (Summer 1982), 122–35.
———. "Integration, Exclusion or Segregation? The Color Line in Kansas, 1878–1900." In *African Americans on the Western Frontier.* Edited by Monroe Lee Billington and Roger D. Hardaway, 128–47. Boulder: University Press of Colorado, 1998.
Worrall, Henry. "Exoduster Illustrations." *Harper's Weekly*, July 5, 1879.

Theses and Dissertations

Aiken, Earl Howard. "Kansas Fever." Master's thesis, Louisiana State University, 1939.

Belleau, William J. "The Nicodemus Colony of Graham County, Kansas." Master's thesis, Fort Hays State Kansas State College, 1943.
Blake, Lee Ella. "The Great Exodus of 1879 and 1880 to Kansas." Bachelor of Science thesis, Kansas State College, Manhattan, Kansas, 1942.
Chartrand, Robert Lee. "The Negro Exodus from the Southern States to Kansas, 1869–1886." Master's thesis, University of Kansas City, 1949.
McDaniel, Orval L. "A History of Nicodemus, Graham County, Kansas." Master's thesis, Fort Hays Kansas State College, 1950.
Schwendemann, Glen. "Negro Exodus to Kansas: First Phase, March–July, 1879." Master's thesis, University of Oklahoma, 1957.
Shaw, Van Burton. "Nicodemus, Kansas: A Study in Isolation." PhD diss., University of Missouri, 1951.
Tolson, Arthur Lincoln. "The Negro in Oklahoma Territory, 1889–1907: A Study in Racial Discrimination." PhD diss., University of Oklahoma, 1966.
Waldron, Nell B. "Colonization in Kansas." PhD diss., Northwestern University, 1932.

Lectures

Bates, Angela. "People of Nicodemus." Black History Month lecture, Fort Hays State University, February 2004.
Siegrist, Ruth A. "Nicodemus." Paper presented at regional Daughters of the American Revolution meeting, Russell, Kansas, May 15, 1982. Located at Graham County Historical Society.

Websites

Kansas Historical Society, www.kshs.org
Kentucky Educational Television, www.ket.org
Minnesota Council on Foundations, www.mcf.org
RootsWeb, www.rootsweb.ancestry.com

Newspapers

Abilene Reflector, 1883–88
American Citizen (Topeka), 1888–1909
American Desert (Millbrook, Kans.), April 1, 1887–June 1, 1887
Anthony (Kans.) Journal, 1879–1925
Arkansas Gazette (Little Rock), 1886–89
Arkansas Weekly Mansion (Little Rock), 1880–84
Atchison (Kans.) Daily Champion, January 1, 1877–December 31, 1890
Atlanta Constitution, 1876–2001
Augusta (Ga.) Chronicle, 1884–present
Benevolent Banner (Topeka), May 21, 1887–October 22, 1887
Bogue (Kans.) Signal, November 29, 1888–November 28, 1890

Boston Herald, 1846–1917
Bridgeton (N.J.) Evening News, 1879–present
Buffalo Park (Kans.) Express, June 3, 1880–July 23, 1881
Buffalo Park (Kans.) Pioneer, April 16, 1885–December 1, 1887
Bull City (Kans.) Post, January 22, 1880–June 24, 1880
Canton (Ohio) Repository, 1878–1913
Chicago Conservator, January 1, 1878–????
Cleveland (Ohio) Leader, 1855–1891
Colored American (Washington, D.C.) 1893–19??
Colored Citizen (Fort Scott, Kans.), April 19, 1878–July 5, 1878
Colored Citizen (Topeka), July 26, 1878–December 31, 1879
Colored Patriot (Topeka), April 20, 1882–June 20, 1882
Commonwealth (Topeka), January 1, 1877–December 31, 1888
Daily Democrat (New Orleans), 1877–80
Daily Illinois State Register (Springfield), 1855–91
Daily Inter Ocean (Chicago), 1879–1902
Dallas (Tex.) Daily Herald, 1873–87
Downs (Kans.) Times, February 19, 1880–June 25, 1890
Ellis County Star (Ellis, Kans.), April 6, 1876–March 21, 1878
Ellis (Kans.) Headlight, May 21, 1881–November 18, 1890
Emporia (Kans.) Daily News, 1878–87
Fort Scott (Kans.) Daily Tribune, 1884–1904
Freeman (New York City), 1884–85
Gate City Press (Kansas City, Mo.), 1880–89
Gaylord (Kans.) Herald, September 4, 1879–February 11, 1892
Golden Belt Advance (Grainfield, Kans.), July 21, 1881–September 10, 1881
Graham County Democrat (Millbrook, Kans.), October 22, 1885–January 14, 1889
Graham County Lever (Gettysburg, Kans.), August 2, 1879–June 10, 1881
Graham Republican (Millbrook, Kans.), August 6, 1881–January 7, 1882
Grainfield (Kans.) Republican, January 28, 1880–December 9, 1880
Harrison (Ark.) Times, 1876–1938
Hays City Sentinel (Hays, Kans.), January 26, 1876–May 27, 1890
Herald of Kansas (Topeka), February 13, 1880–June 11, 1880
Hill City (Kans.) Democrat, July 2, 1887–April 25, 1889
Hill City (Kans.) Lively Times, June 16, 1881–July 28, 1881
Hill City (Kans.) Reveille, August 8, 1884–24 November 24, 1888
Hill City (Kans.) Star, August 2, 1888–April 18, 1889
Huntington (W.Va.) Advertiser, 1874–1921
Independent (Smith Center and Harlan, Kans.), December 22, 1879–November 19, 1880
Iola (Kans.) Register, 1875–1902

Junction City (Kans.) Tribune, 1873–1902
Kansas City Evening News, March 17, 1887–October 3, 1890
Kansas City (Mo.) Times, 1867–90
Kansas Democrat (Topeka), 1886–93
Kansas Free Press (Smith Center, Kans.), October 3, 1879–December 30, 1881
Kansas Herald (Hiawatha) 1878–83
Kansas Jewelite (Mankato, Kans.), 1882–84
Kentucky Gazette (Lexington), January 1, 1877–December 31, 1880
Kirwin (Kans.) Chief, 1874–91
Langston City (Okla. Terr.) Herald, May, 1891–1902
Lawrence (Kans.) Journal, 1885–1911
Leavenworth (Kans.) Advocate, 1889–91
Leavenworth (Kans.) Colored Radical, August 24, 1876–November 16, 1876
Leavenworth (Kans.) Daily Times, 1870–80
Leavenworth (Kans.) Weekly Public Press, 1877–79
Lenora (Kans.) Leader, March 16, 1882–August 30, 1888
Logan (Kans.) Enterprise, 1879–84
Logansport (Ind.) Journal, 1876–78
Macon (Ga.) Telegraph, 1831–1905
Manhattan (Kans.) Enterprise, 1876–1907
Millbrook (Kans.) Herald, May 16, 1882–May 30, 1888
Millbrook (Kans.) Times, July 11, 1879–April 19, 1889
Ness County Pioneer (Clarinda, Kans.), 1879–90
New Haven Evening Register, 1874–1968
New Orleans Observer, 1878
News (Stockton, Kans.), May 3, 1882–March 21, 1883
New York Age, 1887–1953
New York Herald, 1865–1924
New York Globe, 1883–84
New York Times, 1822–present
New York Witness, 1872–88
Nicodemus (Kans.) Cyclone, December 30, 1887–November 7, 1888
Nicodemus (Kans.) Enterprise, August 17, 1887–December 23, 1887
North Topeka Times (Topeka), 1876–83
Norton County Advance (Norton, Kans.), June 6, 1878–November 22, 1882
Norton County Bee (Norton, Kans.), May 7, 1877 (single issue)
Norton County People (Norton, Kans.), July 15, 1880–February 1, 1883
Norton (Kans.) Courier, February 8, 1883–December 25, 1890
Osborne County Farmer (Osborne, Kans.), January 14, 1876–June 25, 1891
Peck's Sun (Milwaukee), May 1, 1874-December 22, 1894
People's Advocate (Washington, D.C.), 1879–84?
Philadelphia (Pa.) Times, 1875–1902

Pittsburgh Gazette, 1863–present
Pittsburgh Post, 1887–1927
Pittsburgh Press, 1887–1992
Plainville (Kans.) News, May 4, 1881–April 26, 1882
Portis (Kans.) Patriot, December 8, 1881–March 29, 1890
Republican Daily Journal (Lawrence, Kans.), November 3, 1877-November 9, 1878
Rooks County Record (Stockton, Kans.), June 26, 1880–December 31, 1890
Roscoe (Kans.) Tribune, June 23, 1880–July 29, 1881
Salina Herald, February 16, 1867–January 30, 1891
Saline County Journal (Salina, Kans.), 1874–91
San Francisco Bulletin, 1855–95
Smith County Pioneer (Smith Center, Kans.), July 27, 1878–May 29, 1885
Squatter Sovereign (Atchison, Kans.), February 3, 1855–December 5, 1857
Star-Sentinel (Hays, Kans.), January 26, 1882–May 6, 1886
St. Louis Globe Democrat, 1852–1986
Stockton (Kans.) News, April 20, 1876–April 20, 1881
Stockton (Kans.) Record, December 6, 1879–June 19, 1880
Summit County Beacon (Akron, Ohio), 1857–1910
Sun (San Diego), 1881–1939
Thomas County Cat (Colby, Kans.), 1885–91
Times-Picayune (New Orleans), 1848–present
Topeka Capital, January 1, 1877–December 31, 1880
Topeka Plaindealer, 1899–1907
Topeka Tribune, June 24, 1880–September 13, 1884
Topeka Weekly Times, 1872–83
Truth Teller (Osborne, Kans.), October 3, 1879–February 23, 1881
Valley Falls (Kans.) New Era, 1880–1916
Vicksburg (Miss.) Herald, 1867–84
WaKeeney (Kans.) Weekly World, 1879–85
Weekly Kansas Chief (Troy, Kans.), 1872–1918
Western Cyclone (Nicodemus, Kans.), May 13, 1886–November 30, 1887
Western News (Stockton, Kans.), July 11, 1883–July 4, 1888
Western Recorder (Lawrence, Kans.), March 17, 1883–November 6, 1884
Western Star (Hill City, Kans.), May 22, 1879–June 10, 1880
Wheeling (W.Va.) Register, 1863–1913
Wichita City Eagle, 1872–83
Wichita Daily Eagle, 1883–90
Wichita Globe, February 17, 1887–October 29, 1887
Winfield (Kans.) Daily Courier, 1873–1919
Worcester (Mass.) Evening Gazette, 1866–1907

Index

References to illustrations appear in italics.

Abilene Reflector, 194, 195
accidents, fatal, 61, 65
Adams, Henry, 26, 27, 29, 39, 98–99
advertising and publicity campaigns, 3, 12, *13,* 16, 22, 53. *See also* flyers and posters
Africa, 98, 99, 222n16
African Methodist Episcopal Church, 18, 56, 70, 111, 144–45. *See also* St. John AME Church, Topeka
Afro-American State League (Kansas), 195
agriculture. *See* farms and farming
aid, charitable. *See* charity
Alabama, 3, 22, 30, 83–84, 86, 87, 88
alcohol prohibition. *See* prohibition
all-black states and territories (proposed), 14, 102, 196
all-black town, Arkansas (proposed), 161
Allen, A. J., 43, 78
Allen, E. B., 194
Allison, Thomas, 61
Allsap, Jerry, 35
AME Church. *See* African Methodist Episcopal Church
American Freedmen's Inquiry Commission, 20
American Indians, 48–49, 65, 96
Anderson, John, 35
Anderson, John A., 177
Anthony, George T., 64, 75
Anthony, Susan B., 183
anti-black violence. *See* racial violence
appointees, black. *See* black political appointees
Arkansas, 89, 161–65, 167

Arkansas Gazette, 162
Arthur, Chester, 165
Atchison, David, 64
Atchison, Topeka, and Santa Fe Railroad, 44, 197
Atchison Daily Champion, 12, 17, 50, 64, 191–92; Hall letters to, 64–65, 129; on McCabe candidacy, 189; on "Mrs. Senator Bruce," 79; on suffragists, 183; view of term limits, 181
Athearn, Robert G., 5, 24
atrocities, 34, 99
Auspitz, Emile, 27

Badger, R. C., 83
Banks, Cage, 43
Banks, John, 18, 19
Banks, J. W. S., 81, 102
banks and banking, 149, 158–60
Barnes, W. H., 158, 160
Bartholomew, Elam, 45, 213n18
Beaumont, Thomas, 51–52, 121–22, 135, 140, 173, 216n9
Beecher, Lowell, 155
Bell, Cyrus D., 103, 105, 106
Bell, Lew, 174
Bell, M. M., *13*
Belleau, William J., 5
Beloit, Kans., 52, 60
Berlin, Ira, 179
Best, Lewis, 59
Bible, 83, 91; as boom literature, 53
biracial people. *See* mixed-race people
bison. *See* buffalo
black appointees. *See* black political appointees

251

252 INDEX

black candidates for office, 70, 71, 76, 77, 78, 81, 82; McCabe, 170, 178–79, 181, 184, 187–89, 193–94
black elected officials: Kansas, 14, 19, 70, 192–95, 198; southern states, 3, 67–68, 78–79, 84–85, 103, 108, 166–67
black emigration, transnational. *See* transnational emigration, black
black expectations, 21, 25, 43, 49, 113, 115, 224n26
black geographic diffusion. *See* racial diffusion
black individual firsts, 7, 14, 56, 71, 79, 84, 144, 163, 192
black labor organizations and conventions, 22, 88
Blackman, Henry, 45, 65
black newspapers, 9, 97, 109, 164, 234n48. See also *Chicago Conservator*; *Colored Citizen*
black political appointees, 67, 74, 80, 81, 82, 146; Hall, 12, 20, 134–35, 137, 151; McCabe, 57, 142, 171–72, 175, 178, 196, 197; Niles, 149, 172, 176; Waller, 72
black separatism, 14, 102, 161, 171, 196
black states and territories (proposed). *See* all-black states and territories (proposed)
black voters, 12, 27, 74, 76, 82, 204; Eagleson appeal to, 79; Hall view, 77; repression, 67; W. R. Hill view, 38
Blaine, James, 193
Blair, Henry William, 4, 27, 28–29, 98, 199, 200–201
"Bleeding Kansas." *See* Kansas-Missouri border wars
Bliss, G. H., 195
Bogue, Kans., 92, 195, 204
Boles, Anderson, 35, 204
bonds, municipal, 37, 38, 128–29, 132, 134
Booker, Rankin, 35
Bosworth, M., 110
Bow Creek, 50, 58, 130
Bowers, F. E., 134, 173
Boyd, L. P., 140, 176, 177
Boyle, I. N., 173

Brewster, Benjamin Harris, 165
bribery, accusations of, 186–87, 192
Brookings, Philip, 42
Brown, Hugh, 35
Brown, John, 3, 24, 25, 108, 162
Brown, John Milton, 67–68, 88, 89–90, 114–15, 193, 194
Broussard, Antoinette, 7
Bruce, Blanche Kelso, 78–79, 103, 166–67
Bruce, Josephine Beall Wilson, 79
Bryant, Sarah. *See* McCabe, Sarah Bryant
Buchan, W. J., 170, 224n26
Buckner, Henry, 35
buffalo, 47, 48, 49, 61
Buffalo Park, Kans., 122
buildings: aid distribution centers, 119; churches, 69; communal, 52; county seats, 142–43; cyclone destruction of, 45; mills, 155–56; promised but lacking, 20, 43; schools, 93
Bullard, F., 173
Burch, John Henri, 88, 89, 96, 128
Bureau of Refugees, Freedmen, and Abandoned Lands. *See* Freedmen's Bureau
Burton, J. R., 194
Butterfield, Dr., 173
Butterfield Overland Despatch Express, 24–25, 126

Caldren, R. D., 123
Campney, Brent M. S., 26, 68
Carey, G. W., 137
Carlos, W. C. Don, 20, 59
Carr, Ben (or Beverly), 35, 211n14
Carter, John, 81
cattlemen and cattle ranching. *See* ranchers and ranching
censuses, 141; racial categories, 179, 180
census taker office, 12, 134, 135, 137–40, 144
Chafe, William H., 67
Chambers, W. L., 31–32; *Niles of Nicodemus*, 39–41, 148, 158, 163, 167
Champion. *See Atchison Daily Champion*

chaplain of Kansas legislature, 81
charity, 47–49, 62, 119, 125, 127; solicitation of, 55–56, 74, 115–16, 119, 120, 121, 122, 126
Chicago, 60; Hall in, 11, 14–15, 56, 84–85, 138, 143, 144, 154; McCabe in, 11, 171, 197
Chicago Conservator, 14–15, 143, 144, 154, 178, 181, 229n55
Christmas, 50
churches, 18, 62, 63, 64; Pittsburgh, 144–45; Salina, 47–48; St. Louis, 111; Topeka, 69–70, 77, 81, 84, 90
Civil Rights Act of 1875, 166
Civil Rights Cases (1883), 166, 167
Civil War, 48, 74, 110; black veterans of, 21, 111
Clarke, Daniel, *13*
clerkships: Graham County, 20, 59, 142, 149, 171–72, 175–78; Hall, 20, 59, 81, 144; McCabe, 56–57, 142, 171–72, 175–78; under McCabe, 149, 172, 176, 181; Niles, 149, 172, 176
Cleveland, Grover, 193
coal, 44, 61
colonists' expectations. *See* black expectations
Colored Citizen, 12, 60–61, 70, 78, 84, 99; cessation, 109; "colored convention" debate, 106; contributors, 80, 81, 103, 105; Douglass and, 100; Embry letters to, 71; Exodusters and, 111, 112, 114; Hall letters to, 61–62; Henderson role, 108; McCabe letters to, 81–82; Nicodemus Colony dissolution, 119–20; Republican state convention and elections of 1878, 70, 71, 74, 76–79; on school segregation, 90
Colored Colonization Society, 98
Colored Men's Conference, Nashville, 1879. *See* National Conference of Colored Men, Nashville, 1879
Colored Men's Convention, Kansas, 1880. *See* Kansas Convention for Colored Men, 1880

Colored Patriot, 181
Colored Refugee Relief Board, 111
color of skin. *See* skin color
Commonwealth (Topeka), 113–14, 115, 116, 117, 185
communal buildings and activities, 52
Compiled Laws of Kansas (Dassler), 142, 172
Compromise of 1877, 27, 211n2
Comstock, Elizabeth, 49, 117, *118*, 119
con artists. *See* swindlers and swindling
Conference of Colored Men, Nashville, 1879. See National Conference of Colored Men, Nashville, 1879
Congress, U.S. *See* U.S. Congress
constitutions, Kansas. *See* Kansas constitutions
Convention of Colored Men (Kansas), 1880. *See* Kansas Convention of Colored Men, 1880
convention of "colored men" (proposed), 105–6
convict labor, 30
Cooper, Hiram, 142
county seat contention, 128–43, 146, 151, 173–75, 178
Cox, Thomas, 70, 115
craftsmen. *See* skilled tradesmen
Craig, Lulu Sadler, 7–8, *8,* 14–15, 19–20, 30–32, 35, 58, *203;* on Christmas, 50; on darkness and heating, 46, 47; Hall and, 16, 59; on isolation of Nicodemus, 44–45; on McCabe's marriage, 177; on Niles, 147–48; reference to lone horse, 54
Craig, Nettie, 49
Crawford (postmaster), 174
Cummings, John, 34
Cummins, William, Jr., 51
currency, 74, 77
Currie, Andrew, 87
Cyclone. See Western Cyclone (Nicodemus Cyclone)

Daily Champion. See *Atchison Daily Champion*

dance party riot of 1880, Roscoe, Kans. *See* Roscoe, Kans.: riot of 1880
Dary, David, 42
Davis, John, 96, 154
Davis, Theodore, 24–25
Davis, Willard, 131, 141, 175
Decatur County, Kans., 157
Declaration of Independence, 63, 64, 69, 108, 117
DeFrantz, Alonzo D., 116
De Green, Caroline, 49, 113
Dell, V., 89
Democratic Party, 45, 80, 132; Kansas, 76, 77, 78, 82, 184, 190, 194, 195; Oklahoma, 197; southern states, 67–68, 89, 201–202
Denney, John C., 158–59
DePrad, John, 11, 35, 149, 152, 173, 175–76, 177
Dick, Everett, 178
Dickson, Moses, 111
Dodge, G. M., 173
Donahue, John J., 81
donations and gifts. *See* charity
Don Carlos, W. C. *See* Carlos, W. C. Don
Douglass, Frederick, 100, *101*, 163, 166
Dorsen, Ben, 35
Dorsey, George, 35, 65
Downing, J. H., 178, 191
draft animals, 48
Du Bois, W. E. B., 14, 30, 52, 77, 219n1
dugouts, 11, 15, 20, 48, 54, 65; design and construction, 46, 47; schools in, 93

Eagleson, James, 109
Eagleson, William L., 12, 70, 71–72, 78, 79, 99, 100, 102; and *Colored Citizen* cessation, 109; on Hall and McCabe, 74; in Oklahoma, 196; on Republican state convention of 1878, 76; on school segregation, 90; statehouse appointment, 81; view of "colored convention," 106; view of Exodusters, 111
Eckles, J. G., 81
Edmunds, William, 35

education, 83–95. *See also* public education
Eggers, L. F., 82
elected officials, black. *See* black elected officials
election fraud, 92
elections: Graham County, 132, 137–38, 142, 143, 152, 172, 173, 175–78; Kansas, 80, 82, 186–93; Mississippi, 68; national, 78, 142, 154, 193. *See also* black voters; third-term candidacy
Ellis, Kans., 37, 45, 46, 50, 58, 60, 62
Ellis County, Kans., 82
Ellis County Star, 35
Ellis Standard, 44
embezzlement charges, 173–74
Embry, J. C., 70–71, 76, 77, 80–81, 85, 102–3, 105
emigrant returns, 16, 42, 50, 121
Emigrants Relief Board, 137
emigration, transnational. *See* transnational emigration, black
employment, 49, 53, 60, 61, 74, 80; Indiana, 97
Emporia, Kans., 7, 32, 190, 195
escaped slaves. *See* fugitive slaves
Exodusters, 3, 7, 22, 34, 110–27, 149, 153, 172; Topeka, 70

farms and farming, 43, 45, 49, 56, 58, 61; Hall on, 62; range wars, 63–64; southern states, 98, 110
fatal accidents. *See* accidents, fatal
federal land offices, 20, 37, 59, 161
federal treasury. *See* U.S. Department of the Treasury
Federal Writers' Project, 144
fees, 37, 94, 172
Fifteenth Amendment, 25, 29
fires, 45, 65, 174
First Kansas Colored Regiment, 18
firsts, black individual. *See* black individual firsts
Fletcher, Jenny, 35, 93
Fletcher, Zachary T., 35, 58, 59, 63, 93, 151
flour, 58, 125; mills, 155–56

Fly, La Barbara W., 5
flyers and posters, 3, 32, *33*, 43, 45
food, 48, 49, 50, 52, 56, 58. *See also* game
Fort Hays, 65
Fort Ogallah, 49
Fort Scott, Kans., 62, 70
Fort Scott Tribune, 194
Fortune, T. Thomas, 164–65, 232n72
"forty acres and a mule," 49, 115, 224n26
Fountain, C., 176
Fourteenth Amendment, 90, 166
Fourth of July. *See* Independence Day
Fraser, Clayton, 5, 46
fraud, 14, 140; accusations of, 48, 119, 122, 126, 135, 141, 142, 172; in elections, 92; by Niles, 148, 158–59, 161; Voorhees Committee testimony on, 147
Freedmen's Bureau, 96, 221n6
Freedmen's Inquiry Commission, 20
Freemasons, 18, 78, 99, 100, 18, 78, 222n16
freemen-freedmen relations, 179, 180
fuel, 44, 46, 47, 61
fugitive slaves, 18, 91–92, 93, 117. *See also* Underground Railroad
Fulbright, L., 150
Furrow, Johnny, 52

game, 47, 50
Gandy, Henry, 51
Garfield, James, 142, 154; assassination, 161
Garland, Samuel, 204
geographic diffusion, racial. *See* racial diffusion
George, A. R., 123
Georgia, 3, 224n26
German Americans, 184, 187
Gettysburg, Kans., 129, 134, 135, 138–43, 151, 152, 157, 175
Gettysburg Lever, 38
gifts and donations. *See* charity
Gillespie, George E., 87
Glick, George Washington, 190, 191, 192
Gordon, James, 173
Gordon, Taylor, 66

Gossaway, Charles, 17
Gould, Jay, 122, 123, 125
Graham, John L., 74
Graham County Aid Association, 121, 122, 123
Graham County Lever, 125, 138, 140, 151–52, 157, 158, 174–75, 178
Graham County map, *17*
Graham County organization, 94, 121, 128–43, 151, 155, 173–75, 178
Graham County schools, 92–95
Grainfield, Kans., 121
grass fires, 45, 65
Graves, Benjamin B. F., 151, 153, 154, 157; county seat fight and, 133–34, 137, 146, 157, 175; Graham County clerkship and, 176–77; on Graham County Republicans, 151; on Hall, 138; Hall relations, 133; McCabe state auditor candidacy and election, 178, 188, 192; *Millbrook Times* launch, 132; on Niles, 153, 154, 160; Niles letter to, 162; on Roscoe riot, 157; view of aid to Exodusters, 121; view of Hill City fire, 174; view of McCabe, 172; view of race, 132
Greenback-Labor Party, 74, 77, 82, 132, 137, 154, 160, 226n17; Eagleson and, 78; federal elections, 80; Graves and, 151, 153, 154, 192; Kansas elections, 76, 190
Greene, Albert, 185
Greener, Richard T., 163

Hahn, Steven, 5, 21
Hall, Abram Thompson, Jr., 4–5, 9–12, 14–15, 18–20, 39, 204–5; as attorney, 59, 139–40; background, 56; census taker office, 12, 134, 135, 137–40, 144; in Chicago, 14, 178, 181; clerkships and clerkship candidacy, 59, 81, 144; conflict resolution, 55; Graham County organization, 128–41, 155, 173, 176; Graham County Republican convention, 173; "higher good of the Commonwealth," 79; on Kansas Convention of Colored Men, 179; letters,

Hall, Abram Thompson (cont.)
59, 61–65, 93, 119, 129, 130–31; later years, 57, 143–46, *145;* marriages and family, 143–46; McCabe compared, 171; on McCabe for state auditor, 178, 181, 191; McCabe partnership, 59, 65, 68, 93, 120, 171, 198; "Needs of the Race," 84, 85–86, 90; Nicodemus arrival, 11, 16, 19, 55; on Nicodemus schools, 92–93; oratory of, 18, 59; racial classification, 180; on Republican Party, 154–55, 179; Republican state convention of 1878, 74, 76, 77; Republican state convention of 1880, 151; in St. Louis, 143, 157; targeted in *Roscoe Tribune,* 176; in Topeka, 68, 69, 81; Townsend relations, 150; views of aid to Exodusters, 127, 119; views of black migration, 106; views of education, 84, 90; views of Niles, 148, 172; views of town company dissolution, 120

Hall, Abram Thompson, Sr., 56
Hall, Charles, 215n1
Hall, Louise, 145–46
Hall, Minnie, 143–45
Hamilton, J. H., 195
Hamilton, Kenneth Marvin, 5, 35, 37, 48, 149
handbills. *See* flyers and posters
Harlan, John Marshall, 166
Harper's New Monthly Magazine, 24
Harper's Weekly, 24, 112, 126
Harris, Bill, 58
Harris, Fred, 131
Harris, Grant, 11, 35, 203
Harrison, Benjamin, 196
Harwi, H. J., 160, 173
hat makers, 60
Haviland, Laura S., 117, *118,* 119
Hayden, Phillip, 11
Hayden, Ruth Kelley, 53
Hayes, Rutherford, 3, 98, 115
Hays City Sentinel, 38, 42–43, 44, 51, 60, 61
Hays Star-Sentinel. See Star-Sentinel

Helena, Ark., 161
Henderson, T. W., 71, 72, 74, 76, 81, 107–8
Henri, Kathyrne, 143
Henry, John, 135–36
Herald of Kansas, 109, 121
Herring, Beverly, 35, 211n14
Hickman, Daniel, 40, 47, 50–51, 52, 136, 148
Hickman, Willianna, 15, 47, 60
high school. *See* secondary education
Higinbotham, George E., 155
Hill, W. R., 30, 34–35, *36,* 37–38, 60, 147, 173–75; flyers, 43; public opinion, 44
Hill City, Kans., 37, 121, 123; in county seat fight, 129, 139, 140, 142, 143, 173–75; Graham County Republicans convention, 151–52. See also *Western Star*
Hillsdale, Kans., 38–39
Himes, James, 121
historiography, 5–6, 202
Hogue, H. S., 140, 151, 157
holidays, 50, 202–3. *See also* Independence Day
Holt, Joel, 186
homesteading, 20, 21, 24, 39, 115; fees, 30; Niles and, 161, 167; "proving up," 94, 112, 177; restrictions, 25. *See also* federal land offices
horses, 16, 38, 39, 54, 58; lack of, 47, 48; legal dispute over, 59
housing. *See* shelter
Howe, Samuel T., 194, 195
Hubbard, Phillip, 18
Hudson, J. K., 116
Humphreys, L. C., 76
hunger, 48, 49, 50
hunting, 47; American Indian, 48, 49. *See also* game

Illinois, 61, 63, 116
illiteracy. *See* literacy
Independence, Mo., 113
Independence Day, 63, 64, 71, 153
Indemnity Party, 161, 162, 163, 165, 166, 167

Indiana, 34, 56, 116; immigrants, 97
Indians. *See* American Indians
Ingalls, John James, 78, 79, 105, 115, 167, *168*, 194; Embry, relations with, 103, 105; St. John, relations with, 182
Ingram, L. W., 173
Inlow, John, 122, 123, 142, 171
integration and segregation, racial. *See* segregation and integration, racial
Iola Register, 187, 195
Iowa emigrants, 72, 159
Irish, 180, 187, 194
Irwin, George, 126
Ise, John, *Sod and Stubble,* 53

Jack, Byron M., 111
Jackson, Margaret, 35
Jackson, Peter, 45, 65
James, C. C., 77
Jefferson, Thomas (Kansas immigrant), 203
Jewellite, 184
Jews as model, 107
jobs. *See* employment
John, Thomas, 35, 203
Johnson, Andrew, 110, 224n26
Johnson, A. S., 44, 46
Johnson, Henry, 35, 62
Johnston, D. J., 159
Jones, J. Pennoyer, 164
Jones, William, *13*
Junction City, Kans., 60
Junction City Tribune, 96
justices of the peace, 59, 131

Kansas, national views of, 3, 24, 108, 112, 125, 126
Kansas Chief. See *Weekly Kansas Chief*
Kansas City, Kans. *See* Wyandotte, Kans.
Kansas City, Mo., 47, 62
Kansas City Times, 78–79
Kansas Colored State Immigration Bureau, 114
Kansas constitutions, 25, 89, 125, 184
Kansas Convention of Colored Men, 1880, 150, 151, 179

Kansas Freedmen's Relief Association (KFRA), 37, 108, 110, 114–15, 116, 117, 119
Kansas Herald, 109, 149–50, 224n40
Kansas House of Representatives, 81–82
Kansas Jewellite, 184
Kansas legislature, 90, 158; black candidates, 78; county naming and boundary-making, 128, 131, 141. *See also* Kansas House of Representatives
Kansas-Missouri border wars, 24, 48, 64, 125–26
Kansas-Nebraska Act, 24, 25
Kansas Pacific Railway 120, 122, 141
Kansas Relief Board, 49
Kansas state auditor position, 170, 178–79, 181, 184, 187–89, 192–95, 198
Kansas state motto, 43
Kebar District, 92, 93, 95
Keeney, James, 58
Kelley, William D., 195
Kellogg, Frank P., 142, 156, 157
Kent, Squire, 148, 149
Kentucky, 29–31; emigrants, 3, 12, 24, 29–32, 35, 37, 43, 45, 47, 91–92, 147; Hill in, 34–35; Lexington, 22, 32, 35; Niles endorsement claim, 17
Kerr, Louise Chaplin, 145–46
Kicking Bird (Milton W. Reynolds), 19
King Solomon Grand Lodge of the Prince Hall Masons, 18, 78, 100
Kirtley, Erasmus, 60
Kirtley, Raz, 47
Kirtley, William, 91
Kirwin, Kans., 20, 37, 69
Kirwin Chief, 60, 188
Knox, John D., 49

labor, convict, 30
labor organizations and conventions, black. *See* black labor organizations and conventions
labor supply, 29, 110, 112, 116
Landis, John, 51, 52, 136, 157, 227

land location business: Hall and McCabe, 59, 65, 68, 81, 93, 120, 171, 177; Singleton, 21, 22; Wall, 98
landlords, 85, 87, 199
land offices, federal. *See* federal land offices
landownership, 97, 202. *See also* homesteading
land redistribution, 21, 102, 110, 163, 169. *See also* all-black states and territories (proposed); "forty acres and a mule"
Lane, James H., 18
Langston, Charles Henry, 69, 72, 151, 194, 195, 196
Langston, John M., 196
Langston, Okla., 14, 196, 197
Langston City Herald, 196
Langston University, 14
Lawlis, Mrs., 38
Lawrence, Kans., 69, 72
Lawrence Journal, 78
Laws of Kansas (Dassler). *See Compiled Laws of Kansas* (Dassler)
lawsuits, 59, 140, 148–49, 197
Leavenworth, Kans., 18, 47, 68–69, 72, 102
Leavenworth Daily Times, 16–17, 74, 111–12, 125
Leavenworth Weekly Public Press, 81
Lee, Jerry, *13*
Lee, Silas, 35, 62, 119
Lee, Willis, 35
Lee Guards, 161
legal disputes. *See* lawsuits
Legate, James F., 158, 169, 191
Leiker, James N., 26, 111
Lemmon, Allen B., 94
Lenze, Jeff, 35
Lewis, Granville, 59, 151, 176
Lewis, J. A., 47
Lewis, John G., 84, 85, 88–89
Liberia, 98, 99, 222n16
lieutenant governor office, 70–72, 76, 194
lighting, 46
Lincoln, Abraham, 31–32, 49, 98, 183

Lincoln Institute, 110–11
Lindsey, Jefferson, 35
literacy, 7, 91–92, 149
literary societies, 69, 81, 84, 90
livestock, 37, 58, 61, 63–64, 203. *See also* ranchers and ranching
lobbying, 80, 102, 146, 195
Lockwood, J. H., 47
Logan Enterprise, 161
Louisiana, 3, 29, 84, 86–87, 88–89, 98
Lynch, John Roy, 108

markets and stores, 44–45, 46, 50, 52, 58, 63; wealth trumps race in, 84–85
Marlow, George F., 22
Martin, Jacob, 35, 54, 58
Martin, John A., 64–65, 75–76, 190, 194
Masons. *See* Freemasons
"massacre of colored people," Caddo Parish, La., 1868, 29
Matthews, John Joseph, 48
Matthews, William C., 193–94
Matthews, William Dominick, 18, 19, 78, 99, 100
McBreen, Tom, 154
McCabe, Edward Preston, 4–5, 9, 14–16, 72, 99, *124*, 149–52, 170–98, 204–5; accused of fraud, 135; as attorney, 59, 139–40, 141; in Chicago, 57; as county clerk, 142, 171–72, 175–78; in county seat fight, 131, 139, 141, 173; death and gravesite, 197; Eagleson calls upon, 106; early life, 170–71; Hall compared, 171; Hall partnership, 59, 65, 68, 93, 120, 171, 198; letter to *Colored Citizen,* 81–82; literary society talk, 84; marriage, 177; Nicodemus arrival, 11, 16, 19, 55; Nicodemus Colony dissolution, 120; Niles trial, 160; as notary public, 20, 123, 131, 171; racial advocacy via legislation and office, 5, 79, 127, 169, 171, 198; racial classification, 180; Republican state convention of 1878, 74, 76; *Roscoe Tribune* relations, 155; state auditor campaign and office, 26, 170, 178–79,

INDEX

181, 184, 187–89, 192–95, 198; St. John correspondence, 122–23, 125, 186; in Topeka, 68, 69, 81
McCabe, Sarah Bryant, 177, 192, 196, 197
McCarthy, Timothy, 194, 195
McComb, J. S., 132
McCoun, J. R., 173
McDaniel, Orval L., 5–6, 38, 49
McFadden, Samuel, 185
McFarland, R. W., 125
McGill, T. H., 135, 143
McGraw, R. W., 142
McNall, Scott G., 54
measles, 15
medical colleges, 56
Memphis and Little Rock Railway, 161
Meyers, Gilbert, 84
Meyers, Jerry, 93
Michigan, 116, 117
migrants' expectations. *See* black expectations
Miles, Maria, 35
Millbrook, Kans., 134, 135, 139–43, 151, 175, 178
Millbrook Herald, 189
Millbrook Times, 51–52, 121, 125, 154; on Hall, 138; on McCabe state auditor candidacy, 188–89; Niles and, 152–53; on race, 132–33
mills, 63, 155–56, 157
Miner, H. Craig, 12, 24, 43, 53, 126
Mississippi, 3, 30, 42, 43, 67–68, 78; press, 113, 117
Mississippi River, 37, 201
Missouri, 24, 25, 68; emigrants, 51, 52, 137, 190; Kansas border wars, 24, 48, 64, 125–26
Missouri River, 37, 68
Mitchell, D. P., 76
mixed-race people, 69, 78–79, 179–80; classification and terminology, 180
mob actions. *See* vigilantism
Mohler, Martin, 185, 187–88, 235n77
Morse, Grosvenor Clark, 86
Mort, A., 142

Moses, A. E., 142, 171
"mulatto" (census classification), 179, 180
municipal bonds. *See* bonds, municipal
municipal township organization. *See* township organization
murder, 50–51, 99, 110, 157
music, 42, 52, 69
Myers, Reverend, 93
Mzhickteno, William, 49

National Colored Colonization Society, 98
National Conference of Colored Men, Nashville, 1879, 105–9, 112
national press. *See* press, national
National Tribune, 143
Native Americans. *See* American Indians
"Needs of the Race, The" (Hall), 84, 85–86, 90
Nellis, D. C., 160
Ness County Pioneer, 138
Nevens, O. J., 142, 171–72
New, John C., 97
New England emigrants, 25, 52, 170–71, 202
New Era, 76
New Religion, A (Niles), 165–66, 167
newspapers, black. *See* black newspapers
newspapers, southern. *See* southern newspapers
newspapers and magazines, national. *See* press, national
New York Herald, 148, 162
New York State emigrants, 56, 132, 155, 170–71
Nicholas, W. T., 185
Nicodemus Cyclone. See Western Cyclone (Nicodemus Cyclone)
Nicodemus Enterprise, 9, 195
Nicodemus National Historic Site, 204
Nicodemus Town Company, 17–18; dissolution notice, 119–20, 172; fees and membership, 35, 37; officers, *13*, 16, 17, 35, 39, 45; prohibition of saloons, 198; promotional posters, *13*
Nicodemus Township, 131–33, 146, 151, 155, 172

Niles, John W., 4–5, 9, 16–17, 18–19, 127, 147–49, 151–67, 204–5; in Arkansas, 161–65, 167; Chambers on, 39–41; clerkship under McCabe, 149, 172, 176; as colony secretary, 13, 39; Craig view of, 39–40; Hall accusations against, 119, 148, 172; Legate and, 14, 158, 169, 191; *A New Religion,* 165–66, 167; Nicodemus Colony dissolution, 120; as night school teacher, 93; oration, 148, 149, 160–61, 163–64; racial classification, 180; as solicitor of donations, 16–19, 39, 40, 55–56, 74, 119, 148, 166; Townsend and, 74; in Washington, D.C., 163–67, 169
Niles of Nicodemus (Chambers), 39–41, 148, 158, 163, 167
North American Review, 105
North Carolina, 83, 97, 98, 99
Northern Cheyenne people, 65
North Topeka, Kans., 119, 126
North Topeka Times, 114
Norton, Kans., 157
Norton County, Kans., 51
notaries public, 20, 59, 123, 171, 210n17

O'Brien, Claire, 6
Ohio, 4, 79, 116, 167, 219n49
Ohio River, 16, 35, 37
Oklahoma, 14, 65, 196–97
Osage Indians, 48, 49
Osborne, Kans., 60, 187
Osborne County, Kans., 185
Osborne County Farmer, 235n77
Ottawa, Kans., 43

Page, Charles, 11, 35, 93
Page, Clarence, 93
Painter, Nell Irvin, 5, 20, 30, 80, 111, 156, 180
Panic of 1873, 110
paper money. *See* currency
Parlor, Edward, 34
patriotism, 64, 69, 153
patronage, political, 72, 74, 196

Patterson, Joe, 61
pay. *See* salaries
Pendleton, George Hunt, 4, 27, 199, 201
pen names, 7, 176, 213n11, 231n42
Pennsylvania, 116
Perry, Samuel L., 97, 99
pestilence, 59
philanthropy. *See* charity
Pinchback, Nina Emily Hawthorne, 79
Pinchback, Pinckney Benton Stuart, 84–85, 108
Pittsburgh, 143–46
political appointees, black. *See* black political appointees
political patronage. *See* patronage, political
Potawatomi people, 48–49
prairie fires. *See* grass fires
Prentiss, Noble, 24, 126
press, black. *See* black newspapers
press, national, 148, 162, 164–65, 183, 189; views of Kansas, 24, 112, 126. *See also* southern newspapers
Prince Hall Masons, 18, 78, 100, 222n16
Pritchard, Lewis, 173
prohibition, 182, 183, 184, 185, 190
Prohibition Party, 193, 195
Promised Land on the Solomon, 5
propaganda campaigns. *See* advertising and publicity campaigns
pseudonyms. *See* pen names
public education, 86, 87, 88–89, 129
publicity campaigns. *See* advertising and publicity campaigns

racial diffusion, 107, 115
racially mixed people. *See* mixed-race people
racial segregation and integration. *See* segregation and integration, racial
"racial uplift," 4–5, 18, 79, 80, 84, 99, 179; AME church and, 69; Embry views, 71
racial violence, 50–52, 59–60; in southern states, 29, 68, 76, 86–87, 88, 99, 110
railroads, 11, 44, 122, 161, 175; bond issues, 128–29; bypass of Nicodemus,

195, 204; as employers, 71; funding, 37; racial segregation, 197
ranchers and ranching, 62, 92; range wars, 63–64
rape, 41, 68, 99, 110
Rapier, James, 87, 88, 107
Rawlins County, Kans., 53
real estate business. *See* land location and locators
Reconstruction, 3, 25, 26
refugees, 109, 110–16, 126, 170
Relief Board of Kansas, 49
religion, 52. *See also* African Methodist Episcopal Church; churches
reparations, slave. *See* slave reparations
"representative colored men," 74, 80, 180–81
Republic National Convention, 150, 196
Republican Party, 4, 27, 105, 132, 157; Indiana, 97; Kansas, 27, 67–82, 149–55, 172–73, 178, 181, 184–85, 187, 189–94; Niles's view of, 161; southern states, 34, 88, 89
restitution for slavery. *See* slave reparations
retail stores. *See* markets and stores
Reville, M. C., 158
Reynolds, Charles, 35
Reynolds, Milton W., 19
Richmond, Robert, 135
Riddle, A. P., 194
riots, 155–57
riverboats, 35, 37, 113
Robb, Mary, 62
Robinson, Charles, 190
Robinson, Mary F. "Minnie," 143–45
Rooks County, Kans., 128, 131, 132, 140, 171, 216n9; Hall clerkship, 20, 59; McCabe appointment through, 171; Niles jailed in, 174
Rooks County Bank, 159
Rooks County Record, 31, 39, 154, 167
Root, George, 40, 50–51
Roscoe, Kans., 45, 155; in county seat fight, 129–30, 137–43, 175; riot of 1880, 155–57

Roscoe Tribune, 142, 143, 155–56, 157, 175, 176, 178
Roundtree, Samuel P., 35, 64, 92, 119, 156, 231n42
Ruby, H., 83, 86–87
Ruede, Howard, *Sod-House Days*, 54
runaway slaves. *See* fugitive slaves
runoff elections, 143

Sadler, Lulu. *See* Craig, Lulu Sadler
salaries, 172, 175, 177, 181
Salina, Kans., 47, 60, 116
Saline County Journal, 116, 193
Samuels, John, 91–92, 93, 177
schools, 35, 38, 69, 71, 83–95; Indiana, 97; North Carolina, 99
Scott, H. J., 173
Scott, John, 35, 93
Scruggs Grove, 52
Schwendemann, Glen, 6
Sears, T. S., 55
secondary education, 94
segregation and integration, racial, 111, 166, 170, 197; in Indiana, 97; mixed views, 80, 88, 90, 102; Niles's views, 161, 163, 164; in Oklahoma, 197
self-protection groups, 63–64
separatism, black. *See* black separatism
Senate, U.S. *See* U.S. Senate
Shaw, John, 62, 132
Shaw, Van Burton, 6, 22, 207n9
Shawnee County Republican Club, 77
shelter, 46, 47, 49, 54. *See also* buildings; dugouts
Shepherd, J. H., 87–88
Sheppard, William, 59–60
Sheridan County, Kans., 131, 140, 141, 213n11
Sherman, Eli, 132
Sherman, John, 14, 167, 169
shootings, 50–51, 59–60
Shorthill, R. S., 132
Shortridge, James, 52, 227n30
Simkins, W. A., 47
Simpson, John B., 83–84, 86, 89

Singleton, Benjamin "Pap," 21–22, 23, 32, 33, 80, 115–16, 180
skilled tradesmen, 29, 60, 70, 84, 155
skin color, 14, 69, 125, 144, 178, 179–80
slave reparations, 5, 14, 21, 127, 153, 158–60, 169, 204
slavery, 25, 29–30, 64, 68. *See also* Freedmen's Bureau; freemen-freedmen relations; fugitive slaves
Smith, A. J. R., 121
Smith, Billy, 61
Smith, C. W., 160
Smith, Henry, 11, 65
Smith, W. H., 17–18, 35, 45, 173
Smith, William, 148
Smith County Pioneer, 187, 189
Smyth, John J., 159
Society of Friends, 117
sod and sod-breaking, 16, 46, 121, 209n7
Sod and Stubble (Ise), 53
Sod-House Days (Ruede), 54
sod houses. *See* dugouts
Solomon River, 11, 16, 19, 141
southern newspapers, 72, 112–13, 117
southern racial violence. *See* racial violence: southern states
Spaulding, Edward, 185
Squatter Sovereign, 64
Stampp, Kenneth, 50
Staples, J. E., 173
Star-Sentinel, 178, 182, 183, 185, 191
state auditor position. *See* Kansas state auditor position
state motto, Kansas, 43
Stemmons, William, 35
Stevens, Jacob, 27
Stevensville, Kans., 130
St. John, John Pierce, 9–10, 76, 136, 198; appeal to Jay Gould, 122; appointments by, 171–72, 178; county seat fight and, 130, 133–35, 137, 138, 139, 140, 141; Exodusters and, 114, 115, 117, 120–21, 122–23; McCabe correspondence, 122–23, 125, 186; McCabe state auditor candidacy and, 186, 187; Niles correspondence, 40, 149; as presidential candidate, 193; prohibition stance, 182, 184, 190–91; Republican state convention of 1878, 75; *Smith County Pioneer* relations, 189; third-term run, 181–84, 190–92, 193; women's rights advocacy, 182, 183
St. John AME Church, Topeka, 69–70, 77, 81, 84, 90
St. Louis, Mo., 49, 111, 113, 143, 157
Stockton, J. S., 113
Stockton, Kans., 59, 60, 131, 148–49, 174
Stockton News, 38–39, 140; Hall letters to, 62–63, 93, 119, 129, 130–31
Stockton Record, 40, 179–80
stores. *See* markets and stores
storms, 45, 50, 53
Stover, L. P., 185
Stringfield, F. M., 67
Strothers, D. L., 194
Stubblefield, Louis, 147
Sunday schools, 62, 63, 84
Supreme Court, U.S. *See* U.S. Supreme Court
surveyors and surveying, 51, 136, 173
swindlers and swindling, 119, 147, 148, 162. *See also* fraud

Talbott, Isaac, 13
Tandy, Charleton H., 34, 110–11
Taylor, W. H., 185
teachers, 35, 93
Tennessee, 3, 12, 24, 29–30. *See also* National Conference of Colored Men, Nashville, 1879
Tennessee Real Estate and Homestead Association, 21, 22, 32, 33
Terrell, N. C., 134, 143, 171, 175, 210n17
Texas, 3, 163
third-term candidacy, 194–95; McCabe, 193; St. John, 181–85, 190–92, 193
Thomas, L., 173
Tillotson, Ida, 134, 227n23
Tillotson, T. T., 134, 160, 216n9
Tillotson family, 134, 139

INDEX   263

Time That Was, The (Hayden), 53
Topeka, 37, 42, 47, 68, 106; AME church,
    69–70, 77, 81, 84, 90; black settlements,
    35; *Colored Citizen* move to, 62;
    Exodusters, 110, 113, 114, 115, 116;
    school segregation, 90; state Republican
    conventions, 185, 194; winter fallback
    location, 50
Topeka Capital, 115, 116, 117, 184, 193
Topeka Tribune, 109
Topeka Weekly Times, 126
Townsend, William Bolden, 18, 19, 72, 74,
    75, 81, 121; literary society talk, 84;
    Republic National Convention of 1880,
    150; views on "colored convention,"
    105, 107
township organization, 130, 131–32
tradesmen, skilled. *See* skilled tradesmen
transnational emigration, black, 96, 98, 99,
    100, 165
transportation, 219n49. *See also* railroads;
    riverboats; wagons; walking,
    long-distance
Trego County, Kans., 122, 174
trials, 158–60
Turner, Frederick Jackson, 53
Turner, John, 111
Twine, William, 29, 194

Underground Railroad, 18, 25, 68, 117
Union Pacific Railroad, 195
universities, 14, 197
*Upon the Past, Present and Future of the
    Colored American* (Embry), 70
U.S. Bureau of Refugees, Freedmen, and
    Abandoned Lands. *See* Freedmen's
    Bureau
U.S. census, 1880, 141
U.S. Congress, 79, 80, 102, 103, 105, 154,
    158, 167. *See also* U.S. Senate
U.S. Constitution, amendments, 25, 29,
    90, 166
U.S. Department of Justice, 165
U.S. Department of the Treasury, 57,
    166–67, 171, 194, 196

U.S. land offices. *See* federal land offices
U.S. Senate, 103, 167, 169, 193–94; Ingalls
    in, 105, 182, 194. *See also* Voorhees
    Committee
U.S. Supreme Court, 166, 167, 197

Vance, Zebulon, 4, 27, 87, 89, 199, 201
Vanduvall, H. L., 157
Van Slyck, Barent, 155
Victor, Kans. (proposed), 129
vigilantism, 99, 174
Viley, Willis, 30–31
Virginia, 12, 34, 196
Voorhees, Daniel Wolsey, 4, 27, 28, 44, 97,
    199, 201
Voorhees Committee, 4, 19, 20, 27, 34,
    97–100, 110; Adams testimony, 26; Allen
    testimony, 43; Brookings testimony, 42;
    Buchan testimony, 170, 224n26; De
    Green testimony, 113; John Milton
    Brown testimony, 67–68, 88, 89–90;
    Knox testimony, 49; majority faction, 27,
    199; minority faction, 27, 103, 199; Rapier
    testimony, 87, 107; Ruby testimony, 83;
    Sears testimony, 55; Singleton testimony,
    21, 80; Stringfield testimony, 67–68;
    testimony against Comstock and Haviland,
    119; testimony on cold climate, 44;
    testimony on education, 83–84, 85, 86–87,
    88; testimony on fraud, 147; testimony on
    partisan politics, 78; Wears testimony, 11,
    14, 25, 100; Wheeler testimony, 45–46
Voorhees Committee Report, 4, 20, 27, 41,
    94, 202; Majority Report, 199–200, 201;
    Minority Report, 26, 28, 199, 200–202
voting rights, 3, 25, 27, 195, 201. *See also*
    woman suffrage movement

wagons, 11, 38–39, 58, 66
Wakeeney (store), 58
WaKeeney, Kans., 38, 61, 122, 173, 174
WaKeeney Weekly World, 178
Waldron, Nell, 5, 22, 211–12n25
walking, long-distance, 37, 53, 58, 60, 61
Wall, O. S. B., 98

Waller, John Lewis, 72, 73, 102, 105
Walton, A. H., 69
Walton, J. L., 173
Warner, Albert, 58
Warren, Charley, 173
Washburn, Henry, 61
Washington, Booker T., 14, 83, 180, 219n1
Washington, D.C., 80–81, 193–94; McCabe in, 196; Niles in, 163–67, 169
water supply, 43, 53. *See also* wells
Wayland Chapel, Fort Scott, Kans., 70
wealth and empowerment, 71, 80, 84–86, 107
Wears, Isaiah, 11, 14, 25, 100
weather, 24, 42, 44, 45, 46–47, 50, 53
Webb, Walter, 66
Webster, Abner, *13*
Weekly Kansas Chief, 179, 183, 188, 191
wells, 43, 58, 61, 63, 64
Wells, Ida B., 229
Western Cyclone (Nicodemus Cyclone), 9, 195
Western Star, 121–22, 125, 136, 138
West of Wichita (Miner), 12
Wheeler, J. W., 45, 49
White League, 86
white supremacists, school destruction by, 86, 87
Wichita, Kans., 116
Wichita Eagle, 75, 187, 192
Wiegand, A., 116
Willard, Francis, 184
Williams, Charles, 35
Wilson, Don W., 9
Windom, William, 4, 21, 22, 24, 27–29, 80, *104;* Embry relations, 103; "forty acres" query, 224n26; "Mississippi Policy" query, 68; Voorhees Committee Minority Report, 199, 200–201
winter, 32, 44, 45, 46–47, 50, 54
woman suffrage movement, 102, 183–84, 190
women house servants, 60
women's rights, 102, 182, 183–84, 190
Woods, C. C., 159
Woods, Randall B., 80
Worcester, Mass., 116
Works Progress Administration, 144
Wright, John W., 69
Wyandotte, Kans., 35, 37, 112–13, 170

Yancy, William, 60